1995–1996

BRASSEY'S MERSHON

AMERICAN
D·E·F·E·N·S·E
ANNUAL

1995–1996

BRASSEY'S MERSHON

AMERICAN D·E·F·E·N·S·E

A N N U A L

The United States and the Emerging Strategic Environment

Editor, Williamson Murray
Associate Editor, Jeffrey S. Lantis
Assistant Editor, Christopher K. Ives

Mershon Center
The Ohio State University

Brassey's
Washington • London

The Library of Congress has cataloged this serial publication as follows: ISSN 0822-1028

Hardcover ISBN 1-57488-037-3
Trade Paperback ISBN 1-57488-038-1

Designed by Sara Leigh Merrey

10 9 8 7 6 5 4 3 2 1

Printed in the United States of America

Contents

Tables

Figures

Acknowledgments

A number of individuals provided invaluable help and assistance in the making of this issue of the *Brassey's Mershon American Defense Annual,* all of whom deserve considerable thanks from the editor. First, Professor Charles F. Hermann, the director of the Mershon Center, has given the editor unstinting and enthusiastic support for the new direction that this issue takes. Second, my three supporting editors, Jeff Lantis, Christopher K. Ives, and Lesley Mary Smith, provided the careful proofreading and textual criticism upon which any edited work must depend. The Mershon Center also owes a special debt of gratitude to Frank Margiotta and the staff at Brassey's, who have undertaken to publish this volume at such short notice. Finally, I also owe my contributors a vote of thanks for providing such challenging and thoughtful pieces. In the end, the credit for whatever success this volume enjoys is theirs; its errors and weaknesses are my responsibility.

Introduction

Williamson Murray

> We have done nothing extraordinary, nothing contrary to human nature in accepting an empire when it was offered to us and then in refusing to give it up. Three powerful motives prevent us from doing so—security, honor, and self-interest. And we were not the first to act in this way. Far from it. It has always been a rule that the weak should be subject to the strong. (Athenian speakers before the Spartan assembly, 432 B.C.)[1]

This issue of *Brassey's Mershon American Defense Annual* represents a significant new direction for the *Annual*. It seemed to the director of the Mershon Center, Charles Hermann, and to myself, the incoming editor, that the ending of the Cold War brought such enormous changes to the strategic environment within which America's defense policy must exist that the *Annual* had to change direction also. In previous years the *Annual* had examined America's defense structure and its national security within a framework that changed little from year to year. We looked at the defense budget, strategic nuclear weapons, U.S. forces deployed in Europe, the military services, manpower, and other issues that easily transferred from year to year.

But then the Cold War represented a period of considerable stability in the international environment, for all of the terrible dangers associated with a potential Soviet-American nuclear exchange. Decreasing that danger, at least temporarily, has not in fact made the world a safer place. Instead of certainty, the governments and policy makers of the world confront uncertainty; instead of ironclad alliances, they face shifting ad hoc coalitions, here today but wholly ambiguous tomorrow. Over the past three to four years, Americans have heard a host of predictions ranging from "the end of history" and the growing happy interdependence of a world dominated by democratic capitalism to a future "clash of civilizations."[2] By and large the former has dominated the intellectual landscape, perhaps because the alternatives are too alarming.[3]

Whatever the parameters of the debate, it seems to us at the Mershon Center that the *Annual* has to do more than provide a report card on U.S. defense capabilities. The crucial questions are not what military capabilities the United States possesses now and how the Pentagon is performing, but how the nation should use its military and where they might be needed—not in the next year, but in the next decade or even the next half century. Such issues lie at the outer reaches of U.S. defense policy; yet they *should* be our central concern. In what kind of world are American military forces going to live in the twenty-first century and how should those charged with America's defense policy respond to the long-range implications of what they are doing with the current American military structure? These are not easy questions, as the range of the current debate suggests, but we have framed the current *Annual* around such long-term strategic issues rather than the more traditional end-of-term report on the state of U.S. defenses. Nor does this year's *Annual* aim to present a consensus: without a serious debate about the future national strategy, the likelihood of making the right choices for the future is slim indeed.

Nothing in America's recent past resembles the international system today. Yet there are profound cultural influences that prevent Americans from looking further back into those decades whose experiences might help us. Henry Ford's statement that "history is bunk" reflects a deeply held American belief about the irrelevance of the past for charting the future.[4] More worryingly, America's political and intellectual elites of the last five decades have increasingly echoed Ford's ahistorical view of the world. What then does the United States do in circumstances when every experience of the past fifty years has little bearing on an international environment in which the United States now has to survive? In a world of uncertainty history may be the best guide, but how then can the American leadership reach for a discipline that remains so far from its interests and understanding?

We have devoted much of the first half of this issue to the long-term strategic implications of the Cold War's end and the potential strategic frameworks for international relations in the twenty-first century. To achieve this change in direction we have asked those with solid credentials as historians to address the larger strategic framework. Their study and research in the past open to contemporary scrutiny worlds in which there were a multiplicity of unevenly balanced powers, just as there are today. Only such pasts can provide useful insights into the emerging strategic environment—one in which it is highly unlikely that there will be even one "superpower."[5]

In the concluding chapters we have moved on to more traditional topics such as current defense policy, the defense budget, nuclear policy, and conventional forces. Finally, lest insularity inhibit us, we have asked a leading European scholar to examine America's strategic course from a foreign perspective. In all of these chapters we have asked the authors to examine where current defense policies might take us and how they might respond, or not respond, to future strategic environments. The result is not an optimistic— nor necessarily a uniform—evaluation either of the future environment or of how our defense establishment is adapting to the new world disorder.

America and the Emerging Strategic Environment

The United States has just won a great war: a war that tested the patience and endurance of a polity that Lincoln termed "the last best hope of earth." The temptation, then, is to rest; and indeed the current international environment may provide Americans with a period of time to reflect on how they need to act on the international stage. The United States has acquired by default a great worldwide empire. That empire is not directly under its sway, and the end of the Cold War has loosened the bonds that tied America's allies to its policies. Even so, the United States, and the United States alone, stands at the center of a condominium that has brought unparalleled peace and prosperity to much of the world. Americans might say of their "empire" as the Athenians said of theirs: "those [the rulers of the Athenian empire, namely, themselves] who really deserve praise are the people who, while human enough to enjoy power, nevertheless pay more attention to justice than they were compelled to do by circumstance."[6]

As the victorious imperium, the United States should have some considerable opportunities to influence and guide the direction that the world may take over coming decades. But the United States will only remain an influential international player if Americans think hard about their national interests, the level of commitment that they can afford *and* will tolerate, and the kind of military that can address the problems of today, *while at the same time* preparing to meet long-term potential threats.

America can only lose from the disintegration of that empire and, in the end, the glue that holds it together and protects it from the challenges of those who would overthrow it must contain the harsh fist of military power. There will, of course, be those who will urge their nation to abandon its responsibilities, to give up all military pretense of having interests in the world. Such a course almost led Britain in the late 1930s to abandon all before the Nazi threat. As Kingsley Martin urged Neville Chamberlain in April 1938, "[t]oday if Mr. Chamberlain would come forward and tell us that his policy was really one of Little Englandism in which the Empire was to be given up because it could not be defended and in which military defense was to be abandoned because war would totally end civilization, we for our part would wholeheartedly support him."[7] Americans will hear much along these lines from both the right and the left in coming decades, and in the face of economic and social problems at home such oratory will be welcomed. They should do their best to ignore such siren calls, but their commitment to do so will greatly depend on how well their leaders cast U.S. foreign policies.

The American victory in the Cold War rested on the ability of the United States to keep together a great, worldwide coalition of industrialized and industrializing powers. The resulting diplomatic and strategic success not only buttressed America's military and economic power with greater depth and resiliency but created a web of economic and financial interrelationships that have made the present era one of unparalleled prosperity.

The early days of the Cold War cast the strategy that won the Cold War.[8] But there was nothing inevitable in the course that the United States pursued or in its eventual victory. The documents of the early Cold War pinpoint how tenuous were the initial American moves against the expansion of Soviet power and how considerable was the opposition to a strong stand in Europe.[9] Moreover, only the most extraordinarily inept and mischievous behavior on the part of the Soviet leadership could have kept the United States in the contest to the end. By the late 1960s America's intellectuals, particularly the younger ones, had joined Europe's in a desperate desire to believe and hope for the best from the Soviets while at the same time thinking the worst of their own side. There were, of course, those in the West's community of scholars, the Ulams, the Conquests, a small number reinforced by the dripping contempt of Alexsandr Solzhenitsyn, who kept the crimes and the nature of Soviet tyranny before those willing to read beyond the current myths of "Soviet studies."[10]

In the end, the ineptitude of Soviet policy allowed the United States and its industrialized allies to lurch to victory. But if it was difficult—and it was—to keep the United States in the long-term competition with the Soviets, then how much more difficult is it going to be to keep the United States focused on many of the critical issues shaping the emerging strategic environment of the twenty-first century—especially when it will not be entirely clear for years, if not decades, who exactly its potential opponents might be?

How then can one use the past to suggest policies and defense structures to deal with the uncertain future? On the highest strategic level, the United

States has gained enormously by the creation of this informal empire in Europe and Asia. What Americans should not forget is that the specter of Soviet power was as important in shaping this coalition as the policies of the United States. It has been, and should continue to be, central to U.S. policy that this state of affairs continue as long into the next century as possible. The longer the United States keeps the industrialized world together, the less it has to fear a resurrection of something like the nightmarish challenge that the Soviet Union and its military represented for much of the Cold War. Unfortunately, as memories of the Cold War recede, it will be harder and harder over the coming years and decades to justify to the American people the military commitments that underpinned that empire.

At the same time Americans should not lose sight of the fact that the international economic order, as it currently exists, is fragile, as recent events in Mexico underline. Consequently, the United States must make clear to its European and Asian allies that it is willing to support their continuing security and to devote some effort and degree of sacrifice to the protection of the common good—that is, to the strategic and economic interests of the industrialized, democratic world as a whole.[11] But that does not mean that the United States should not expect its allies to do *their* share in maintaining forces necessary to help in protecting the larger interests of the industrialized world.

Americans cannot assume that the current world order will remain on a relatively benign course—at least in terms of the relations between the major powers. They must remember that past international orders have changed with astonishing rapidity. Paul Kennedy, in comparing the differences between British strategic policy making in the 1930s with that of America during the Cold War, has underlined the stunning shift that occurred in the balance of power in the period between the world wars:

> Perhaps the greatest difference between British net assessment in the 1930s and American net assessment in (say) the 1960s was the extraordinary fluidity and multipolarity of the international scene in the earlier period. At the beginning of the 1930s, the British widely regarded the Soviet Union as the greatest land enemy of the Empire, while in naval terms the chief rivals were the United States and Japan; they saw Mussolini's Italy as temperamental, France as unduly assertive and difficult (but not hostile), and Germany as still prostrate. Five to eight years later, Japan appeared as a distinct challenge to British interests in the Far East, Germany had fallen under Nazi rule and was assessed as the "greatest long-term danger," and Italy's policies appeared aggressive and hostile, whereas the United States was more unpredictable and isolationist than ever, Russia had become somewhat less of a strategic threat (but remained an ideological foe), and France's weaknesses were more manifest than its strengths.[12]

Kennedy goes on to point out that even the immediate short-term balance can shift with startling swiftness:

> In April 1938 the Foreign Office, discussing the "revised terms of reference" for the Joint Planning Sub-Committee, listed the "principal new developments" since the previous assessment, in the autumn of 1936, as "(1) the consolidation of the Rome-Berlin-Tokyo axis; (2) the existence of a state of war between China and Japan; (3) the development of the Spanish Civil War; (4) the temporary weakness of the Soviet Army as the result of the recent (and continuing) 'purge'; (5) the annexation of Austria by Germany; (6) the dangerous state of Anglo-Italian relations and the attempt now being made to improve them; (7) the progressive deterioration of our position in the Middle East as a result of events in Palestine, with the consequent risk to our oil supplies and communications with the east."[13]

Great shifts may not happen, but they *can*, and Americans must not forget that fact in thinking about their defense and strategic policies. They must balance in realistic fashion the threats of today against the greater long-range threats of the twenty-first century. They *must* be willing to take risks today to avoid disasters tomorrow.

Britain's great role in the nineteenth century as an imperial policeman suggests a similar role for the United States as long as the international environment—at least in a macro sense—continues on a relatively benign course. There is, however, a warning from Britain's continuing belief in its imperial role after World War II, when an economy shattered by the two terrible struggles against Germany could no longer support *any* imperial structure. Well into the 1960s Britain struggled to maintain as much of the ramshackle framework of empire as possible. The results were the often bloody loss of provinces, international ridicule, empty coffers, and an economy that had enjoyed little of the investment that Britain's competitor economies received throughout the period. In the early 1970s all that remained was for Britain to go cap in hand begging membership in the European Economic Community from the French and Germans. The United States obviously does not confront as bleak a choice; but failure to place defense spending and the costs of "engagements" within the larger context of U.S. economic security could have serious consequences.

Two crucial points flow from this analysis. First, American policy makers, civilian as well as military, must recognize the limits that America's politics, current economic situation, and military capabilities place on the nation's capacity to intervene in the troubles that have emerged throughout the world. The Vietnam War carries a salient lesson. On one hand, the American people *will* bear extraordinary burdens and pay an extraordinary price if required to do so. But the war in Vietnam made no strategic sense, and eventually the

American people saw through the facile arguments of their leaders and brought an end to the conflict. The ensuing anger in the American population came close to bringing about an American withdrawal from the Cold War: only the huge Soviet military buildup and the Kremlin's provocative strategic policies kept the United States engaged.

Second, continued frittering away of the American military in mindless, badly thought-out interventions in the Third World creates two dangers. The United States risks abandoning decisions about where to intervene to the latest public outcry fueled by the visceral impact of television pictures of the newest world disaster—starving, mutilated children, the grim visages of war, the shattered remnants of collapsing societies. Following such media hype blindly will lead to ill-thought-out, under-planned commitments like those in Lebanon and Somalia. In the long run, that risks destroying the willingness of Americans to countenance any overseas interventions. U.S. policy stands in real danger of pushing the American people into that very isolationism that so many feared at the end of the Cold War but that has yet to exert any great influence on American foreign policy.

Indeed, one would be foolish not to recognize that American isolationism, both on the right and on the left, is alive and well. The pre–Gulf War debates in the House and the Senate—as well as H. R. Perot's comments on television and the letters that Jimmy Carter was sending to the world's leaders in the weeks before the Coalition attack on Iraq—suggest that isolationism is an attractive theme to many Americans. Certainly, if one could not see Kuwait as deserving of U.S. attention—especially with the danger that its surrender would place the Gulf's oil under the ominous shadow of a dictator with megalomaniac dreams—then what conceivable situations would be worthy of U.S. intervention?

This combination of factors poses a serious danger to vital U.S. interests. If isolationism prevails, even in modified form, the United States will not be able to intervene early enough to prevent regional problems from turning into international crises. In a critical conflict the same pressures may mean that U.S. intervention is so late and ill-prepared that American national interests are profoundly threatened.

The great danger is that the Clinton administration's strategy of "engagement" risks creating a national mood of disengagement from international affairs. Only if the United States picks the right crises and does not simply involve itself and, more important, its armed forces, in every catastrophe that looks bad on CNN or captures the popular imagination, is there some possibility that the United States will continue as the guarantor of a measure of international order.

The American military already exercises a considerable impact on the world's trouble spots, as U.S. peace-keeping forces in the Sinai suggest. But peace keeping demands very different military forces than we currently possess—the deployment of a carrier battle group to Haiti in 1994 hardly represented a force tailored to meet the complexities of local conditions. The current force structure and culture of the American military are largely unsuited to deal with "operations other than war."[14] The Pentagon has insisted on tailoring its forces for the past rather than for the present and the future. The United States could pay a serious price in both strategic and operational terms for its unwillingness to change with the times.

What then does the United States need to do with its defense policy? In the largest sense Americans should recognize that for the present they do not confront any great, *immediate* threat to the security and welfare of the world condominium of industrialized democratic states. The United States still remains a superpower and therefore has an obligation to lead; it may be able to do so to a lesser extent than during the Cold War, but in fact that means that it requires wise, sophisticated leadership—one with some understanding of other nations and other cultures.

The requirement of leadership also requires that the United States exercise restraint. It cannot afford, nor will the American people allow, U.S. military forces to serve as the world's policemen in every international quarrel or tragedy. The United States will have to pick where it chooses to intervene with a sense that there are limits on what military intervention can conceivably achieve. Second, American foreign policy must retain a sober sense that the United States confronts great challenges at home. Victory in the Cold War did not come cheaply, and the nation must therefore repair much of the damage that the strain of that conflict imposed on civil society.

The Military and the New World

The United States must tailor the organization and structure of its military to address a complex, difficult, and ambiguous world—the future world, not the world of the past. Unfortunately, the downsizing of the U.S. military since the Gulf War—as typified in President George Bush's Base Force and President Bill Clinton's Bottom Up Review—has represented a major effort to save as much as possible of the old force structure at the expense of future capabilities and new force structures.

The Pentagon is presently tailoring its forces entirely on the basis that they must be ready to fight *two major regional contingencies at the same time*. This basic assumption, which is driving current as well as future defense budgets, has no basis in American historical experience. The United States fought three major regional conflicts in the period from 1946 through 1991. In the first two, Korea and Vietnam, it also confronted the Soviet Union with its great military capabilities. Yet the Soviets failed in fact to take advantage of America's situation to strike with their forces—or those of their allies— against other U.S. commitments. If history suggests anything, it suggests that the chances of American military forces engaging in two major regional contingencies at the same time are so minimal as not to be worthy of serious consideration. Yet that assumption may well be gutting long-range prospects by wrecking current procurement programs as well as the research and development crucial to American success on battlefields two decades hence.

Consequently, the Department of Defense needs to set a more realistic strategic assessment for the current force structure. Such an assessment would posit that *at most* the United States will confront *one* major regional conflict. As a corollary, it is clear that even in the case of a major contingency, it is inconceivable that the United States would commit its forces *without substantial Allied forces fighting at their side*. A second major regional war breaking out at the same time as the first, even under the conditions of the Clinton review's force structure, would demand a massive mobilization of America's civil as well as its military potential.[15] The belief that under the present economic and political circumstances the United States can afford the luxury of preparing for the unlikely contingencies of two major wars not only is politically naive but also carries with it extraordinary dangers to the long-range stability of the forces and to the political support on which their viability must rest.

The strategic assumptions discussed above suggest that for the short term—for the next decade and perhaps even the following one—the United States needs substantially fewer of the forces that typified the military structure of the Cold War. But depending on the attitudes of the American polity, the United States requires forces specially trained for the "operations other than war" that apparently will characterize intervention situations over the immediate future. These forces would look, equip, and prepare themselves in a very different fashion from the forces that the United States deployed throughout most of the Cold War.

Such specialized units might be removed entirely from the regular force structure and placed under a command that aimed to train its forces largely for the peace-keeping mission. For example, in the early 1960s the U.S. Army created special task forces for "operations other than war," FLAGs (Free-World Liaison and Assistance Groups).[16] The 8th Special Forces Group, activated in Panama, was supposed to serve as the model for such a group; it had its own organic engineers, military police, and psychological operations and civil action elements. Such an expansion of "peace-keeping" capabilities would allow a substantial portion of "operations other than war" to devolve on those prepared for the mission rather than bleed the regular conventional forces over into a mission for which they have little training and that will serve only to debilitate their regular combat skills. But above all, the political masters of the Pentagon must decide *what is essential and what is not essential* when committing American forces. And that will require *hard* choices.

The new force structure would certainly need fewer carrier battle groups, fewer conventional army divisions, and fewer air force fighter wings. Some of the decreases in heavy, conventional strength could go into the preparing of specially trained and prepared forces for peace-keeping missions. But the Pentagon should not continue to believe that it can easily translate heavy conventional forces into politically sophisticated units prepared to handle the complexities and ambiguities of "operations other than war." To ask regular forces to fulfill the peace-keeping mission and *at the same time* to prepare seriously for combat may well result in a situation where they can perform neither mission well.

There is another crucial problem that the changing security environment has brought about. The present reality is that American forces are coming home from the great Cold War deployments. And nowhere has the Pentagon addressed this problem with sufficient focus or emphasis in any of its projections and budgets for the future. The United States may leave residual forces in Europe and in the Western Pacific; the Pentagon may even be able to maintain some considerable logistical infrastructure throughout Western Europe and the Western Pacific, although only if the United States maintains its close relationship with its current allies.

The return of U.S. forces to North America suggests a different set of priorities in how the United States should fashion its forces. It means above all else that the services require sealift and airlift to deploy their forces—and that will be the bulk of the U.S. military—from the great island continent on which they are stationed to the war or crisis that threatens American interests. In other words, for the foreseeable future the priorities of the navy and air force must be very different from those in the Cold War. The troop-carrying airlifters of Air Mobility Command must rank equally with, if not more highly than, the bombers and fighters of Air Combat Command—not just in terms of support but in the money devoted to new aircraft. On the part of the navy, attack transports, pre-positioning cargo carriers, and other support vessels should receive first place in naval budgets above carriers and the combat vessels that support them. The Pentagon might even consider, as it decreases the carrier fleet, retaining one or two additional carriers to serve as transports to move the army's heavy armored units to trouble spots such as the Middle East in as expeditious a fashion as possible.[17]

If the long-range sealift and airlift does not exist to transport the ground forces and the support structure for air units deploying overseas to meet a sudden crisis situation, then the Pentagon can no longer justify those ground and air forces stationed in the continental United States, unless, of course, it believes that Mexico and Canada will sometime in the near future appear as significant threats to the security of the United States.[18]

The Pentagon should tailor the forces that the United States deploys outside of the United States for two purposes: to work closely with our allies in multilateral operations and for the initial move to a crisis area. They, as well as the marines and the army's XVIII Airborne Corps, and certain picked fighter units (designated in all three services) would serve as intervention forces for the heavier forces that the army and air force can eventually bring to bear.[19]

The German seizure of Norway in 1940 suggests how the American military should think about the next major regional contingency. It is highly unlikely that U.S. forces will possess the airfields and ports of a Saudia Arabia to sort their gear out over a five-month period. Instead, U.S. forces are probably going to have to seize, in major combat operations, ports and airfields at the same time against considerable resistance. And the seizure of port facilities will demand the over-the-beach capabilities of the marines as the critical element. Such potential operations also require intervention capabilities unique to the army (XVIII Airborne Corps) and the marines (amphibious capabilities), working in the closest cooperation to achieve the basis from which larger U.S. and allied forces could fight if necessary. One capability without the other is a sure recipe for military catastrophe.[20]

The American military must also rely on marrying up its ground forces with pre-positioned equipment ships located around the world—ships that have the capability for immediate amphibious operations against hostile shorelines. If the contingency is large enough the Pentagon will have to rely on committing the reserves to combat at an early point in the fighting.[21] It will have no other choice.

As the Gulf War underlined, airpower must play an essential role in any conflict in which the United States involves itself in the future. But that airpower must reflect the lessons of the Gulf War, and the one overwhelming lesson of that conflict was that stealth aircraft and precision-guided munitions are *force multipliers*.[22] Cruise missiles, one method of precision attack, are expensive and of relatively small utility against hardened targets. On the other hand, there is little evidence that air force F-16s and navy and marine F/A-18s hit much of anything, because few were equipped to drop precision munitions.[23] Consequently, aircraft with the ability to drop precision-guided munitions should represent the heart of U.S. airpower capabilities. The United States requires both the supplies of precision-guided munitions and the manufacturing capabilities to produce the weapons that an extended air campaign might require. Unfortunately, the air force's predilections, perhaps driven by choices made higher in the Pentagon, have not suggested a heavy emphasis on precision-guided capabilities.

Above all, in tailoring U.S. conventional forces for the next century, the Defense Department needs to remove redundant capabilities that stretch the Pentagon's resource base to the breaking point. Is it conceivable that the United States will deploy ground forces into areas where the air force and navy will not have already established air superiority?[24] If it is not, then the army should delete its air defense branch, except for those portions that might roll into a limited anti–ballistic missile capability. Do we need long-range, expensive land-based missiles for the army to attack targets that are the responsibility of air force and navy attack aircraft? Do the marines need to buy a fighter aircraft, the F/A-18, that contributes relatively little in direct support of their ground troops but rather seems more designed to help the navy man the twelve carrier battle groups it seems so loath to discard?[25]

Turning the question around on the maritime front, for example, one might underline that no threat presently exists to the control of the world's oceans by the U.S. Navy and its allies. Consequently, the navy, presently structured to control the world's oceans, is not prepared to meet the challenges of the intervention mission. Navy planners argue that carrier battle groups provide "presence," but they miss the fact that the carrier battle group possesses virtually no capability to intervene unless backed up by considerable marine forces on navy support vessels. But the navy's desperate attempt to maintain twelve carriers has been starving the marines of the vessels and structure needed to execute their intervention mission. In the past the marines have provided the support for the larger strategy of the navy. In the current strategic environment, however, the roles should be reversed: the navy should exist to support marine—and army—expeditionary interventions. In other words, the navy should be sacrificing carriers to build amphibious carriers, LHAs and LHDs, for the marines. Not surprisingly, it is not.

The Pentagon is also going to have to change the way that it does business. For much of the Cold War, the American military placed a reasonable emphasis on the technological superiority of its weaponry. The Gulf War certainly provided justification for that decision, but with the current trends in defense spending the best may well be the enemy of the good. The F-22 may be the best fighter foreseeable for much of the first half of the twenty-first century, but can the air force afford an aircraft that threatens to put the procurement of everything else in jeopardy? The C-17 may be a wonderful transport aircraft, but can Air Mobility Command afford it, when the air force could buy Boeing 747s at substantially lower cost and with the added advantage that 747s can be fixed virtually anywhere in the world? What the Pentagon buys has to be integrated into the larger context of the cost of all other systems.

Finally, the United States needs to think about substantive changes in the culture of its military services. Ironically, professional military education played a crucial role in the U.S. victory in World War II, but that education came to be devalued in the military services during the Cold War. In the late 1980s Congress carried out an extensive study of professional military education in the United States. Not only did it offer substantive criticisms, but it also seemed willing to consider and support substantial changes. The marines and the air force did make major changes to their command and general staff colleges, but by and large the general reaction in the U.S. military appears to have been a contemptuous disbelief that education might play any role in the preparation of the officer corps for the next century. The navy, for example, with the best war college in the world, persists in sending captains with twenty-nine years of active-duty service to school just before they retire. The institutions of professional military education must prepare the services for the next century, and this area deserves the greatest attention.

The fundamental question that the services confront is that consenting to any abandonment of the Bottom Up Review's force structure means that they must scupper another great wave of those men and women who answered their country's call. The services deserve some sympathy for their unwillingness to tell those who have placed their lives on the line that they are no longer needed; the army, the marines, the navy, and the air force are not IBMs. The consequences, though, of holding onto an obsolete or unaffordable force structure could be dangerous. First, given the harsh realities of budget deficits, cuts are going to occur anyway. By delaying or prolonging such cuts, the services will drive out the best and keep the mediocre. Second, by committing scarce resources to maintaining an unrealistic force structure and by underfunding the future, the services will ensure that sometime and somewhere in the future young Americans will die in needlessly high numbers.

Conclusion

In the early 1980s Ronald Reagan was elected president of the United States. With the enormous threat of the Soviet military in mind, he set in motion a vast program of defense spending to redress that balance. There was, however, little effort to provide a strategic framework to guide the services into a coherent and thoughtful buildup of American forces that would complement each other rather than exist in independent universes. The U.S. military is now paying a price for that lack of strategic forethought.

The United States confronts the need for further downsizing of its forces. The Bottom Up Review attempted, but failed, to provide a strategic framework for the direction of our defense policies. At least it has provided the starting point for the debate: a debate that must consider both America's strategic role in the world and the size of forces that the nation can afford.

The United States will continue to require some of the great conventional capabilities that the Pentagon developed for the Cold War. It will need to hone those capabilities to the same sharp edge that characterized the U.S. forces that so thoroughly deconstructed Iraqi military forces in the deserts of Mesopotamia. That alone is the major reason why the Pentagon must come down substantially from the totals in the Bottom Up Review. Better a well-prepared force, two thirds the size advocated by the review, than a force hollowed out by lack of training, maintenance, and support. Such a force also offers the prospect that the Department of Defense can invest in research and development for the future and procure sufficient weapons for the present. For those "operations other than war" the United States needs new forces, trained in a very different fashion from the present conventional heavy forces; and the Pentagon should not kid itself that there is any easy transmission between these very different missions.

In thinking about the continued downsizing, the services need to think along the lines of their *core competencies*. What do they need that is essential to the larger operational capabilities that will allow the U.S. military to meet national strategic objectives? What is *not essential*—no matter how much has been invested or even if there are deeply felt institutional roots—must go. Such an approach may put whole communities out of business, but in saving the core, the services will also save those elements of their force structure that they will absolutely need for reconstitution should the United States confront a greater threat sometime in the next century.

The Department of Defense needs to address two crucial questions in adapting to the momentous changes that have occurred over the past decade. What kind of forces can the United States afford that will provide some current security without jeopardizing the long-term survivability and combat potential of its forces? And how best might the services inculcate innovative thinking into the cultures of officer corps that have not had to deal with great changes in military technology or the strategic landscape over the past half century? Both of these questions represent momentous tasks, and if the nation fails in answering them, it will jeopardize its security and perhaps even its fundamental values. We hope that this issue of the *Brassey's Mershon American Defense Annual* will contribute to the necessary debate on the future course of U.S. defense policy.

Chapter 1

What History Can Tell Us About the "New Strategic Environment"

MacGregor Knox

T he owl of history is an evening bird. The past as a whole is unknowable; only at the end of the day do some of its outlines dimly emerge. The future cannot be known at all, and the past suggests that change is often radical and unforeseeable rather than incremental and predictable. Yet despite its many ambiguities, historical experience remains the only available guide both to the present and to the range of alternatives inherent in the future.

The nature and direction of the "new strategic environment" that has followed the sudden and almost universally unforeseen collapse of the Soviet empire are a puzzle that will only yield, if at all, to analysis based on knowledge of the past. That knowledge can help explain the underlying character and dynamics of the world's major regions and states. It can tell about the enduring features shared by all state systems so far recorded. And it can give some grasp of the past and continuing effects on the relationships between states of ideology, of technology and economics, and of demography, the dynamic forces that have propelled the sweeping changes of the past two centuries.

The Weight of Culture and History

Cultural characteristics and internal dynamics, the first of the three levels of analysis employed in this chapter, are vital above all in understanding

1

the strengths, weaknesses, and possible futures of the existing great powers—
powers that are great above all by virtue of their ability to fight great wars.[1]
Analysis of the cultures and historical trajectories of the world's major regions
and societies may also help to anticipate the rise of new great powers, the
transformation of old ones into revolutionary rogue powers intent on destroying the international order, and the appearance of the lesser but still tan-
gible threats posed by small and mid-sized "crazy states."[2]

Culture and history have so far ruled out the rise of great powers in at
least three of the world's major regions. Most of Africa south of the Sahara
has regressed economically since independence in the 1960s, and some of its
states have disintegrated or threaten to disintegrate amid ethnic or religious
warfare. Literacy rates were and have remained too low, economic and scientific rationality too foreign, tribal allegiances too strong for the successful
construction of modern states and economies—and political power has come
too exclusively from the proverbial barrel of a gun. Escape from suffering
seems unlikely except for a few exceptionally well managed and lucky small
states; the emergence of dynamic and externally ambitious small or mid-sized
powers seems unlikely for a long time.

The states of Latin America, despite far greater economic success than
those of Africa, remain hobbled in most cases by societies stratified by race
and political cultures formed by centuries of rule by native priest-kings and
despotic colonial officials, generals, and *caudillos*. Even the most powerful
Latin American states—Brazil, Argentina, Chile, Venezuela, and Mexico—
as yet lack the internal cohesion and the effective armed forces and bureaucracies needed for emergence as great powers or mid-sized rogue states
anytime soon. For good or ill, racial stratification has also so far largely inhibited the growth of fierce loyalties on the European nationalist pattern except to some extent in Mexico and Cuba, where proximity to the overmighty
United States has acted as a stimulant, and perhaps in Argentina and Brazil.

In the Middle East, control of oil and pan-Arab ideology seem to offer
the basis for the advent of an Arab superpower, but culture and religion have
so far almost precluded the necessary unity, internal stability, and effectiveness in the modern world. Not the state, but the Arab or Muslim world at
one end of the scale and the family or tribe at the other presently dominate
the loyalties of the societies that stretch from Morocco to Iran. The majority
religion's origins in worldly conquest and its consequent wrathful rejection of
a world dominated by Western knowledge and power have so far limited the
ability of the Middle East's societies to gain a share of that knowledge and
power.

Government remains either tribal monarchies imperfectly equipped with modern attributes of sovereignty thanks to oil and/or Western patronage, or dictatorships that range from lamentably inefficient (Egypt) to totalitarian rogue states (Iraq, Syria, Libya, and theocratic Shia Iran). The "secular" dictatorships have built on the region's long history of despotic rule a succession of syncretic authoritarian or totalitarian ideologies and military–secret-police regimes merrily derived from the sometimes publicly acknowledged examples of Mussolini, Hitler, and Stalin.[3] The most extreme of these "Arab models of totalitarianism" and their militant theocratic competitor in Iran have so far failed to create larger units than the ones assembled in 1918–23 from the wreckage of the Ottoman Empire. Despite Iraqi success in building the infrastructure for production of nuclear weapons and ballistic missiles, and feverish Iranian activity toward that same end, these states have so far failed in their single most burning ambition: acquisition of the power to exterminate each other, the Jews, and the West. But that failure is merely provisional.

South Asia has not one but two aspirant great powers. Pakistan's military-parliamentary regime, perched precariously over a society rent by communal and tribal divisions, shares many of the disabilities of the states of the Middle East. Should internal or external shocks end its sham-democratic interlude, its possession of nuclear weapons and delivery systems will offer perhaps irresistible temptations to new theocratic or totalitarian rulers. The paramount power on the subcontinent—India—suffers from divisions of language, caste, and religion that far surpass in number and depth even the cleavages of Pakistan and inhibit enterprise even more than the morass of corruption and bureaucratic confusion that was the major legacy of the naive academic socialism of India's founding fathers. Religious-ethnic division poises India perpetually on the edge of massive violence, while the growth of religious-ethnic extremist movements threatens, at the limit, either the subcontinent's breakup or its rule through a "Hindu model of totalitarianism." Until now Indian ambitions have extended only to the domination of Pakistan, the Himalayas, and the Indian Ocean. But a new nationalist-extremist India, its ambitions backed by its existing and future arsenal of "peaceful" nuclear weapons, might easily clash with an equally ambitious China for the mastery of Southeast Asia or seek to extend its "security zone" westward toward the oil of the Middle East.

East Asia, the region of fastest economic growth from the sixties to the nineties, has by far the strongest and most powerful non-Western states, ruling societies that of all the non-Western world have fitted most easily into the Western mold. Indeed, their very national cohesion and economic prowess make at least some of these states candidates for mutation into that most strategically significant of all animals in the international arena, the rogue great power.

Mao's new regime after 1949 replicated many unpleasant features of the imperial old order; not for nothing did the dictator reportedly treasure biographies of the cruelest of his predecessors, beginning with China's pitiless unifier, Ch'in Shih Huang Ti. That same millennial tradition of sinocentric despotism has remained alive and well in post-Maoist Beijing. Yet China's rulers have confronted the same mortal threat that autocrats of backward countries have faced repeatedly since Peter the Great. Military competition in the external arena in the end requires a market economy and Western ideas that threaten the autocracy, while failure to compete externally invites military defeat with even more drastic and immediate domestic consequences.

China's post-Mao leaders intended their answer to that threat, "market Leninism," as the road to the superpower status promised by China's population and resources. Like the Meiji oligarchs of neighboring Japan before them, they introduced capitalist economics not as a complement to democratization, but as a means of resisting it. Their eccentric marriage of capitalist development and communist police state has so far squared the circle, but only so long as their peasant army remains willing to shoot. And development, given its regional concentration in the south and on the coast, has also apparently begun to prize apart a Chinese imperial structure imposed over two millennia ago on regions and linguistic groups that despite a common written language have always maintained strong individual identities. Social turmoil and mass migration, as Maoist village and block-level controls have crumbled, also pose major threats to internal stability. Party leadership rivalries, commonplace in the past, hold the same potential for destroying a regime under stress as do regional divisions of the nation. And the putrefaction of the Maoist idea, manifest despite persistent official attempts to embalm it,[4] also seems to threaten the regime's long-term survival, as the decay of Soviet Marxist dogma foreshadowed Soviet imperial collapse.

Yet China's history and political and economic dynamics suggest a potential for external self-assertion as well as for implosion and disintegration. The impressive continuity, despite intervals of chaos and division, of territorial unity and bureaucratic rule over more than two thousand years remains a powerful precedent that was absent in the Russian/Soviet empire. China's modern nationalism, heir to Imperial China's tradition of extreme cultural contempt for outsiders and shaped by Western and Japanese encroachment as well as by Mao's adaptation of Leninism, has emerged strengthened rather than chastened from wars against Japanese and Americans. China's party elite, despite the immense corruption engendered by literal application of the slogan "to get rich is glorious," remains the only wielder of political power. China's military remains committed to modernization, especially of its nuclear, air, and naval forces. Its foreign policy aspires to regional hegemony and control of the South China Sea and of its oil. And its overseas minorities offer a ready-made pretext, should one be required, for intervention in the affairs of many smaller neighbors. China's combination of sheer size, autocratic power, nationalist-Leninist ideology, capitalist economic dynamism, and politico-economic crisis resembles on a far larger scale conditions in Wilhelmine Germany—the capitalist-authoritarian state that wrecked both the European balance and world order for three decades after 1914 at an ultimate cost of up to 100 million dead. The China of Mao's successors may yet become the most dangerous of all rogue states.

Nor has post-1945 Japan been free from the consequences of its history. Indeed nowhere is the power of culture to give entirely different meanings to formally similar political and economic arrangements more visible. The parliamentary and legal façade that MacArthur imposed after 1945 sits uneasily upon the authoritarian bureaucratic-industrial core of the Meiji state and the "power in the guise of culture" that has maintained it.[5] The resulting regime remains peculiarly vulnerable; much in this seemingly placid and pacifist society eerily resembles preconditions of the National Socialist dictatorship in Germany. Both countries possessed, and Japan still has, a deeply nativist traditional culture commandeered by nineteenth-century nationalist intellectuals and spread to the masses through the same universal schooling that underpinned economic success. Both developed in the nineteenth century a tradition of nationalist self-pity stemming from weakness in the face of more developed societies, and in part exorcized bloodily—or in Japan's case not exorcized at all—in the twentieth.

Despite a 1941–45 defeat only a hair less total than that of Germany, consensus reigns in Japan that while war is perhaps deplorable, Japan was victim rather than perpetrator of the Pacific War.[6] Myths of the alleged uniqueness of the Japanese brain and of Jewish world-conspiracies intersect with immense technological-industrial power, growing scientific sophistication, the persistence of much of the bureaucratic machinery that once blindly propelled state and people toward conquest, and slowly increasing prominence for Japan's "self-defense forces." And the system itself—as before 1945—lacks a center, an identifiable and accountable political leadership and a legitimacy based on principles rather than success.[7] Any sharp check to economic expansion and national self-esteem may well destroy "Weimar Japan" and with it peace in Asia and the world. And across Japan's sea, similarly fierce feelings of national victimization, mostly at Japanese hands, have marked the societies of the two Koreas, of which one has a modern industrial economy and the other a disproportionately large army, ballistic missiles, and (despite disclaimers breathlessly ratified by the United States) probably rudimentary nuclear weapons as well.

The Russia emerging from the ruins of the Soviet Empire bears a historical burden as heavy as anything afflicting China or Japan. Despotic rule from the Mongols to the tsars, the absence of a middle class before the mid-nineteenth century and after 1917–21, the immense weight of a peasantry that made up three-quarters of the population well into the twentieth century, a quarter century of messianic autocracy, terror, and mass murder under Stalin, and almost forty years of "failed totalitarianism" thereafter molded a society with strong antidemocratic and anticapitalist instincts. Key institutions from the old regime, above all the KGB, army, strategic forces, and military-industry, have retained much of their power. Crime, formerly the domain of the state, has been privatized; the resulting breakdown of social order, inevitably given Russia's past, has renewed popular yearning for a ruler with an iron hand. Nationalist prophets have railed at alleged Western and Jewish responsibility for the collapse of the empire and have demanded forceful measures to tame the 27 million non-Russians within Russia and to rescue the 26 million Russians marooned in the new states on Russia's periphery. The prospects for lasting democracy and peaceful external behavior in Russia seem notably poorer than those (retrospectively) of Weimar Germany, which post-1991 Russia, like post-1945 Japan, resembles in its emergence from imperial collapse, in its structure as a composite of new elements and powerful old-regime institutions, and in its underlying anti-Western inclinations.

The Western European democracies survived the crises of the Cold War era. Yet even they have suffered and continue to suffer from dangerous weaknesses. Their traumatic passage through the "Second Thirty Years' War" of 1914–45, their apparent rescue by the United States in 1944–49, and the chastening of Britain and France at Suez in 1956 imposed on their liberal-democratic governing classes an apparently lasting loss of external self-confidence. Britain and France, as ex-colonial and nuclear powers, have sporadically roused themselves to defend by force their own narrowly conceived interests, from Chad and the Falkland Islands to the Second Gulf War of 1991. Yet when broader and less concrete but no less vital Western interests have been at stake, even Europe's fighting military powers have often quailed, sought refuge behind the fig leaf of "humanitarian intervention," or displayed barely disguised nationalist resentment directed at the United States.[8] On issues ranging from the survival of the Jewish state in 1973 to the punishment of Libyan-sponsored terrorism in the 1980s to the creation of an effective Balkan balance of power in the early 1990s, the Germans and the lesser powers, for their part, have paraded a pacifism as virtuous in theory as it was strategically evasive in practice.[9] Only small right-nationalist minorities have remained outside this pseudo-pacifist consensus, but the wars they prefer are wars against rather than for the interests of the democratic West.

Internal fragility, despite—or because of—fifty years of relative peace, is a widespread complement to Western Europe's external diffidence. High levels of structural unemployment, political fragmentation except in Britain and Germany (where the electoral systems repress or discourage it), a stunting of political leadership, the culturally and politically corrosive effects of intensifying exposure to television, and boredom—a powerful though much-neglected force—have weakened and may yet destroy an internal order resting on prosperity as much as on deeply felt democratic principles. And since the oil shocks of the mid-1970s, prosperity has become ever more seemingly precarious and ever more dependent on forces and conditions outside Europe itself.

Finally, the remaining superpower, the United States, has also fallen on hard times. Two principal inherited disabilities have long hampered it in the world leadership role thrust upon it in 1941–45: radical unfamiliarity with and lack of curiosity about the languages, cultures, and politics of the outside world, and a guileless moralism and legalism in its public discourse about—although not necessarily its practice of—international politics. It has in addition suffered since the 1960s from a growing crisis of culture, values, social cohesion, economic effectiveness, and governance. In the international arena the two principal results of that crisis have been discontinuity and disarray in policies and leadership, except to some extent during the Reagan years, and a failure to keep pace in relative terms with the explosive economic growth of Japan and East Asia. Despite the long-proven resilience of the United States' institutions, internal crisis may ultimately endanger democratic government as well.

The World of Sovereign States

However powerful their internal driving forces, the world's societies and cultures also interact continuously with the outside world—the system of sovereign states. Like its predecessors stretching back to the ancient Middle East and the warring states of the Greeks, the twentieth-century state system has shown a staying power and consistency at least as great as those of the characteristics of the units within it. It has expanded its membership radically over the century; a flock of new states in Eastern Europe and the Middle East joined it after World War I, and after 1945 membership in the charmed circle of sovereign states swelled even more dramatically, from the fifty-one founders of the United Nations in 1945 to the 180-odd members of the early 1990s. Yet this inflation in numbers has concealed a degree of continuity in great power status that is remarkable, given the convulsions of the century. By the end of the Cold War era only one of the seven great powers of 1900—Austria-Hungary—had vanished; two, Britain and France, had sunk to a second-class status imposed by economic and demographic relative decline; and four, Russia, Germany, the United States, and Japan, remained powerful, although only the United States and perhaps Russia were still great powers defined by military might.

Neither the defeat of Germany and Japan in 1945 nor the advent of nuclear weapons fundamentally changed the nature of international politics, despite fearful or hopeful claims that the "absolute weapon" had revolutionized or would revolutionize statecraft. Power has remained the central element of international politics. Arms, alliances, and the "perpetual quadrille of the Balance of Power," not strategically illusory notions such as collective security, remain the system's central elements.[10] Fear and ambition remain the dominant motive forces of states, the "cold monsters" (in de Gaulle's trenchant phrase) that inhabit the international arena. Force, whether threatened or employed, has remained—from the Berlin crisis of 1948–49 to the Second Gulf War of 1991—not merely the ultima ratio but a normal tool of statecraft for the great powers.

In 1944–45 and after, the Soviet autocracy stepped by force into the shoes of its former partner in Eastern Europe, National Socialist Germany. Stalin, however cautious, had in his long career frequently betrayed a messianic ambition. In the 1920s he had envisaged replacing "capitalist encirclement" with a ring of satellites. He had helped overthrow the European balance of power in 1939–40 in quasi-alliance with Hitler, while apparently looking forward to a final confrontation with the United States. In 1950, after patiently preparing North Korea's forces, he gave the green light to Kim Il Sung's attack on South Korea. And in January 1951 he directed his satellite leaders—after MacArthur's catastrophe on the roads to the Yalu had suggested irremediable U.S. weakness—to prepare for an all-out attack on Western Europe to be launched within the following three to four years.[11]

The vehemence with which his successors of the 1960s and 1970s marshaled their westward-facing tank armies and SS-20s and the interest that Moscow's "Marxist theoreticians" showed in war with China in 1969 scarcely testified to any weakening of the will to power.[12] That will, and the even more frenetic urge driving Stalin's former partner, National Socialist Germany, has served as a standing affront to the Western "neo-realist" theorists of international politics who have insisted that the state system's Hobbesian-anarchic character make the quest for mere security the overriding concern of *all* states equally.

Yet will alone was not enough to ensure Soviet triumph. Like the similar ambitions of Imperial Germany and its National Socialist successor, Soviet ambitions ultimately provoked U.S. counteraction. After Stalin's miscalculation in Korea the United States again acquired an army capable of fighting a great war in Europe. The global quasi hegemony of the naval, air, and economic power of the United States countered Soviet quasi hegemony in Eurasia. To describe the resulting Cold War era as "bipolar" was and remains misleading. The mismatch in relative power and global reach rendered bipolarity fortunately "imperfect," and thus relatively stable.[13] The power challenging the system remained, despite its ever-increasing armaments, too weak to risk force against the central interests of the United States, of its European and Japanese allies, and of the West's newfound ally in Beijing. The system of sovereign states survived the Soviet attempt at universal domination as it had the earlier challenges from Imperial Germany, Revolutionary and Napoleonic France, and Imperial Spain. And the world economy coterminous with the international system, after the crises of the Thirty Years' War of 1914–45, recovered with a swift and unprecedented expansion, unbroken until 1973, that underwrote the world political and military balance of power throughout the Cold War era.

The post–Cold War state system has yet to reach the blissful new equilibrium widely foretold as the Berlin Wall fell in 1989. In the projections of the optimists, a continuing global economic revolution will soon complete a process purportedly begun in the early decades of industrialization: the replacement of a world of warring sovereign states by a pacific global economy. "Trading states," multinational corporations, international financial agencies, the inexorable growth of mass communications, ever-increasing economic interdependence, and transnational demographic and ecological forces have ostensibly abolished the economic autonomy of the nation-state, have increasingly undermined its freedom in both foreign and domestic policy, and ultimately threaten its extinction.[14]

Few signs of that extinction are visible. The Second Gulf War of 1991, whatever else it may have proved, demonstrated beyond doubt the continuing centrality of force not merely to relations between states and societies, but to the global economy itself. As the critics suggested—thereby destroying their case for redoubled appeasement of Saddam Hussein and others like him—the war was indeed about control of oil. It was a war to preserve— among other things—the stability of the world market from the unpredictable *economic* consequences of ceding that control to a totalitarian, terrorist state. And despite Western failure of nerve in defining aims that would convert military decision into abiding political victory, the war accomplished its overriding immediate purpose handily at relatively low human cost to the Western attackers.

The warring peoples of former Yugoslavia, the mutual hostility between most of the remaining tribes of East-Central Europe and the Balkans, and the mortal quarrels that ring the newly assertive Russian republic likewise suggest no slackening of the will to affirm national sovereignty and to oppress one's neighbors in its name. The movement for European unity, a prize exhibit of those claiming obsolescence for the nation-state, appears stalled by the very national peculiarities and antagonisms that are supposed to be disappearing. Neither the contradiction between deepening the unity of the core members and broadening the European Union into Scandinavia and East-Central Europe, nor that between the economic centrality of Germany and its military reticence ("for obvious historical reasons," as German spokesmen obliquely put it), nor those between the traditional and highly individual foreign policies of Germany, France, and Britain, seems likely to disappear soon. It could scarcely be otherwise given that the states of Europe have pursued economic integration out of national interest, not supranational ideology.[15] And were the European Union actually to develop as touted by its enthusiasts, it would simply become a European superpower under German leadership, a German-European nation-state.

In yet another respect the international system has behaved in ways that suggest that little in its underlying mechanisms has changed. The cohesion of the West, especially the vital tie between Western Europe and the United States, has swiftly frayed with the disappearance of the Soviet common enemy. Only Russian nationalist outbursts and united Germany's reemergence as an aspirant great power, "contained" within the European Union for now but secretly feared by its neighbors, have reminded those neighbors of their continued need of the United States. But if Germany, despite its habit of sudden self-assertive lurches, remains democratic and—in its own national interest—"European," then Europe's need of the United States is likely to decline further, and European rejection of U.S. leadership is likely to grow. That development will bring with it the danger of fatal Western indecision in the face of future external challenges.

Even more threatening to the long-term stability of the system than divisions within the West is the gradually declining external power of the United States itself. The dissolution of its Soviet rival and the absence of an immediate great-power threat have led to a perplexity about the United States' world role symbolized by its brief attempt in Somalia to lend its forces to the inept and corrupt United Nations. The continuing inability of the U.S.

political elite, regardless of party, to distinguish between war—the purpose for which armies, navies, and air forces are recruited, organized, equipped, and trained—and international social work, for which such forces are wholly unsuited, gives grounds for foreboding.[16] And regardless of its skill in policy and strategy and even of its continued technological and scientific prowess, the relative economic decline of the United States as East Asia and other areas industrialize further seems certain to continue.

The Forces of Change

The persistence of culture and the durability of the state system suggest that any consideration of the "new strategic environment" must weigh the consequences of the past. But the forces for change that constitute this chapter's third level of analysis are likewise vitally important in determining outcomes. The three greatest forces that remade the West after the mid-eighteenth century, and the world thereafter, were secular ideologies, technology and economic growth, and demography.

Modern mass politics, created in the American and especially the French revolutions, provided the field within which the secular ideologies could develop and prosper. As messianic faiths, they were distinct from and often hostile to the prosaic or seemingly unprincipled practice of democratic or parliamentary government found above all in Britain and the United States. In continental Europe and beyond, they filled the void that had gradually opened in popular and elite loyalties with the slow decay of religion. And social and political democratization strengthened rather than weakened their grip on the popular imagination.

The revolution in Paris drove out or killed monarch and nobles. That apparent example of revolutionary class struggle, the new inequalities between factory master and factory hand in the Manchester and Birmingham of the early Industrial Revolution, and Marx's Hegelian determinism then combined to create the secular religion of class. In its long career from Marx's worktable in the British Museum reading room to the regimes of Stalin, Mao, Ho Chi Minh, Kim Il Sung, and Pol Pot, it showed remarkable power for mobilizing Western intellectuals and non-Western masses. Yet its greatest successes in creating parties and states resulted from alliances with the far greater force of nationalism.

That force took practical shape in the international arena after 1789, when the French, by the same blows against aristocracy and monarchy that established the myth of class struggle, also created the *nation* of equal citizens. French ideological fervor and the career open to talent in war ultimately conquered much of Europe. That compelled all others, especially France's German neighbors, to follow. Their nationalism developed as a reaction against French culture and conquest, and by the first decades of the nineteenth century that reaction had formed a body of ideas of unique explosive potential, a compound of anti-Western resentment and quasi-racist ancestor worship. By 1848–49 German ideas and German expansionist ambitions had galvanized Poles and Czechs in fear and emulation, and set the example for would-be nations to the east and south.[17]

Nationalism, despite an intellectual pedigree stretching far back into the Middle Ages, was in politics almost entirely new.[18] Before the 1790s, Europeans had killed each other and outsiders for the power of their overlords or for the greater glory of God, but rarely—or rarely primarily—over language and ethnic allegiance. Now these became a matter of life and death.[19] The ideal-typical core of the nationalist faith consisted of three essential and interrelated propositions. First, according to nationalist intellectuals, humanity was divided into quasi-biological *segments* by blood—as evidenced, in general, by language and culture. Second came a "theory of political legitimacy" that dictated that every people, every *Volk*, should or must have their state; in the natural order of the world, blood, culture, and borders coincided.[20] And if they did not, then they must be made to do so. Finally, nationalist ideologues proclaimed that individual self-realization and personal freedom were only possible through total devotion to the *Volk* and its state.[21] This was from its origins, and has remained, a system of belief that by its inner logic, and like its Marxist analogue, drives its adherents inexorably toward genocide.[22] Only religious, cultural, and intellectual forces that preempt, override, or weaken belief in the ethnic-cultural segmentation of the species can deflect nationalist peoples and states from the extermination of their neighbors.

In Britain, the United States, and even France, political, cultural, and religious restraints were strong enough to prevent the development of nationalist doctrines with much coherence and staying power, although these restraints were usually too weak to inhibit violence directed at peoples deemed ethnically or racially inferior. Among the "Anglo-Saxons," ethnic heterogeneity and the Lockean preoccupation with the "pursuit of happiness"—"possessive individualism" to its detractors—undermined calls for loyalty based on blood and sapped the nation-state's claim to monopolize individual self-fulfillment. In France, the notion of 1789 that individuals had rights, however frequently and cheerfully ignored in practice both internally and in France's foreign conquests, fulfilled a similar braking function, as did the failure of French racialists to define the French convincingly as a race.

And in Italy and Russia, the salience or predominance of illiterate peasantries opposed an almost impenetrable barrier to the "nationalization of the masses" in the nineteenth and early twentieth centuries.

But in Germany no such obstacles existed, and its history from the nineteenth century to 1945 was one long demonstration of the absence of built-in limits to nationalism's destructiveness, even—or especially—in those highly developed societies often considered the embodiment of "progress." Despite its late start, Germany surpassed Britain, the first industrial nation, in total industrial power soon after 1900. Its population had by that point, despite large Polish, French, and Danish national minorities, achieved a literacy rate approaching 99 percent *in German*. The Prussian Protestant population that formed the core of the empire created in 1871 had acquired a consciousness of national uniqueness and power through the proselytizing of its nationalist historians, pastors, and poets, and the battlefield prowess of its army. And long before the advent of Darwin in the early 1860s, German Protestant intellectuals had irrevocably defined the national essence in quasi-racialist terms: what was German was that which was not Jewish. And blood—not religion or culture—defined that which was Jewish.[23]

German nationalism's road led to a Thirty Years' War that culminated in a genocide unique even in a century unparalleled for frequency and magnitude of mass murder. Western European and Anglo-Saxon commentators, bemused by the apparent incompatibility of German *Bildung* and German barbarism, usually failed to see their obvious connection.[24] But it was precisely the exemplary thoroughness with which the Prussian and German schoolmaster had done his duty and the very modernity of Germany that helped make possible the wide diffusion of and fanatical devotion to the "National Socialist Idea" impelling the German regime and masses to conquer and murder.[25] And it was the wide diffusion of knowledge and expertise in German society that also gave resonance to the most powerful of Hitler's social appeals, the "career open to talent." Nazi and *Wehrmacht* careerism, the explosive personal as well as national ambitions that the regime had unleashed, gave its troops the élan that crushed France and almost destroyed the Soviet Union. Thereafter, the fanatical belief in German superiority inculcated by the educational system and *Hitler Jugend*, along with a measure of terror, guaranteed resistance of unparalleled fierceness to the bitter end.

What the German example (and the contrast between German industrialized fanaticism and the lesser commitment to war and conquest of Mussolini's partly peasant followers) suggests is that the spread of literacy and the processes of social democratization that are still under way may encourage rather than inhibit nationalist extremism, even in relatively "advanced" societies: the more democracy, the more nationalism. That was a sobering lesson already implicit in the French revolutionary experience; France's breakthrough to equality generated violence, both internal and external, on a scale hitherto unparalleled in Western Europe. Far from bringing peace, the democratic emancipation of previously subordinate social groups and the triumph of national "high cultures"[26] over regional and local loyalties actually permit a mobilization of hatred against outsiders far more organized, widespread, and efficient than possible in earlier ages. All that is needed, as the German case suggests, is a national mythology of sufficient potency and a political leadership with the belief and will to transmute that mythology into military-bureaucratic-industrial reality.

Nor is the force of nationalism necessarily spent even in its former core areas in Western and Central Europe. Germany indeed reemerged after 1945 divided and impotent. A defeat demonstrably more total than that of 1918 radically altered its political culture, while its crimes and those of its Soviet partner and foe had redrawn the ethnic map of East-Central Europe to eliminate some of the many irredenta upon which lesser nationalisms had fattened. Yet far more important in imposing limits upon Europe's nationalisms than the fact of defeat were two factors that were contingent rather than permanent in their operation. The first was political and strategic. Hitler had for the moment destroyed or radically weakened Europe's traditional powers, including his own, and deprived Europe's nationalisms of plausible great-power vehicles. The U.S.–Soviet Cold War that filled the vacuum he had created froze Europe's nationalisms in place. The second underlying factor was the immense prosperity of the postwar era, which for a time replaced with private satisfactions the collective enthusiasms that Europe's muzzled and leashed nationalisms could no longer provide, and legitimated Western Europe's parliamentary regimes.

But neither the muzzling of nationalism nor the effects of prosperity were inevitable consequences of the order of things. It was the unprecedented and perhaps temporary European and world engagement of the United States that kept the most powerful fragment of Germany anchored in the pacific West, imperfectly remade Imperial Japan, and underwrote the swift economic revival of Western Europe and the unprecedented broadening and deepening of the world market from the late 1940s to the 1990s. Soviet power likewise kept Germany divided and the lesser nationalisms of East-Central Europe from one another's throats; the Warsaw Pact was indeed a WARPACT on its westward face, but on its own turf it served as a crude successor to the Hapsburg order.[27] Yet unlike the power of the Hapsburgs, Soviet power rested squarely on ideological terror. And once Stalin's pygmy successors showed that they lacked his messianic will to use that terror, the system Stalin had built was doomed.

The slow decomposition of the Marxist-Leninist religion of class from 1953 until its final collapse in the 1980s left a power vacuum in the arena of global ideological conflict resembling the void left by Soviet collapse in the state system. In the West, lesser ideologies—founded like Marxism and nationalism on the moral superiority and historic mission of allegedly oppressed groups—have momentarily taken over Marxism's role as vehicle for the hatred of intellectuals for Western society. But in Eastern Europe it has been the real thing, historic nationalism itself, that has profited most from the vacuum.

From Kaliningrad/Königsberg and the supposedly eternal German-Polish border in the north, to the ethnic-religious mutual slaughter in former Yugoslavia in the south, to the Crimea, the Caucasus, ex-Soviet Central Asia, and the non-Russians within Russia itself, irredenta new and old fester. The collapse of the Soviet system has intensified rather than ended the socioeconomic crisis that helped destroy that system and has created wide audiences for nationalist prophets and causes along Russia's periphery. Ex-Communist rulers from Russia to Serbia, Croatia, and Romania have exploited the post-1989 outpouring of national fanaticism to legitimate their own power. That outpouring, like the barely contained mortal enmity between the Greek and Turkish republics, has also threatened the cherished claim of the optimists that liberal parliamentary regimes do not go to war with one another. The occasional and far from resolved conflicts over the fate of Pakistan and over weapons proliferation between the United States and the paramount power in South Asia, democratic India, likewise suggest that nationalism may again disprove the optimists' equation of government "by the people" with perpetual peace.[28]

In the societies of East Asia, which of all those in the non-Western world most resemble the Western nation-state model, nationalism likewise appears to be growing in force. To reach the extremes achieved in Western and Central Europe before 1945, it requires a society sufficiently literate—or sufficiently exposed to television—that national myths can be forcefully inculcated. China, preceded by smaller states such as South Korea, has now crossed that threshold.

Nationalism's one remaining competitor in the international arena is not the presumed ideological concomitant of the optimists' "borderless world," internationalism. That ambiguous notion has so far failed the most elementary tests of a political faith, numbers and commitment; its adherents are confined to the Volvo-driving classes and are rarely willing to die for their beliefs. Nationalism's principal ideological challenger is instead religion, or rather the youngest and most militant of the great world religions, Islam. The failure, from the sixties to the nineties, of Middle Eastern "secular" regimes to deliver prosperity, the destruction of the Jews, and the defeat and humiliation of the West has opened the road for antiregime, anti-Jewish, and anti-Western religious fanaticism as an alternative to Arab state-loyalty. Political movements pledged to the creation of "Islamic states" throughout the Middle East and North Africa have maintained their momentum despite the best and most savage efforts of secret police forces and armies in states such as Egypt and Algeria. Further democratization of these societies—as in France after 1789 and Eastern Europe after 1989–91—seems almost certain to increase rather than decrease extremism and external violence, on the pattern of the "Islamic Republic of Iran."

Islam's Middle Eastern and South Asian borders have also long since proved themselves as a source of interstate and terrorist conflict. The massive brutality that erupted after 1990 along the Balkan boundaries established by Ottoman conquest in the fifteenth century has given concrete political shape to the long-standing mortal hostility between Islam—the Bosnian and Albanian Muslims—and the Orthodox Slavs. The "Christian" West's inability or unwillingness to intervene effectively, to shed blood to protect Muslims, has inevitably further poisoned Islamic opinion against the West. And the multiple religious-ethnic conflicts of the Caucasus and ex-Soviet Central Asia have yet to reach their full potential strength.

Despite the Islamic world's fragmentation into states and tribes and sects, Islam may also eventually serve as the foundation for an imperial ideology for generalized revolt against the West. For far more likely than the world unity proclaimed by the optimists is the coalescence of regional units, based on cultural and religious affinities—for which Islam offers the most potentially powerful basis.[29] And like Marxism's symbiotic relationship with nationalism, Islam in the Middle East may also ultimately intertwine with a genuine and effective pan-Arab nationalism, locked in war or cold war with the West across the Mediterranean and with the Persian Shia across the Tigris and Euphrates.

Yet ideology is only one of the powerful disruptive forces that have shaped the recent past. The permanent revolution of technology and economic growth has given to nationalist (and communist) extremism ever newer and more powerful weapons. Machines and economic growth have multiplied manyfold the disparity in power between societies that have industrialized and those that have so far failed. They have also eroded—by progressively abolishing time and distance—preexisting barriers to surprise attack and have undermined the claim of the defensive to be the "stronger form of war."[30] In 1914, except for a few pessimists, both attackers and attacked expected to be home by autumn. The peculiar 1914–17 balance between the technologies of transport and those of destruction, and between the economic weight and geographic position of the opposing alliances, froze both fronts and opposing fleets in place. But by 1939 the technologies of transport had won: the internal combustion engine and electronics had restored swift movement to land and sea warfare alike. The result was *Barbarossa* and Pearl Harbor. Thereafter, still newer technologies perfected the machine age's potential for strategic surprise: the marriage of the German ballistic missile and the American nuclear bomb.

Far from exerting the pacifying effect sometimes ascribed to it, the bomb initially provoked pacifists such as Bertrand Russell to demand its immediate use on the Kremlin. Then its acquisition by the Soviets and its perfection in the form of thermonuclear devices capable of destroying much of humanity led to provisional stalemate that reinforced the rough Cold War balance between Soviet land-power in Eurasia and U.S. sea and air power around its fringes. The prematurely christened absolute weapon, once wedded to the ballistic missile, was a weapon against which no defense existed. It could thus with a certainty hitherto unimaginable guarantee reciprocal damage disproportionate to virtually any political objective.

Possession of the bomb generated abiding—and continuing—efforts to make destruction less certain and thus make war more possible through the creation of a defense. Remaining intangibles—the numbers and size and accuracy and responsiveness and survivability of delivery systems and the survivability and effectiveness of surveillance and targeting and command systems—generated intense competition. At the newly renamed level of "conventional" warfare, the stalemate imposed by the bomb and by U.S. global air and sea power partially neutralized Soviet tank army superiority. The European wars the Soviet Union might have launched ultimately migrated to the periphery, to Korea and Indochina and the turbulent frontiers of Brezhnev's second Soviet empire.

Further revolutionary technologies—those of cryptography, imaging, lasers, electronic reconnaissance, miniaturization, and data processing—slowly began to return to the defensive some of the advantages it enjoyed in earlier centuries. But those advantages have not yet been great enough to offset the offensive threat of nuclear surprise attack with ballistic missiles. And the "conventional" offensive at least partially kept pace, thanks to electronic countermeasures, radar-defeating aircraft geometry and materials, advanced inertial guidance and satellite navigation, and cruise missile propulsion and airframe breakthroughs. The new defensive advantages in conventional warfare have accrued only to states with an advanced military-industrial base—in practice, during the Cold War era, only the United States, favored allies, and in part the Soviet Union. For states without satellite imaging, signals intelligence, or the latest radars, the new technologies meant a further confirmation of inferiority in all-out war, for they partially neutralized the weight of numbers, the greatest asset of would-be great powers in the non-Western world.

But technological change has also imposed great and continuing checks on the greatest powers. Seemingly ever-growing Western superiority in the new technologies and in the science that underpinned them contributed to the terminal demoralization of the Soviet ideological and military elites, just as new techniques of communication, from worldwide satellite television to the lowly facsimile machine, rendered porous the hard shells of many of the totalitarian states. But the ten- or twentyfold leap in intensity and breadth of worldwide communications from the 1960s to the 1990s has also had consequences for the Western powers and for their relations with non-Western societies, as has the gradual seepage of advanced technologies outward from their Western countries of origin.

Global competition between Western television networks for instantaneous news has given and will increasingly give new openings for attack to forces deeply hostile to the West. The explosion of terrorist violence from the late 1960s through the 1990s was predominantly *violence for media effect*—effect on and through the Western media. The lure of immediate worldwide coverage encouraged myriad groups with real or imagined grievances, from the Palestinians to Moluccans and Croats and Armenians and Islamic extremists, to attack targets or take hostages in the West. In some cases the terrorists publicly announced that publicity was their goal: "We saw Arafat at the UN. He was succeeding, and no one even knew about us," said the Moluccans who hijacked a Dutch train in 1975 and killed a civilian hostage for the cameras. In other cases that aim was merely implicit. And the television networks vied with one another for exclusive coverage that magnified terrorist achievements, mightily increased their renown, and—because the U.S. media were the most fiercely competitive and all-pervasive—maximized the temptation to target U.S. citizens. Fraudulent protestations of devotion to the public's right to know masked the ceaseless quest for the video scoop well described in the breathless commentary of a *Washington Post* "media critic": "ABC news scored the most sensational journalistic coup of the six-day [1985] hostage crisis: exclusive videotaped interviews with the pilot and two of his crew aboard hijacked TWA flight 847 as it sat on the Beirut airport runway."[31] Soviet collapse dampened terrorist activity by removing the most important paymaster and supporter of anti-Western attacks, but the temptation to use television as guerrilla theater in the literal sense will remain strong.

Terrorist groups have not been the only adepts at the manipulation of opinion in open societies through those societies' media. Governments have taken and will continue to take a hand; television has given the Potemkin villages that earlier dictatorships showed to selected visitors a new mass audience. Despite rivalry from powers such as Iran and Iraq, the rulers in Hanoi have so far proved the undisputed masters of the genre. Perhaps recognizing that their own dour countenances made for less effective video than the earnest and beguiling faces of sympathetic Western actresses, they made masterful use of surrogates who could project a public image of friendliness and flexibility to "the American people" as opposed to that people's allegedly evil and unrepresentative government.

The Ayatollah Khomeini likewise made effective use of Western television in consolidating his own rule through the U.S. embassy hostage crisis, in striking down the "Great Satan's" political leadership in the 1980 election, and in spreading the gospel of Islamic world revolution. And despite a degree of obtuseness bordering on pathology in his dealings with foreign powers, Saddam Hussein nevertheless used CNN, through the exclusive live coverage from Baghdad that he conceded, as a highly successful conduit for his propaganda throughout the Second Gulf War.

In all these efforts, the nature of the medium itself and the attitudes of its journalistic masters have played and will continue to play a powerful supporting role. Television's unique ability to command emotion through images and symbols, shocking immediacy, and built-in selectivity of presentation make it the most perfect instrument yet devised for the political manipulation of mass audiences. The wartime images of the death and devastation that it can convey, even when not deliberately selected for propaganda effect, are often powerful enough to sap the confidence in victory and conviction of righteousness of viewers in advanced countries. The death, devastation, and further decades of tyranny that may result from *enemy* victory are of course never on view—either in advance or when they come to pass. And the built-in hostility to one's own government, the conviction of moral superiority even to democratically elected officials that by the mid-1970s had become the most salient characteristic of the U.S. media, has smoothed the path of totalitarian media handlers from Hanoi to Baghdad.

The penetration of Western media into the non-Western world, whether by direct broadcast or by videotape, has also had powerful and ever-intensifying consequences. It has combined in psychologically devastating fashion three powerful forces. The first is the so-called "demonstration effect," the generation of burning feelings of inferiority, envy, and hatred by televised visions of Western opulence, well-being, and power. The second, which interacts with and often reinforces the first, is the high visibility given to all-pervasive violations of powerful non-Western religious, sexual, and cultural taboos—especially those of the Islamic world. Finally, the Western habit of sometimes obsessive self-criticism, when viewed (literally, thanks to television) by societies where criticism has neither moral standing nor legal protection, has generated astonished contempt and furnished endless raw material for the construction of anti-Western polemics and conspiracy theories.[32] The result of these forces has been a worldwide nationalist and cultural-religious reaction that has generated entirely new pressures on the West and within it, for many Western intellectuals have long argued that non-Western enmity is a natural consequence of and fitting recompense for their own societies' purported historic crimes.

Videotape and satellite television have scarcely been the advanced economies' only exports to the wider world. Like the rum and Bibles of an earlier era, they too have arrived in the company of arms. The Cold War impelled the superpowers and their allies to compete in weapons "aid" and trade targeted to bolster allies and clients and undermine enemies or friends of enemies. But superpower competition was merely one source of the marked international democratization of the means of mass destruction from the seventies to the nineties. It was above all the inexorable and seemingly natural processes of foreign trade, the very "globalization" of commerce hailed by optimists as the precursor of eternal peace, that led a West German chemical firm to supply a nerve gas plant to Muammar Qaddafi, Dutch concerns to sell high-speed uranium-separation centrifuges to Saddam Hussein, a French aerospace combine to celebrate in its advertisements the combat testing of its antiship missile by Argentina against the ships of a close French ally, or Italian exporters to flood the world market with cheap, largely undetectable, and exceedingly nasty plastic antipersonnel mines. The denials, evasions, and excuses of Western governments and firms, when challenged, have been only slightly less impudent than the fierce opposition from commercial interests and foreign trade bureaucracies to even the feeble and inadequate restrictions that the West under U.S. leadership placed for a time on sales to the Soviets, their satellites, and their clients.

The end of the Cold War, contrary to the anticipations of the optimists, has brought little respite. Quite the contrary: Soviet collapse has opened a rolling bankruptcy sale in which everything from top-of-the-line Soviet/Russian armor and aircraft to nuclear reactors and know-how tempts eager clients from Algeria to Iran and China.[33] And cutbacks in U.S. arms sales to friends and clients has in no way inhibited other states, from Britain and France to Chile, Brazil, and Israel, from entering the market or seeking to expand their share. Two of the three remaining Asian Leninist despotisms, North Korea and China, have combined in their prolific arms exports the pursuit both of foreign exchange and of strategic advantage. Every missile or strategic weapon or component exported to Libya, Syria, or Iran compounds Western or Israeli difficulties and undermines the global quasi hegemony of the United States. China's export of missiles and nuclear know-how to Pakistan has likewise served the eminently strategic goal of bolstering a mortal enemy of India, China's principal rival along with Japan for paramountcy in Asia.

The overall Western advantage in total war may nevertheless have increased since 1945. The high-technology arms of the 1980s and 1990s—at least when employed in deserts against militarily and politically incompetent adversaries—have so far more than offset the international democratization of weapons of mass destruction fostered by international trade. But in "peacetime," or even in times of confrontation, technologies of mass destruction that will soon include the products of the molecular biology revolution offer even weak states means never before available to strike great power adversaries at the heart, in their own capitals and homelands.

Except in the unlikely event that the industrial democracies entrust their security to the goodwill of powers such as Libya, Iran, Iraq, North Korea, and China, the result of new forms of offense reaching the hands of aspiring non-Western powers will in all likelihood be renewed Western emphasis on defensive systems. Even the absolute weapon runs the long-term risk of a loss of status—except when delivered anonymously by suitcase or truck rather than missile. And the new high-technology and high-precision "conventional" offensive weapons linked to global sensor and navigation systems may make possible entirely new forms of preemption, retaliation, and punishment that partially neutralize the nuclear, chemical, and biological weapons in the hands of smaller powers. The new high-precision offensive systems are also wielded by increasingly small groups of supremely expert professionals, rather than the mass armies of citizen-soldiers of the era stretching from 1792 to the 1980s. The advent of a new elite of machine warriors, a tendency certain to be further intensified by the advent of robot combatants, has already visibly diminished post–Vietnam War inhibitions in the United States against using force. The reprofessionalization of war has so far helped widen the post–Cold War divergences between the United States and its European allies, who remain wedded to the old model of warfare. But military high technology may yet lower the barriers to international violence in all Western industrial societies and thus—as with many other factors already mentioned—cause the realm of perpetual peace to recede yet further into the future.

As in the past, the ceaseless and restless processes of economic growth and decay likewise offer additional powerful sources of internal and international instability.[34] Even in the West, where it originated, the seemingly limitless and accelerating economic "progress" unleashed by the industrial revolution massively increased social and political disorder, fostered extreme ideologies, and assisted their breakthrough to power in the first third of the twentieth century. The disruptive effects of growth on non-Western or partially Western societies, from Imperial Japan to Imperial Russia to Pahlavi

Iran, have correspondingly been even more marked. The very processes of economic globalization hailed by the optimists have intensified and will in all probability continue to intensify beyond all previous historical experience the speed and intensity of disruption. That in turn will foster the creation of yet more extremist movements and rogue states.

And even in the developed West, the corrosive effect of growth has not ceased with the achievement of industrial societies in the early to mid-twentieth century. Economic interests and commercial mass media unfettered by any commitment to established values, above all to the democratic civic or constitutional patriotism that still provide the Western industrial powers with much of their cohesion, mock on a daily basis all claims that history has reached or will reach a democratic-capitalist "end."[35]

In the international arena, the economic rise of East Asia and the corresponding relative economic decline of the United States ultimately threaten U.S. global military dominance; in a far shorter term they threaten an end to the already precarious stability of the post-1945 international economic system—and hence of international order. The role of economic hegemony acquired from Britain, refused with catastrophic consequences by the United States in 1917–44, and grudgingly accepted thereafter, now seems once more in doubt. Yet no other power has anything remotely resembling the leadership capacity of the United States at its height, a capacity founded on diverse but mutually reinforcing strengths: economic primacy, military superiority, and the power of democratic capitalist ideas reinforced at least provisionally by material success.

Japan and Europe, the obvious potential successors, are each crippled. Japan's ethnic introversion and fiercely nationalist economics preclude the emergence of anything remotely resembling an idea that might legitimate Japanese leadership of the world market. And were it to develop such an "imperial idea," the lack of accountable leadership and clear-cut decision making within Japan's "stateless society" itself would almost guarantee its continued incapacity to lead others.[36] Europe's limitations seem on first sight less daunting: deep political and economic fractures even between its core powers, economic division into prosperous northwest and lagging south and east, and an apparent slow decline in high technology relative to the United States, Japan, and the small East Asian "tigers." But neither Japan's nor Europe's difficulties seem capable of easy remedy, nor is the increasing power vacuum at the core of the capitalist world economy one that once and future rogue great powers such as Russia and China can hope to fill.

In the short term this growing absence of a world economic hegemony may not matter; perhaps the world market ties of the 1990s are so much thicker than those of the 1920s that the world economy, like the Internet, can hope to expand indefinitely in a state of blissful anarchy. But economic history suggests that repeated and often highly dangerous structural crises punctuate even periods of growth. And the seamless global financial market that the optimists hail seems more rather than less susceptible to sudden catastrophic panic than the old self-contained national economies.

The history of international politics also suggests that power vacuums rarely go unfilled for long. In the absence of a leading power willing and able to guarantee the world market's stability, the likely outcome in the event of global financial panic and economic crisis is the division of the world into mutually hostile blocs—a Japanese "greater East Asia co-prosperity sphere," German-Europe, and the Americas under U.S. hegemony. Economic frictions between the blocs and over their relationships with China and Russia would in all likelihood not remain purely economic for long. And the unresolved ethnic conflicts and potential conflicts ringing Eurasia—from Siberia, poised precariously between China and European Russia, to the South China Sea, South Asia, Arabia and the Gulf, North Africa, and the terrified small powers between NATO and Russia—suggest that the international system of the near-term and medium-term future will be at least as conflict-riven as that of the recent past.

One further and enormously powerful force for conflict between states and societies remains: the press of numbers. European expansion from the fifteenth through the nineteenth centuries was demographic as well as technological, military, and economic. The expansion within Europe of revolutionary France after 1792 was likewise the expression of a demographic exuberance ultimately quelled by 1.8 million French war deaths. But the subsequent demographic contraction, as Europe's new industrial societies matured in the course of the nineteenth century, was both relative and—after the end of the post-1945 baby boom—even absolute, as births in parts of Northern and Western Europe and European Russia fell below replacement rates. The result has been the apparent realization of the worst "yellow peril" nightmares of *fin de siècle* European ideologues and their dictatorial successors. Birthrates in the industrial societies have reached their nadir just as the West's well-meaning donations of insecticides, vaccines, and modern medical technologies have encouraged an almost asymptotic rise in the population of the non-Western world.[37] Demographic analysis, the most predictively accurate of all forms of historical knowledge, suggests that the demographic transition to slower growth in most of the non-Western world will take place between 2030 and 2100. Yet the Western industrial democracies by the early 1990s made up a mere 12.3 percent of world population. Barring the unforeseen, that proportion will fall to 11.4 percent by 2000, 9.1 percent by 2025, and decline even more steeply thereafter.[38] That development suggests the long-term precariousness of Western power, of the role of Western ideas in the wider world, and even of Western survival.

Swift population growth has also massively increased the internal strains in the non-Western world, has intensified pressure on food and water resources, and has generated huge surpluses of unemployed young males, the most turbulent and potentially warlike segment of any population. In some areas, especially sub-Saharan Africa, extreme poverty, environmental and epidemiological catastrophe, lack of social cohesion, and external dependence almost preclude successful aggression except against neighboring states in equally sorry condition. But in the oil-poor states of North Africa and the Middle East, as well as in South and East Asia, growing resource shortages, environmental degradation, and huge surpluses of males between 15 and 25 coincide with state and military structures increasingly capable of using those males in bids to overturn the regional or even global balance of power.

Conclusion: The Horoscope of the Age?

Neither the cultural and political dynamics of the world's major regions and states, nor the unchanged and unforgiving nature of the international system, nor the great driving forces of ideology, technology and economics, and demography suggest that the "new strategic environment" will in the medium term be more benign than in the Cold War era. States and societies with long despotic traditions have not mutated, and seem unlikely to mutate soon, into liberal-capitalist democracies. Their adoption of capitalist economics, whatever its long-term effects, seems most likely in the medium term to create expansionist capitalist-authoritarian powers analogous in domestic character and international consequences to Wilhelmine Germany or interwar Japan. Self-doubt, internal weakness, and relative economic decline will in all likelihood continue to enfeeble the Western industrial democracies.

In the international arena, the state remains the basic political unit. It alone can dispense the "cash payment" of international politics, which— however regrettably—remains force. Claims made for the present or future supremacy of multinational corporations, the global market, or "trading states" increasingly resemble a naive Anglo-Saxon version ("those with the gold make the rules") of the Marxist dogma that economics is the base and all else the superstructure. And the Western solidarity that blocked Soviet expansion and underwrote militarily the post-1945 capitalist world economy has eroded swiftly in the apparent absence of a common enemy.

The principal forces for change retain all the terrifying power revealed between 1914 and 1945. Ideology still inspires messianic movements and crazy states. Self-proclaimed alternatives to Western democratic capitalism exist in "Weimar Japan," elsewhere in East Asia, and in the Islamic world. Communism has crumbled, but its disappearance has created a vacuum filled with nationalist violence. Regional integration on the model of the European Union seems powerless to transform nationalist exclusiveness into the optimists' "borderless world"; either integration will remain primarily economic, or new—nationalist—superstates will result. Religion and culture have gained new salience as powerful sources of conflict.

The globalization of trade, finance, and mass communications, far from establishing perpetual peace, has democratized weapons of mass destruction and inspired fantasies of anti-Western violence. Within states, economic growth continues to inflame social and ethnic fractures, generate messianic beliefs, and help those beliefs to power. Externally, the slow erosion of the United States' relative military power and its far swifter relative economic decline are opening the road for the emergence of rogue great powers that may include "market-Leninist" China, a resentful and racially exclusive Japan, and a resurgent nationalist Russia. Finally, the explosive pressures of demographic growth promise ever-greater internal and international turmoil in the non-Western world, while further diminishing the industrial democracies' already meager share of the human species.

The West's consolations are few. It retains for the moment the preponderance of armed might that served so well in the Cold War. Its economic power and latent strength remain great, if slowly diminishing. The military-technological revolution has provided and seems likely for a time to continue to provide new and powerful methods of deterring, punishing, and defending against attack even by weapons of mass destruction. And as in the past, the West may be able to rely on ideologically inspired enemies to misread its incessant self-criticism and self-doubt as cowardice and to overreach—the fatal error of Hitler, Stalin, and Saddam Hussein. Yet as the end of the twentieth century approaches, the industrial democracies face a prospect increasingly resembling the one Hitler described chillingly in a speech of November 1930 and did his best to realize thereafter:

> To the multitudes who now preach that we are entering an era of peace, I can only say: my dear fellows, you have badly misinterpreted the horoscope of the age, for it points not to peace, but to war as never before.[39]

Chapter 2

American Strategic Policy for an Uncertain Future

Brian R. Sullivan[1]

But all historians . . . have impressed on us that the soundest education and training for a life of active politics is the study of history and
that the surest and indeed the only method of learning how to bear
bravely the vicissitudes of fortune is to recall the calamities of others.
(Polybius, *Histories*, Book I)

In a remarkably short time, the sense of optimism and self-confidence
that permeated America's view of the world and its place in international affairs in the period 1989–91 has largely evaporated. In the space
of two years, the United States had enjoyed a series of remarkable diplomatic
and military victories: the end of the Cold War, major nuclear and conventional arms reduction treaties with the Soviet Union, reunification of Germany within NATO, liberation of Eastern Europe from Soviet domination,
the collapse of Soviet communism, disintegration of the Soviet Union itself,
reinvigoration of the United Nations, settlement of major regional conflicts in
Central America, Southern Africa, the Middle East, and Cambodia, and victory of an American-led coalition over Iraq. But the general feeling of euphoria, symbolized by the victory parades in New York and Washington in
June 1991, had disappeared within a year.[2] Over the next several years, a growing realization that the United States had won the Cold War at the cost of
neglecting deep-seated problems within American society replaced the facile
idea that history had ended with a permanent triumph of American values.

The feelings of gloom, fear, or even rage that afflicted many Americans throughout the 1992 presidential campaign contributed to George Bush's defeat. This popular mood hardly reflected a sense of the decline of America as a world power. Rather, it arose from the painful realization that victory in the Cold War had brought peace unaccompanied by prosperity. This was particularly true for those without the education or talents to succeed in the emerging economy of the 1990s. For them it was not enough, to use Secretary of Defense Richard Cheney's words, that "the peace dividend [was] peace." Even if they could not articulate the idea, it was as if many Americans had expected material rewards in the form of plunder to accompany victory over the Soviets. Instead, the country lay in the grip of the most serious downturn since the Depression. But even the recession's end in the early 1990s failed to bring significant economic improvement to the lives of most. The income of the majority of American workers has remained virtually stagnant or suffered decline since 1973.[3] There were few signs that major improvements lay ahead if Bush's economic policies had continued.

New Directions in American Foreign Policy

In early 1991, Bush had made sound arguments in favor of the United States assuming leadership of what he termed the "new world order."[4] In effect, he advocated the realization of an international, liberal, and democratic vision, similar to those of Woodrow Wilson and Franklin D. Roosevelt. But the election of William Clinton in November 1992, as well as the votes for H. Ross Perot, demonstrated that Americans were more interested in their lot at home than in protecting democracy or furthering self-determination throughout the world.

This did not necessarily equate to a return to isolationism. With remarkably little debate Americans accepted the departing president's December 1992 commitment of an army and a marine division to the United Nations' humanitarian mission in Somalia. Nor did they object to the ongoing protection of the Kurdish enclave in northern Iraq, the stationing of an army battalion in the Sinai, and rotation of sizable air units through Saudi Arabia. In addition, they accepted the new administration's doubling of U.S. forces guarding the northern border of Macedonia in March 1994, military participation in relief operations for Rwandan refugees beginning in April, occupation of Haiti in September, dispatch of major air and ground forces to Kuwait in October, not to mention various blockades and humanitarian operations off, over, around, and inside Bosnia. While understandably concerned about the possibility of a major regional war, Americans still backed Clinton when he considered the use of military forces to resolve the nuclear crisis with North Korea in spring 1994. In early 1995, they appeared willing to accept the stationing of U.S. forces on the Golan Heights if that would facilitate a peace settlement between Israel and Syria.

But Americans did demand withdrawal of their forces from Somalia in October 1993 after the loss of a dozen soldiers in a firefight in Mogadishu and showed little enthusiasm for Clinton's proposals for U.S. involvement in Bosnia. The distinction appears to be that they support the use of their military forces in humanitarian and peace-keeping operations where such operations involve limited expense and few casualties. They were also prepared to suffer major losses to repulse clear threats to American interests. One can define such interests as the prosperity and security of the United States and its allies in Western Europe, the Middle East, East Asia, and the Pacific and the general tranquillity of the Western Hemisphere. But, to employ another well-worn phrase, Americans were refusing to allow the United States to become "the world's policeman." Neither did they seem willing to adopt active measures to prevent incipient problems from expanding to major crises. Instead, as the 1992 and 1994 elections demonstrated, Americans wanted their government to concentrate on domestic economic and political issues.

Traditionally, long-term American foreign and strategic policies have rested on the basis of ad hoc responses to the great international crises that have confronted the United States. The isolationism that characterized American attitudes toward Europe until 1916–17 originated in the policies of Washington, Adams, and Jefferson in reaction to the wars of the French Revolution. America had to avoid wars with great powers until the nation had become a great power itself. Likewise, American internationalism during the Cold War represented President Harry Truman's adaptation of Roosevelt's response to the Nazi, Fascist, and Japanese threats of the late 1930s and early 1940s. Of course, in turn, Roosevelt had adapted to his own purposes Wilson's internationalist policies established to deal with the crises of 1917–19: that, having become a great power, the United States had moral and practical imperatives to defend both its interests and its ideals against threats from other powers, great or small.

Similarly, Bush based his response to the Gulf crisis on the precedents created by Roosevelt and Truman. At the same time, he attempted to build upon his Gulf policies to create the foundation for a post–Cold War strategic policy. But he failed. Rather than the prelude to a new era, the American people appear to have considered Desert Storm the final act in the internationalist era of 1941–91. In part, Bush was at fault for his failure to persuade the American people with his derivative, nostalgic rhetoric. Admittedly, it was not unreasonable for a man of Bush's generation to liken Saddam Hussein to Hitler or to respond to Iraq's aggression against Kuwait with words and actions that the British and French should have used against Hitler's early aggressions.[5] But to recall such precedents in 1991 in order to advocate a "new world order" only suggested plans for a continuation of a past the American people wished finally to escape. While Bush encouraged dreams of a future of hope and freedom, he unintentionally evoked a vision of a United States reshackled to the same old burdens.[6]

The defeat of Iraq, especially when the Soviet Union's collapse followed six months later, seemingly offered Americans what they had longed for after World War II, only to be cheated of by the long years of the Cold War. In 1945 they had not wanted world domination or even world leadership. Now, again, they wanted only to concentrate on matters at home, especially after the disappearance of the Soviet threat. They hardly conceived of an international crisis that would demand their attention. Quite the contrary. And only a great new foreign threat to American well-being seems likely to refocus their attention on strategic issues and foreign policy. Certainly, the American people found altogether uninspiring Clinton's July 1994 advocacy of a policy of "engagement and enlargement."[7]

The Emerging Economic World

Unfortunately for Americans, the current, highly advantageous international situation of the United States in the mid-1990s is unlikely to endure for more than several decades. In fact, thanks to the economic and military influences of modern technology, the balance of world power is shifting at an unprecedented rate in history. As a result, the United States will almost certainly not experience anything like the century of world primacy that Britain enjoyed between its defeat of Napoleon and World War I. It is possible that in as few as twenty years, a new world crisis will burst on the American consciousness due to radical realignments in the international order. This would force Americans to develop a new set of foreign and strategic policies in response. But in 1995 they remain clearly disinterested in considering such hypothetical situations. Instead, they appear determined to focus their attention on domestic affairs while foreign policy drifts in an incoherent compromise between isolationism and internationalism. American unwillingness to allow their government to take preemptive action abroad has been and continues to be one of the great strategic weaknesses of the United States. Meanwhile, the world is changing rapidly.

To understand the speed with which modern rates of economic growth in the 1990s are transforming the international system, one might best consider a comparison between the economic performance of Britain and Germany between 1870 and the outbreak of war in 1914. During that forty-odd-year period, the Germans first astounded, then frightened, Europe by the speed with which they came from behind to match and then exceed Britain's economic power. But during that period, the growth of the German gross national product (GNP) was relatively modest by late twentieth-century standards; it averaged only about 2.8 percent a year. Nonetheless, that growth rate significantly exceeded that of Britain, which averaged only 1.8 percent annually. In other words, while Germany's yearly economic growth exceeded Britain's by approximately one percentage point, the resulting increases compounded year after year. And it was that compounded advantage in economic growth that allowed Germany to become the greatest military power in Europe and simultaneously challenge Britain for superiority at sea early in the twentieth century.[8]

It is easy to understand why the United States surpassed both Germany and Britain as an economic power during that same period; America's GNP grew at an average annual rate of 3.8 percent between 1870 and 1930. Britain suffered so much economic damage from its participation in World War I that its economy had barely recovered to 1914 levels in 1929 just before the collapse of the Great Depression. After recovery from the Depression, the British economy grew at an average rate of barely 2 percent between 1940 and 1990. But the American economy averaged annual growth of 3.2 percent during that same fifty-year period. The difference in the average economic growth rates of the United States and Britain between 1870 and 1990—only about 1.9 percent annually in favor of the United States before World War I and about 1.2 percent in America's favor after 1939—produced dramatic results. In 1870, U.S. per capita income was 15 percent below that of Britain. By 1990, per capita U.S. income surpassed that of Britain by 50 percent. Still, the U.S. rate of growth has lessened. Between 1959 and the present, average annual growth of the American GNP has been slightly over 3 percent.[9] The American economy may enjoy higher growth rates in the future thanks to a boost from information technologies, a sector that the United States presently dominates. But that remains to be seen. For the moment, most economists doubt that American economic performance over coming decades will increase above the levels at which it has performed over the past thirty years.

In striking contrast, China's GNP grew at 13 percent in 1992, 13.4 percent in 1993, and a projected 11.5 percent in 1994. Estimates place China's average annual rate of growth at 8–9 percent between 1978 and 1993 and 10 percent or higher since 1984. The Chinese GNP, already estimated by the Central Intelligence Agency as having surpassed that of Japan in purchasing power, is now about 40 percent of that of the United States and growing rapidly. The United States overtook Britain as an economic power before World War I by growing at an average annual rate approximately 100 percent greater than Britain's in the period 1870–1914. In the 1870–1990 period, the United States enjoyed advantages over Britain of only 1–2 percent in its average annual GNP growth. China, however, has been surpassing the United States' GNP growth rate in the period from 1987 to 1993 by annual rates 5–11 percent higher, that is, by an economic performance superior by some 250 to 450 percent. At continued present rates of economic growth, China's GNP will surpass the United States' by approximately 2005 and reach a size 50 percent larger by the second decade of the twenty-first century.[10] In terms of both speed and scale, Chinese economic growth over the 1980–2010 period could far surpass anything previously witnessed in history.

Of course, nothing guarantees that China will continue to grow at such astonishing rates. The Chinese lack a modern legal system and a respect for property rights that the functioning of an advanced capitalist economy requires. Increasingly, they have had to purchase goods on the international market at world prices. These factors may inhibit the further explosive expansion of their economy. But Chinese economic success during the previous two decades still provides a striking example of the rates of economic growth possible under optimum conditions in the modern world economy. When one considers the recent performance of Singapore, Malaysia, Thailand, Indonesia, South Korea, Taiwan, and Hong Kong, as well as the possibility that the Filipino and Vietnamese economies may reach similar or even higher rates, it becomes clear that Chinese economic growth is not an aberration. Rather, it indicates how quickly East Asia is gaining in economic power, and great economic power often translates into political and military power in the cold world of states.

There are indications, moreover, that Argentina, Chile, Brazil, and Peru may join the ranks of the expanding powers by adopting many of the economic policies of successful East Asian states.[11] If nothing more, in a period of a decade or more, the United States may produce a significantly smaller percentage of the world's wealth than at present; consequently, it would count for considerably less in the international balance of power. Quite possibly, it may also confront political and military challenges to its world primacy from new and unexpected directions.

However rapid and sustained their economic growth, countries like Singapore or Chile are unlikely to pose serious threats to American interests. But countries like China, Indonesia, and Brazil, with their extensive territories, populations, and ample resources, might well present such challenges once their economies reach sufficient size. Meanwhile, other great powers might emerge. In twenty to thirty years' time, the list of other significant powers might include a European confederation, a revitalized Russia, India, and Japan. The restructuring of the Russian and Indian economies in the 1990s could conceivably allow them to grow at sustained annual rates significantly higher than that of the United States for decades to come. While Western Europe's and Japan's economic growth rates will almost certainly be lower, both are already rich enough to offer theoretical challenges to American power. Already, the combined GNP of the fifteen states of the European Union is reaching parity with that of the United States.[12]

There is no certainty that any one of these states (or the European Union) will emerge as a future world power. There is no reason to believe, a priori, that any of these nations would become hostile to the United States and its interests. As difficult to estimate as potential opponents are the causes that might lead hostile relations to develop. Nevertheless, the dynamics of the international system do appear to make such clashes likely. What Thucydides wrote concerning the world of the Greek city-states over two millennia ago has remained a classic text because his observations about power relations among countries reflect basic verities. By their very nature, states seek to expand their power. Stronger states dominate weaker ones and in the process, the interests of the strongest necessarily collide and provoke wars.[13]

Emerging Challenges in the New Century

In the euphoria attendant on the collapse of Soviet communism and the establishment of democracy in many previously authoritarian and totalitarian nations, political scientists have suggested that an era of universal peace might have dawned.[14] They advance the argument that democracies do not fight democracies. That supposed fact, combined with new respect for national self-determination, human rights, and a reinvigorated United Nations, offers some the hope for the prevention of major wars and the rapid settlement of minor ones. Democracy, however, is a system for the regulation of domestic politics. It provides no mechanism for the resolution of international disputes. To insist that the spread of democracy means the spread of peace is reminiscent of the Marxist-Leninist idea that establishment of classless societies would end international conflicts.[15] Such arguments about democracy ignore the wars among the ancient Greek democracies, between the British and Dutch republics in the seventeenth century, between the American and French republics in the 1790s, and between the American republics in the Civil War.

To be sure, many of the nations involved in these conflicts were far from perfect democracies. Mature democracies, such as those in Western Europe and North America, do seem capable of resisting the blandishments of demagogues like Henry Clay or psychopaths like Benito Mussolini. Democracies seem unlikely to go to war with each other without serious cause, but democracy does not alter human nature. It will not suppress avarice, foolishness, ambition, pride, selfishness, or other causes of conflict between groups of human beings.

Recent events in the Balkans, Cyprus, Gaza, the Caucasus, Kurdistan, and Kashmir have also tarnished the hopes invested in universal acknowledgment of the right to national self-determination and in the proper functioning of the United Nations. Self-determination serves well as the foundation for sovereign states where linguistic, ethnic, or geographic boundaries and national identity are clear, such as in Western Europe or East Asia. But experts seem to have forgotten that such distinctions between Germans and French, Italians and Austrians, Thais and Cambodians, and Chinese and Vietnamese were drawn only at the cost of centuries of warfare. Where history has yet to achieve such demarcations, acceptance of the principle of self-determination can actually ignite conflicts, such as those between the Armenians and Azeris, the Russians and Chechens, the Kurds and their Turkish, Arab, and Persian neighbors, or even in such places as Kashmir and East Timor.

When the United Nations has attempted to resolve such disputes, the national interests of the permanent members of the Security Council in protecting or expanding their power at the expense of collective security or regional tranquillity have hampered its efforts. Too often, either too few interests are involved to motivate sustained intervention in the face of human suffering (Somalia, for example) or the presence of such interests divides the permanent members, preventing their cooperation (Bosnia and the Caucasus, for example). Such failures have obscured major successes by the United Nations in Cambodia, Namibia, Mozambique, El Salvador, and elsewhere. But, for all its successes in resolving conflict, the United Nations remains restricted by the will of its members, particularly the permanent members. The latter have repeatedly demonstrated that they will not surrender significant portions of their sovereignty to an international organization. As a result, national interests continue and will continue to determine international relations. Thus, war among the powers, small as well as great, will not disappear as the ultimate arbiter of international disputes. If, as appears likely, China, a European confederation, or another great power challenges the economic and political primacy of the United States, war—even a third world war—may not be an inconceivable result.

This is not to predict that the United States will engage in a conflict of catastrophic proportions some time in the twenty-first century. True, the majority of Americans have indicated that their government should focus on domestic priorities. This will make it difficult for the United States to take the necessary steps to prevent or reduce serious threats to American interests. Both Bush and Clinton have done a poor job of articulating how much American prosperity depends on the security of the United States and its allies. Future American presidents *may* offer more persuasive arguments. Furthermore, there are practical foreign policy initiatives that could lessen the dangers of major war over the next two to three decades. None would require vast expenditures or the diversion of other resources from America's domestic problems.

The United States needs to decide what kind of Europe it wants and the degree to which the majority of Europeans share its wishes and then take action in support of mutual goals. During the Cold War, the United States supported the unification of Europe to strengthen the continent against the Soviet threat. If the reemergence of a Russian threat to Europe seems a danger, then the United States needs to work with its European allies to widen and strengthen the European Union. But a united Europe would roughly equal American strength. If the rise of a European superpower threatens American interests, then the United States should withdraw from NATO and balance itself between Russia and Europe. Alternatively, it might even encourage the emergence of an independent, renationalized Germany. As it is, American policy toward Europe is drifting indecisively. On the one hand, it risks the reemergence of a powerful Russia to threaten a divided Europe, one already abandoned by the United States. Alternatively, it risks Europe's uniting without American support, rejecting the Atlantic connection, and assuming equidistance between Russia and the United States.

If China emerges as a rival early in the twenty-first century, the United States would gain from having India and Japan as allies to balance Chinese power. If no such Chinese threat materializes, it would still benefit the United States to promote India as a force for stability, prosperity, and democracy in South Asia. India presently faces considerable impediments to its development: low levels of public sanitation threaten not only India itself but the world with the danger of epidemics. High birth rates and illiteracy hold India back from realizing its economic and social potential. Tariff barriers, bans on imported consumer goods, large numbers of unprofitable state-owned businesses, and a tangle of government regulations hobble the Indian economy. Finally, residual misunderstandings and hostilities left over from the Cold War mold Indian public opinion against the United States and inhibit economic cooperation between the two countries.[16]

The United States could help India deal with these problems to the mutual benefit of both countries. Washington needs to bring American business leaders and Indian government officials together to discuss how to encourage investment and improve trade. Taking advantage of new local government councils, the United States could initiate relatively inexpensive pilot programs in hygiene, literacy, birth control, and farming, each of which would cost only a few tens of millions of dollars. The United States could also embark on a diplomatic effort to get India and Pakistan to acknowledge their nuclear arsenals, sign the Non-Proliferation Treaty, and clarify their policies on the use of such weapons. This would, hopefully, increase trust, decrease the danger of nuclear war in the region, and create the possibility of further American/Indian security cooperation.

For all its flaws from an American viewpoint, the United Nations remains a useful tool. Indeed, with the collapse of Soviet power, the United Nations has emerged even more as an instrument of American policy than the League of Nations was for Britain and France prior to the Italian-Ethiopian War. But by demonstrating the United Nations' subordination to American leadership, as in the 1990–91 Gulf crisis and Somalia, the United States has reduced the effectiveness of the organization. It hardly serves long-term American interests to demonstrate too blatantly how the United Nations sometimes serves as a mechanism for extending American power.

Furthermore, the United States has also undermined the United Nations' credibility by delaying a necessary and inevitable reorganization of the Security Council. The council continues to include as permanent members only the great powers of 1945. Thus, it cannot guide the world in the twenty-first century with a permanent membership that does not contain Germany, India, China, and Japan while its membership suggests that Britain and France are great powers. Admittedly, reconstitution of the Security Council remains a delicate matter since it raises the question of the right of Britain and France to continue as permanent members. But, if addressed successfully, council reorganization could greatly benefit American interests. After all, the two likeliest new permanent members would be close allies: Germany and Japan.

The above discussion represents only three foreign policy initiatives that could strengthen American national security early in the twenty-first century. Other initiatives might include aiding the Turks to negotiate solutions to their problems in Cyprus and Kurdistan, encouraging development of political and economic independence in the Central Asian republics, facilitating the entry of the Indochinese states into ASEAN, and supporting the continued democratization of South Africa in the post-Mandela years. Many such initiatives would cost little save patience and persistence. But they would also require imagination, flexibility, and, above all, understanding of local conditions. Assisting India to overcome its problems might cost only several hundreds of millions of dollars annually. Unfortunately, given the present antipathy among the American population to any foreign assistance programs and its suspicion of new foreign commitments, it appears unlikely that the United States will attempt any of these courses of action for the foreseeable future—that is, unless successive American presidents display imaginative, strong, and inspiring foreign policy leadership. To limit the influence of isolationist tendencies, America's leaders need to underline repeatedly to their people that their prosperity depends on the security of their trading partners and the expansion of that partnership to include ever-larger numbers of other prosperous, cooperative nations.

If the previous speculations are at all reasonable, then it would also be prudent for the United States to take other precautions to help ensure its national security. As the Romans said, if one wishes peace, then one should prepare for war. That raises the question of U.S. defense spending. Despite the present prodefense Republican majority in Congress, it is probable that American defense spending will continue its notable decline from the high levels of the mid-1980s. Certainly the current positions of both national parties on federal spending are hardly compatible with significant increases in defense spending. Barring an unexpected international crisis that threatens the United States directly, American defense spending in the late 1990s may well drop to the percentages of GNP allocated in the late 1940s, perhaps even to the 3.6 percent of GNP agreed to by the Bush administration in August 1990.

Even without additional cuts in force levels, under present plans the active-duty forces by the end of the decade will reach a total lower than the 1,460,000 under arms in June 1950, when the Korean War broke out. But it remains unclear whether such reductions in and of themselves are cause for alarm. Without a demonstrable threat to American interests, there are good arguments that addressing contemporary American domestic problems should take precedence over defense spending, even in the perspective of enhancing national security. Furthermore, given a fourfold increase in America's economy since the Truman presidency, even if defense budgets declined to 1950 levels in percentage of GNP, they would still provide approximately four times as much in real terms for forces that would be substantially smaller than the levels of 1948–50.[17]

More relevant to American defense spending is the near certainty that neither the American people nor their representatives will support significant military budget increases for the immediate future, especially lacking a palpable threat. Both have demonstrated repeatedly that they support major defense spending increases only after real, or perceived, security crises provide the motivational fear. For the time being, lingering images of victory in the

Gulf, grave concern over the erosion of the U.S. standard of living, and awareness that the United States has won the longest and most expensive struggle in its history largely shape American attitudes toward national defense.[18] Americans are not likely to accept cuts in entitlement programs, tax increases, or increased budget deficits to fund a defense buildup until the wolf howls at the door.

But while such attitudes may cause concern, they hardly provide reasons for alarm. After all, the Soviet Union and its military threat have vanished. Ten years ago, the Reagan administration warned that Soviet funding for military programs in the 1980s effectively exceeded that of the United States by 35 percent and that the Soviet military was receiving 15–17 percent of the Soviet Union's gross national product. It argued that Soviet armed forces not only threatened to dominate Eurasia and Africa but even posed significant threats to the security of Central America and the Caribbean.[19] In 1994, however, the Central Intelligence Agency estimated that the Russian remnant of the Soviet empire had a gross national product 12 percent of that of the United States, and even that figure represented a 12 percent decline over the previous year (compared to an American economic growth of 3 percent).[20]

Thus, even if the Russians could return their military spending to the unsustainable levels of the 1980s, not only would they complete the destruction of their economy, but they would also fail to match even the greatly diminished American defense outlays of the mid-1990s. Furthermore, the Russians have lost their Soviet empire and their military allies, and now confront the possible breakup of the Russian Federation itself. Even the centuries-old Russian advantage in manpower has evaporated. Ten years ago, the population of the Soviet Union exceeded that of the United States by tens of millions. Today, Americans outnumber Russians by a ratio of better than 5:3 and are increasing with a growth rate five times higher.[21] In addition, America has preserved its NATO, Middle East, and Pacific alliances. The populations and armed forces of U.S. allies exceed, and their defense spending nearly matches, that of the United States. (In 1993, U.S. defense spending amounted to $297.3 billion, that of its allies $284 billion.)[22]

Admittedly, Russia's armed forces still possess a formidable nuclear arsenal, although one can question its continued utility except as a symbol of national greatness. But one can gauge the power of Russia's conventional forces by its surface fleet rusting at anchor, an army struggling to maintain order in Tajikistan and to subdue Chechnya, and a widespread refusal of tens of thousands of conscripts to report for military service. Given the problems afflicting the economy and society, it seems doubtful that Russia will pose a significant military threat to American interests for decades to come. In contrast to the $485 billion spent by the NATO allies in 1993, the Russian defense budget came to a paltry $77 billion for the same year.[23]

China's military potential, however, presents a challenge of a different magnitude. At present, Chinese defense spending remains well below that of the United States. While the CIA declines to make public its estimates of annual Chinese military spending, experts calculate that China's defense budget has not surpassed $50 billion a year and may be as low as $27–30 billion. Consequently, it certainly remains under 2 percent of the Chinese GNP.[24] But if the more optimistic forecasts of economic growth prove correct, then it is entirely conceivable that the Chinese military will enjoy larger budgets than their American counterparts within fifteen years or so. Given the technological lead that the United States presently holds over China, it would still take the Chinese military a considerable period of time to match the quality of American military equipment. But China might be in a position to contest American military primacy in twenty years and certainly to contest U.S. interests in Asia even more quickly.

On the other hand, a number of experts cite a wide array of constraints on a long-term continuation of Chinese double-digit economic growth. Others argue that the economic expansion of the past fifteen years has already weakened Beijing's control over the prosperous coastal provinces and that even if its leaders preserve a formal national unity, China may fissure into a de facto confederation over the next decade.[25] In such circumstances, the United States might not confront a "peer competitor" for the foreseeable future. Barring the rise of China to superpower status, other large powers appear less likely to match American military power in the first quarter of the twenty-first century.

But as the history of the past century demonstrates, a nation need not match U.S. economic power to present a significant military threat. In the late 1930s, the combined incomes of Nazi Germany, Fascist Italy, and Imperial Japan were only approximately 40 percent of that of the United States. Throughout the Cold War, the Soviet GNP never reached even half that of the United States.[26] Apart from China, the only countries with economies from one-quarter to one-half the size of that of the United States are presently American allies. Admittedly, while it remains a process with which Americans are culturally and intellectually unfamiliar, history contains numerous examples of yesterday's allies becoming tomorrow's enemies, sometimes swiftly and unexpectedly. One might identify Japan or a European confederation as hypothetically the most powerful potential enemies of the United States sometime in the twenty-first century. But the democratic nature of Japanese and Western European societies would require both a major cause and a lengthy period—perhaps thirty or forty years—in which the national polities developed a consensus in favor of hostility against the United States. Furthermore, both Japanese and Europeans would confront an array of daunting obstacles (Japan's aging population and lack of strategic depth, Europe's lack of a strong executive and unified military force) to achieving the military power necessary to challenge the United States. For Americans to begin a major armament program at the present time to deal with such eventualities not only is politically impractical but also might turn such hypotheses into tragic, self-fulfilling prophecies. Thus, China seems the only nation that might emerge as a peer competitor to the United States over the next several decades.

Even if China were to rise to a position of rough military equality with the United States by the year 2015, it is hardly inevitable that an American-Chinese rivalry of the kind that characterized American-Soviet relations in the Cold War would result. Marxism-Leninism seems certain to end up in the trash bin of history in the next few years even in China. Any other ideology that Chinese rulers are likely to adopt, even extreme nationalism, would not provide the sort of arguments to justify world conquest such as the Soviets or Nazis professed. If China's exaggerated claims of national superiority threaten its neighbors, an encircling defensive alliance of Japan, Indonesia, India, Russia, and smaller powers, backed by the United States, would likely result. Such a coalition would be more formidable than that erected against the Soviet Union in the 1940s and 1950s. But it hardly seems sensible at present to seek the creation of such an alliance.

In any case, even if the political leaders could persuade the American people to rearm now to deal with a peer competitor twenty years in the future, it is difficult to see what advantages would accrue from such a premature effort. In fact, given the cycles of alarm and complacency that characterize American defense spending, it would seem wiser to wait until a potential foreign opponent's spending patterns suggest aggressive intent and its behavior becomes provocative before beginning major rearmament in response. In the meantime, devotion of such resources to economic growth would better serve U.S. security. This would be especially wise if the American growth rate remained significantly inferior to those of other major powers, as suggested above. The strongest possible economy would provide the best foundation on which to rearm against a major opponent, should that ever become necessary. Furthermore, such a national focus on the economy would benefit the United States even if foreign threats failed to materialize.

Emerging Military Challenges

While the United States is unlikely to confront a major military opponent for the next fifteen years, other serious threats seem likely to emerge. These dangers would not arise as much from the clash of national interests as from the spread of existing technologies and developments of new ones and from certain misconceptions about the future of conflict. Such emerging threats over the past forty years would almost certainly have prompted increases in American defense spending, but given the likely constraints of federal budgets over the next several decades and growing demands of an aging population on entitlement programs, the armed forces may not receive allocations as generous as those during the Reagan administration, even in the face of potential crises. That makes it particularly important to understand the dimensions of such threats in order to craft the most effective responses from limited resources.

Most current speculation about an emerging military revolution—one in which American armed forces supposedly enjoy a commanding lead—centers on information-based warfare and deep-strike, high-precision weapons. Whether these developments indicate a revolution over coming decades or the culmination of technologies introduced to warfare in the first half of this century remains unclear. To describe the perfection of signals intelligence and pilotless aircraft technologies of World War I and the radar, computer, and ballistic missile technologies of World War II as "revolution" in the 1990s deprives the word of meaning. The apogee of military developments often indicates their impending obsolescence, as in the case of defensive warfare in the period 1914–17. In any case, such debate obscures the signal import of the military revolution that has been taking place over the last several decades.

However laudable, American-led efforts to prevent the proliferation of nuclear weapons have failed. In particular, the half-century-old technological and scientific revolution pioneered by German, American, and Soviet applications of nuclear and ballistic missile developments to warfare is finally spreading to a growing number of relatively smaller powers. If South Africa, Pakistan, and North Korea can acquire such weapons, it seems certain that virtually any country willing and able to spend $10–15 billion can do the same. Given the possibility that a number of medium-sized powers will enjoy double-digit rates of economic growth in the coming decades, such expenditures would hardly prove prohibitive, especially if spread over a decade. There is good reason to fear that twenty to thirty countries will possess nuclear-tipped ballistic missiles by 2010.[27]

The consequences of such a spread of nuclear and ballistic missile tech-nologies extend far beyond the dangers of regional nuclear war or a small or medium-sized nuclear strike against the United States or its allies. Acquisi-tion of deliverable nuclear weapons by smaller states implies a revolution in international relations akin to the revolution in military tactics brought on by the development of firearms. Just as possession of the arquebus by small men negated most of the advantages previously enjoyed by large men on the bat-tlefield, a relatively small nuclear arsenal will allow small states to behave in many ways as great powers do.

For centuries, the equality of sovereign states has only been true in the-ory. In reality, the ability of great powers to impose their will on the world of weaker states through the threat or use of force has made the great powers more equal than others. But during the period when the Soviet Union and United States struggled, military developments imposed limits on the power such supremacy could confer. At least in retrospect, as early as 1949 when the Soviets exploded their first atomic bomb, nuclear weapons transformed and equalized the relationship of a weaker Soviet Union with the more powerful United States. Total war in the Clausewitzian sense—that is, the destruction of the enemy's armed forces, occupation of its territory, and the breaking of its will—ceased to be practical between the United States and the Soviet Union. Even in the period between the detonation of the first Soviet atomic weapons and Soviet parity in strategic nuclear weapons in the late 1960s, the logic of mutual deterrence already prevailed. What remained was a choice between Clausewitz's theoretical "absolute war" (for the United States alone until about 1967 and for both powers thereafter) and limited war. Even the latter seemed safe only if waged by proxies, as in Korea, Vietnam, and the Middle East.[28]

The extension of this balance to conflicts between the great powers and smaller states appeared in the political-strategic relationship between the So-viet Union and Israel after the latter acquired the means of striking Soviet territory with nuclear weapons in the early 1970s. Not only were Israel's Arab enemies effectively prohibited from attempting its destruction, but the Sovi-ets lost any reasonable option of supporting a total war by the Arabs against Israel.[29] Only in the last several years, however, has a similar theoretical in-hibition on American military actions moved close to reality. As private re-marks by government and military officials across North Africa and South Asia suggest, the leaders of medium-sized powers have drawn the lesson from the Gulf War that smaller states can challenge the United States militarily--but only if they possess nuclear weapons.

The markedly different responses by the United States to the crises pro-voked by Cuba and North Korea in mid-1994 underline this point. Both states acted in response to roughly the same motivation: fear of the collapse of the ruling regime due to the loss of Soviet economic aid. The far more gen-erous offer that Washington extended to Pyongyang than to Havana was a result of the probable possession or near-possession of nuclear weapons by the former. Thus, the utility of nuclear weapons for blackmail, as well as deter-rence, was clearly apparent. Aside from other compelling reasons, any gov-ernment anticipating a clash of interests with a great power has received persuasive arguments for the utility of nuclear weapons. That is why it is likely that several dozen will acquire them in the immediate future. When this re-ality dawns on Americans, one of their periodic periods of alarm is sure to fol-low. As Colin S. Gray has recently noted, "[I]t is how the United States one day assuredly will obtain a multilayered strategic defense system."[30]

But more than panicked public opinion would promote the creation of systems to defend the United States against limited nuclear strikes. The same motivation that is driving small states to acquire nuclear weapons will com-pel the U.S. government to do what it can to neutralize such threats. Hav-ing just defeated the Soviet Union in a struggle for world primacy, it is unthinkable that the United States would allow a severe diminution of its position by the passive acceptance of the ability of states like Iran and Libya to obliterate American cities. Of course, U.S. leaders will pose official justi-fications for the building of strategic defense systems in less stark terms. But the propensities of the Tripoli and Teheran regimes and their ilk are depress-ingly familiar.

Proponents of a new Strategic Defense Initiative would have little trou-ble in combining the idealistic and pragmatic arguments traditionally re-quired to persuade American public opinion to fund an expensive defense program. A new Strategic Defense Initiative could probably justify itself on the grounds that it would defend democracy against tyranny, dissuade would-be aggressors from starting nuclear war, and provide Americans with a high degree of security against annihilating attacks. Since the American GNP will likely reach an annual level of over $10 trillion early in the twenty-first cen-tury, $100 billion or so, spent over ten years, to create an effective strategic defense for the United States would almost certainly be acceptable to the American electorate.

Such a defense program would provide the intersection of the nuclear/ballistic military revolution of the 1940s and 1950s with the still-emerging information-based warfare technologies of the late twentieth and early twenty-first centuries. Certainly an effective defense against nuclear mis-siles would revolutionize international relations, if not warfare itself, by countering current trends. But advances in information-based warfare—even detached from nuclear weapons—suggest even more profound alterations in the general nature of war. Such advances (major improvements in targeting, weapons lethality, training, and the tetrarchy of command, control, communications, and intelligence) suggest an increasing vulnerability of large weapons platforms such as ballistic missiles, manned aircraft, tanks, and surface warships, particularly carriers. That growing vulnerability results from the constantly improving ability of information-based warfare systems to locate and identify objects, subsequently to target them, and finally to strike with ever greater precision and destructiveness.

But large weapons platforms are the means with which the American armed forces have become accustomed to wage offensive warfare. If even immobile and hidden weapons platforms become increasingly defenseless, then moving and exposed platforms will be even more susceptible to destruction by information-based technologies. The future ineffectiveness of its large platforms would present the United States with enormous difficulties in projecting power at acceptable cost. Worse yet, as such technologies improve, smaller objects on the battlefields, perhaps even individual infantrymen, will become extremely vulnerable to precise targeting and easy annihilation. If these trends are correct, then the early twenty-first century would witness one of those periodic pendulum-like swings in the basic nature of warfare. The defensive would regain the advantages it lost in the final year of World War I.[31]

To use the phrase of Andrew F. Krepinevich, the Gulf War may have been a "*precursor war*—an indicator of the revolutionary potential of emerging technologies and new military systems."[32] For example, the military applications of technological developments that played a crucial role in shifting the advantage in land warfare from the offensive to the defensive in the last century had made a widespread appearance by the 1850s. The Crimean War and the Second War of Italian Independence involved the use of the telegraph, railroads, rifled artillery, artillery shells, and rifles with percussion caps and minié bullets. These innovations did not cripple the offensive, although they did produce appalling casualties on the attacking side. In retrospect, battles like Inkerman and Solferino indicated the increasing advantages that defenders would enjoy at battles like Cold Harbor, Plevna, Mukden, and eventually Verdun, the Somme, and Paschendaele.[33]

It is certainly true that, thanks to the technologies adopted in the 1970s and 1980s, American forces defeated the Iraqis in the Gulf War in one of the most one-sided triumphs in military history. But consider the losses the Kuwaitis could have inflicted on the Iraqis in August 1990 had they possessed the arms, knowledge, and will that American armed forces possessed in 1991.

Moreover, consider the possible alternative outcome of the Gulf War had the Iraqis possessed the technological capabilities and training of their American opponents in January 1991. Admittedly, if forty-year-old nuclear weapons and ballistic missile technology is only now spreading throughout the developing world, considerable time may pass before the technologies possessed by American armed forces in 1990 become widely available.

In the meantime, the American military should be able to make considerable advances. But a number of large and medium-sized states are likely to acquire great wealth in the next few decades and, thus, the means to buy the most modern military technologies. Furthermore, if the general trend of warfare benefits the defensive over coming decades, improvements in American military capabilities might parallel only those made between 1864 and 1914—to the further advantage of the defense. As a result, if the American military were to take the offensive against the forces of a major power, or even a medium power, in twenty years or so, the United States might confront the prospect of casualties ranging from tens of thousands to millions of dead. Fear of the political reaction to such losses might well preclude action.

For these reasons, solutions to the problem of defensive-dominant warfare might present the U.S. military with greater challenges over the next several decades than the task of creating a strategic defense system. Indeed, the inevitable acquisition by other states of the technologies for constructing strategic defense systems would greatly reduce the offensive capabilities of American strategic nuclear forces. The ramifications of such limitations as well as others imposed by the rise of the defense would affect the basic premises of U.S. statecraft and national strategy.

By pure good fortune, the United States fought its Civil War, expanded its national economy to the world's largest, and transformed North America into a sphere of influence during a period (1861–1914) when the defense was ascendant. Assisted by ocean barriers surrounding its continent and its isolationist foreign policy, the United States preserved its unity and expanded its power with little danger of foreign military interference after 1815. By another coincidence, the military actions through which the United States rose to world preeminence in the twentieth century began with the end in 1917–18 of the cycle of defensive-dominant warfare. As a result, in both world wars, Korea, Vietnam, and the Gulf as well as in smaller crises, campaigns, and engagements of the 1917–91 period, the United States projected its power across the oceans, through the air, and inland from the shores of foreign territories within an acceptable time limit, and at a relatively low cost in terms of casualties. But if over the period from 1995 to 2015, or 2025, the defense gains superiority over the offense in warfare, the United States would face serious strategic difficulties in projecting its power.

True, Americans could enjoy a high degree of security within their own national territory, particularly if defended by antimissile systems. But in an age of defense-dominant warfare, the United States could project military power only at a high, perhaps prohibitive, cost in lives or resources. Of course, the same consequences of military technology would affect other countries. But, with the exception of Brazil, other potential world powers rest on or near the Eurasian landmass. Moreover, the majority—Russia, India, China, Indonesia, and Japan—impinge on each other in East Asia, the region that may well be the center of world power in the twenty-first century. The geographic barriers to their projection of military power against each other are considerably less than for the United States. Two of the potential world powers, India and China, will have populations in excess of one billion each and could sustain military casualties, if necessary, at levels that the United States could not, particularly with an American population far more aged than at present.

To a certain extent, this vision of the future recalls the strategic situation of Britain in its relationship to Europe in the period 1854–1914. To complete the analogy, Brazil might assume the strategic significance to the United States that the United States did to Britain between the Crimean War and World War I. In such a case, so long as a balance of power remained stable in Eurasia, the United States could avoid military involvement in its quarrels. But if a power threatened domination over the "world island," the United States would confront a strategic situation similar to the one Britain faced in the period immediately preceding World War I. The great danger, of course, would be that the United States would suffer Britain's fate in the Great War.

It is, of course, unrealistic to suggest that history will repeat itself in such a mechanistic manner. The one prediction that a strategist can safely make is that the future will be filled with surprises. Nonetheless, while the United States could well escape the gloomy scenario outlined above, a combination of geographic reality, the possibility of defense-domination of warfare, the wide proliferation of nuclear weapons, and the likely rise of Eurasian states to high levels of power in a relatively short time would present the United States with daunting strategic challenges. Above all, America could confront the threat of one power dominating all Eurasia, and the projection of American military power necessary to defeat such a danger might cost the American people the lives of millions of their sons and daughters.

In part technology might solve these problems. The American military might devote the limited funds available for research and development over the next several decades to improving the means for projecting force through space or underwater. It might also address the problems of closing with an enemy in the face of formidable defenses by developing pilotless aircraft and computer-driven vehicles and military robots.

Reliance on technological superiority has constituted a central pillar of American strategy since the Mexican War. Repeated successes have reinforced this characteristic, although there has been a tendency in the U.S. military to ignore failures, particularly when American military technology offered few advantages, such as in Vietnam and Somalia. If rapid alterations in the patterns of world power occur, the present leads in military technology enjoyed by the United States might not last for long. After all, that is what the Germans accomplished with regard to the French Army and the Royal Navy before 1914, thanks to the considerable increases in Germany's economic strength in the decades before World War I.

Fortunately for the United States, some within its armed forces have discovered the crucial importance of strategy, as opposed to operations and technology, since the defeat in Vietnam. The American-led victory over Iraq and retrospective appreciation of the successful national strategy that helped lead to the defeat of the Soviet Union in the late 1980s have demonstrated the value of such an approach.[34] So long as this intellectual approach remains strong within the U.S. military, it may offset the tendency to rely excessively on technology as the solution to strategic difficulties and to a possible loss of American material superiority.

America and the New Century

The American advantage over its rivals, in peace as well as war, has been psychological and cultural as well as material. Americans generally consider themselves morally superior to others, particularly their enemies. Partially as a result of Puritanism, partially due to the fortunate course of American history, partially as self-justification for national prosperity by a people heavily influenced by Christian ideas about divine providence, Americans have seen themselves as a chosen people. They have conducted their wars as crusades and seen their national mission as the spread, both by example and conquest, of American ideals. Such attitudes proved of incalculable value in the American Revolution and to the Union in the Civil War. These ideas provided justification for expansion across the continent and deep into the Pacific. They motivated Americans in two world wars and sustained the United States in its long struggle against the Soviet Union.

However, as suggested at the beginning of this chapter, Americans' self-confidence has weakened at the moment of their greatest victory by the seriousness of the economic and social ills besetting American society. Ironically, the United States is a relatively less prosperous society and one more afflicted by fears of crime, loss of faith in the political system, growing divisions in its social structure, and concerns about a decline in educational standards and moral conduct than at the nadir of its Cold War experience in the second half of the 1970s. Yet simultaneously, the United States enjoys more influence throughout the world than ever before. This influence arises not so much from military or economic power as from the influence of American higher education and the extraordinary attraction of American culture, for better or worse.

American-educated elites guide most of the economically successful states in East Asia, South Asia, and Latin America. In Mexico, for example, 1994 witnessed the Harvard-educated president appoint a Yale-educated successor after his previous choice, educated at the University of Pennsylvania, had been assassinated. Men and women with American educations dominate East Asian and Indian electronics industries. Executives trained in American business schools have increasingly influenced even West European and Middle Eastern business cultures. In France, officially hostile to the influence of American culture and ideas, articles in journals devoted to economics, defense, and international affairs mostly cite American publications in their footnotes. Furthermore, an increasingly large number of foreign generals and admirals have graduated from American schools of professional military education. The education and off-campus experiences of such men and women have not necessarily made them pro-American, but American attitudes have heavily influenced them.[35]

Meanwhile, American popular culture, projected by a variety of ever-more-invasive electronic means, has bombarded the average non-American for years. Of course, as is inherent in the nature of entertainment, what Americans broadcast are not their realities but their dreams and nightmares. Given the more traditional values of the majority of the world's population, particularly in Islamic countries, contemporary American fantasies often prove highly disturbing, even grossly offensive. In effect, American popular culture is carrying out a form of illegal immigration against which neither states nor religious imams can erect effective barriers.[36] Ironically, negative foreign reactions to the images Americans project have reinforced many of the doubts Americans feel about themselves.

But, as Lincoln observed, we cannot escape history. At a time of unprecedented global influence, American fears, hopes, beliefs, and realities are spreading with revolutionary results throughout foreign societies. In spite of the insistence of some Cold War critics, far from being a counterrevolutionary nation, the United States remains a profoundly revolutionary polity. While opponents of American popular culture may couch their outrage in moral tones, what really threatens many foreigners are American political and philosophical beliefs: equality of all before the rule of law, the sovereignty of the people as the basis for legitimate government, protection of property rights from government interference, freedom of speech, of assembly, of the press, and of conscience, and all the implications of the Declaration of Independence, the Constitution, and its amendments. However unconscious or unintentional, these ideas pervade American television programs, motion pictures, music, books, and even the way in which American companies package and market their consumer products. The result has been the spread of revolutionary concepts and thus the promotion of violence, either in support of or in opposition to such ideas. This is hardly what Americans wanted or expected from victory in the Cold War, but uprisings and conflicts will nonetheless be the likely consequence.

Indeed, this has already happened in South Korea, China, the Philippines, South Africa, Eastern Europe, Mexico, and Central America. The spread of American ideas about democracy, civil rights, self-determination, and racial equality was not the only cause of these troubles. Nor, as in China in 1989, did they always prevail. These ideals, however, have constituted a major factor in creating such turmoil. The Middle East, North Africa, and the Caribbean seem likely to undergo similar unrest as a result of American influence in the near future. The consequences may not be altogether pleasing to Americans. This is the natural result, after all, of the global victory of a country founded upon ideas, rather than territory or ethnicity. American successes inevitably have resulted in the spread of its ideas more than the expansion of its political dominion. So, while Americans undergo a crisis of faith, the values upon which their society rests inundate the rest of humanity—but to be interpreted as they, not Americans, see fit.

The results are unpredictable. If American ideas gain universal acceptance, will Americans come to view their country as no more than typical? What if, at the same time, American prosperity continues its decline and the distribution of wealth grows still more inequitable? Would that end the American notion of their country as the "city on a hill" and undermine the American political system in a fashion similar to the collapse of communist faith that resulted in the disintegration of the Soviet Union?[37] Contrarily, what would occur if the spread of American ideas provokes widespread chaos and hostility against the United States throughout the world? Would Americans fight to ensure the victory of their beliefs? Or would they lose faith in the American dream if liberal democracy proved altogether more revolutionary in its effect than they had anticipated?

These questions bring us full circle, back to the reasons for the current American unwillingness to play a more prominent role in world affairs. When American citizens are unsure about the worth and effectiveness of their core values, they are likely to be reluctant to defend their national interests. This uncertainty, far more than a tendency toward greater isolationism or reductions in defense spending, is the real problem affecting American strategy in the mid-1990s. Such a problem, in turn, arises from the basic nature of the American political system.

Only a president possessing a clear strategic vision and substantial popular support can develop and conduct an effective national security policy. The Constitution, the nature of American democracy, and historical traditions allow no alternatives. Such a partnership of president and people requires unusual leadership. A president who fails to persuade Americans of his vision or who loses faith in his ability to achieve that vision will suffer Lyndon Johnson's or George Bush's fate. Even when a president is sure of the direction in which he wishes to lead, he cannot force the pace. He must inspire his people, rally their courage, and promote their self-confidence, and he must convince Americans that the ends on which they have agreed are just, beneficial, and worthy of the sacrifices entailed in their accomplishments. That was the genius of Franklin Roosevelt. In essence, to be a successful leader in the fields of foreign affairs and national security, an American president must combine the attributes of elected king and secular prophet.

What remains to be seen is whether a system of government that served the United States well in its rise to primacy can sustain it through an indefinite period of world leadership. American society will have to produce men and women equal to such tasks. Americans themselves will have to exercise the wisdom to choose such individuals as their leaders. If the speculations in this chapter prove even remotely accurate, history will offer little forgiveness for error on the part of either presidents or people. The verdict of history will be a judgment on democracy. Its successes in the past are no guarantee that the final judgment will be favorable.

Chapter 3

How to Think About Defense

Eliot A. Cohen

How Did the United States Get Here?

Great struggles leave their marks on the institutions that wage them. The ambience of the Cold War saturated every element of the American defense establishment, including the defense intellectual establishment that grew up around it. America's ways of thinking, its assumptions about the world, its view of statecraft and of its role in the world— all still bear the imprint of the duel with the Soviet Union and its minions. American defense planners have found it easier to scrap the Cold War's hardware than its software, the intellectual algorithms for thinking about defense. When staff officers prepare briefings, justifying items in the defense budget with carefully constructed scenarios of an Iraqi invasion of Saudi Arabia, they do so within a frame of reference shaped by the Cold War, even if the Soviets no longer figure as the enemy. When administration representatives discuss the need to "contain" regional opponents, they think in categories concocted by George Kennan and Paul Nitze at the onset of the contest between East and West. When defense contractors offer the Defense Department studies on "deterrence after the Cold War," they unwittingly perpetuate concepts of American strategy that have decreasing relevance to the new age. It will be years before conscious examination of the intellectual legacy of the Cold War and the smack of reality contradicting its precepts will breed new ways of thinking.

While liberals often read into American military history brutality and ve-
nality, conservatives are no less prone to read into it folly and neglect. In fact,
the story is more complex. From colonial settlement through the founding to
the nineteenth and early twentieth centuries, the United States never really
disengaged from world politics; it adopted strategic postures congruent with
available resources.[1] Its strategic record is better than commonly supposed
and is certainly superior to that of most of the European states with which it
contended.

One of the Cold War's least fortunate consequences was the oversimpli-
fication of America's strategic history. As the contest with the Soviet Union
was indeed ideological as well as political, and as its moral (as distinct from
geopolitical) dimension was so pronounced, American military history became part of a morality play. As a result, when American strategists first considered new strategic postures for the period after the Cold War they invoked
a distorted view of the nation's past and, in particular, the specter of rapid and
complete demobilization. President George Bush's secretary of defense,
Richard Cheney, warned against repeating the cycle of precipitate demobilization that supposedly had undermined American strategy in the past:

> ... historically we've always gotten it wrong. We've never done it right. You
> can't find a time in this century when we've been through one of these cy-
> cles where we did, in fact, take the force down in an intelligent fashion.[2]

In making such an assertion he merely echoed the anxieties of those at
the onset of the Cold War, who wrote of a "cycle" evident in the "prelimi-
naries, developments, and immediate sequels" of the world wars:

> (1) prior to the war, insufficient military expenditures, based on the public's
> prewar conviction that war could not come to America; (2) discovery that
> war *could* come after all; (3) a belated rush for arms, men, ships, and planes
> to overcome the nation's demonstrated military weakness; (4) advance of
> the producing and training program, attended by misunderstandings, delays,
> and costly outlay, but gradual creation of a large and powerful army; (5)
> mounting successes in the field, and eventual victory; (6) immediately there-
> after, rapid demobilization and dissolution of the army as a powerful fighting
> force; (7) sharp reduction of appropriations sought by the military estab-
> lishment, dictated by concern over its high cost and for a time by the re-
> vived hope that, again, war would not come to America.[3]

The so-called cycle of armament/disarmament disintegrates on close inspection. In the immediate aftermath of World War I, for instance, the
United States deployed a military almost twice its prewar size. The army num-

bered 92,000 in 1912, 149,000 a decade later; the navy 51,000 in 1912 and almost twice as many, 100,000, in 1922; while even the marines grew from under 10,000 to some 21,000. American forces in 1922 included, one should note, a technologically advanced navy close to parity with that of the world's greatest maritime power, Britain.[4] American diplomats subsequently used arms control treaties to dismantle the one alliance (between Britain and Japan) that could possibly have endangered U.S. security. America's serious interwar military troubles only began in the late twenties and early thirties, when the Depression struck.

More recently, the American military has found itself transfixed by four uses of force, three failures and one success. The failures are Vietnam, Lebanon, and Somalia; the success, the Persian Gulf. Many officers (and not a few civilians) have read into the cumulative experiences the following half-truths, or, in some cases, falsehoods: (1) the United States can win wars easily if the civilians will set clear objectives and then get out of the way; (2) the press is invariably hostile to the military and, where possible, the Defense Department should exclude and manipulate the media; and (3) the American people lack the stomach for casualties and consequently will support only wars that the nation conducts with the utmost speed.

Careful reflection suggests a more complex set of truths. First, the military in Vietnam had more discretion (particularly in the war in the south) than is often realized. When the use of force has political repercussions (and this is surely almost always the case), some measure of civilian control *is entirely* appropriate. Second, the press is no more hostile to the military than to every other institution of government or private enterprise; it is, in any event, an inescapable feature of modern life. Third, the sensitivity to casualties in the Gulf War stemmed more from military sensibilities (for a variety of reasons) than from an American public whose sons and daughters had no fear of conscription to induce fear of bloodshed. An air force general uttered the remark "no target is worth an airplane" during the Gulf War, not a politician.[5]

The first task in rethinking American strategy after the Cold War, then, is to develop a healthy mistrust for the shibboleths and folk wisdom of the American national security debate. To do so requires not merely an attempt to illuminate our future, but a careful, dispassionate examination of our past, no small task. Unfortunately, most American policy analysts and decision makers have little interest in a serious, as opposed to a clichéd, study of U.S. history, while too few strategic historians think they have much to contribute to a present debate about the future.

❦

The Strategic Environment

The rethinking of American strategy should be all the easier given the benign nature of the current environment. For many living outside the United States, the world is indeed a dismal place; the atrocities in cities from Bihac to Aden and from Sukumi to Kigali remind us of that. The trends elsewhere, where Japan anxiously eyes a Korean peninsula soon to be kitted out with nuclear weapons, or where ethnic Russians are thinking of secession from an economically moribund Ukraine, are not terribly encouraging. But from a purely American view, the world is, and will be for some length of time, more secure than during the Cold War. Conceivably, that judgment may change, but for now Americans have the luxury, as few do in history, of rethinking the fundamentals of their national security.

The new strategic order has three dominant characteristics: international disorder, a revolution in military affairs, and a crisis of demotic culture. The Cold War imposed an order on international politics and provided a strategic rationale for American behavior. It imposed a global logic on U.S. defense policy: the essential decisions were decisions *not* to engage the Soviet Union and its clients in a direct military conflict. Although American leaders distinguished between areas of greater and lesser importance to the United States, they often did so on the basis of criteria resting on the balance with the Soviets rather than any intrinsic interest. Since 1989, American interests have become altogether hazier; they have also contracted. During the contest with the Soviet Union, Somalia and Yugoslavia, to take only two cases, had some importance as *points d'appui* for military power. The United States could not remain indifferent to these countries because of repercussions on regional balances of power. Even if the immediate *military* consequences of a shift of such countries from one camp to the other remained limited, the *psychological* and hence political effects were not.

Today, the United States has no immediate strategic interest in either country. Its prestige does not ride on the outcome of clan warfare in Mogadishu or Sarajevo, at least as long as Washington policy makers refrain from foolish pronouncements about what the United States will do in either place. Its interests in the resolution of such civil conflicts are primarily humanitarian and only secondarily strategic. In the long run, the consequences of the Yugoslav civil war may prove exceptionally ugly in the Balkans, but such possibly tragic outcomes should properly concern the inhabitants of Berlin, Paris, and Rome more than the residents of Atlanta, St. Louis, or Los Angeles.

The stumblings of the Clinton administration conceal a deeper problem in the conduct of American foreign policy than the error of particularly inept politicians. The geopolitical challenge after World War II was simple: the emergence of Soviet power, political and military, and the ambitions of Soviet leaders. The economics of that configuration were also straightforward: the American economy accounted for a staggering 50 percent of global production, while Western Europe had most of the human resources necessary to rebuild its shattered economy. Even so, it required several direct challenges, including communist coups, for American statesmen to devise suitable responses (containment, the Marshall Plan, and the rearmament prompted by NSC-68 and the Korean War). The calls often heard at home and abroad for "vision" along the lines of containment in the Cold War miss the point. It is unlikely that anyone can or will respond. The contrast between the situation now and forty-five years ago reflects more than the superiority of U.S. statesmen early in the Cold War (a fact, to be sure). It reflects the greater ambiguity of a world that confronts less direct and for the moment less ominous challenges to its fundamental stability than those of 1945–50.

Today, the geopolitical problems are more diffuse and the remedies less obvious. There is, and can be, no global scheme for American foreign policy, save for the vague objectives of promoting an environment conducive to international trade and open communications. Moreover, the United States takes on the tasks of devising foreign policy in this new world at a time when its economy, though thriving, commands barely a quarter of world gross national product—a portion likely to shrink as economic growth spreads in Asia, a continent that includes a China whose gross national product may pass that of the United States early in the next century.

A second broad development bearing on American defense policy is what defense thinkers call "the revolution in military affairs." It appears that we are in the early stage of a transformation of warfare driven by the new technologies of information. Until quite recently, military technologies essentially resembled those of World War II, albeit improved and upgraded. But the advent of the microchip and advanced materials (e.g., for construction of stealth aircraft) promise radical changes in the conduct of war. Armed forces in advanced states can now discern a future in which unparalleled capabilities to see and track opponents and to deliver precise conventional fire will transform warfare. Global positioning systems, for example, put accurate navigation within the grasp of humans almost anywhere on the planet. Satellites, unmanned aerial vehicles, and remote sensors—acoustic, infrared, and others—have transformed intelligence. Above all, the integration of military organizations by electronic communications and computers will drastically improve even as it creates opportunities for warfare by electronic means as varied as electromagnetic pulse weapons (that disable electronic devices by brute force) and computer worms or viruses (that do the same by guile).

War in the twenty-first century will look very different from warfare today.[6] Periods of covert warfare involving electronic sabotage will precede active operations. Fighting may consist of barrages by accurate, long-range cruise and ballistic missiles, while mobile forces such as ships or tanks may find themselves caught in webs of "intelligent" minefields. Rather than fighting as individual platforms, ships and planes will increasingly fight as networks, and the high ground in such contests will be advantages in information as much as in terrain. Efforts to hide, through the use of camouflage and deception, will accompany attacks on command posts and the other side's "eyes."

Such a revolution in military affairs will enable new competitors to the United States to amass certain kinds of military power relatively quickly. For example, until recently, satellite pictures that could discriminate among objects twelve inches in length were the stuff of supersecret intelligence organizations of the major powers. Today, they are on the verge of routine availability in commercial products from American and overseas space vendors. In the Gulf War, only the United States had in any quantity receivers that could allow precise location using global positioning systems. Such receivers are already widely available commercially and within a few years will fit comfortably in a shirt pocket. Furthermore, the ending of the Cold War has opened the vast pool of scientific and military research talent in the former Soviet bloc to exploitation by those with sufficient funding. As some countries, particularly in Asia, become wealthier, they have acquired a taste for the latest military hardware. In the 1970s the Northrop Corporation could sell at considerable profit the reliable but relatively low-technology F-5 fighter to America's allies, but not its own air force. Today, countries like Malaysia will only buy the latest in American military technology.

A further consequence of the military revolution will be the radical transformation of units of account—the military chess pieces, as it were. The division, for example, an organization of fifteen thousand or more soldiers, has its roots in the late eighteenth century and emerged in its current form in World War I. It is probable that it will yield to smaller units networked in ways that supersede traditional hierarchies. The navy's carrier battle groups, which date back to the period between the world wars, may go the way of battleship lines. These developments do not necessarily undermine America's military edge, however.

The American defense budget still towers over all others. At approximately a quarter of a trillion dollars a year it is roughly seven times that of major European countries such as France or Germany and approximately six times that of Japan. Minor troublemakers such as Iran and Iraq spend less than 5 percent of what the United States spends on military power. Furthermore, the United States amassed during the Cold War a vast capital stock in military weapons which retains considerable value. Its constellation of intelligence-gathering systems in outer space and on earth, its massive platforms such as aircraft carriers and ships, and its technological establishment of astounding sophistication are unparalleled. Moreover, only the United States possesses the know-how and logistical assets (including such mundane items as transport and refueling aircraft) to conduct global military operations.[7] In this respect analogies drawn with the late 1940s are erroneous, for America's lead in military technology is more extensive today than it was fifty years ago at the end of World War II. It is highly unlikely, for now, that any of the major developed powers will spend the resources to catch up. Advances in, and proliferation of, civilian technology may eventually subvert that lead, but whether that will occur depends largely on decisions made over the coming decade.

Strategists rarely discuss the cultural dimensions of strategy, but these are in fact a third and conditioning element in the strategic environment of the United States. The willingness to use military power and the capacity to amass it depend to a great extent on a country's culture. During the Cold War, strategic planners could take for granted the willingness of Americans to engage in world politics and contend with the Soviet Union. Even if they were not, in John F. Kennedy's words, willing to pay *any* price, or to bear *any* burden, they certainly accepted burdens unprecedented in their national history. These burdens included assigning between 4 and 10 percent of gross national product to defense (the historical norm was between 1 and 2 percent), peacetime conscription, creation of a vast military establishment, and acceptance of real and potential infringements on civil liberties. These latter included laws to protect secrets and the creation of governmental agencies that possessed the ability to spy on Americans overseas and, to a lesser extent, at home.

The price was surely worth it, but a price it was. Now, with the ending of the Cold War, Americans have shown little eagerness to shed such burdens and structures. This may represent one of the lesser surprises of the post–Cold War world. America has become accustomed to world power and has no intention of giving it up. But it is equally true that Americans will look on global responsibilities with a colder eye, particularly if exertions of American military power result from allies too miserly or timid to fend for themselves. At the same time, however, the United States, and perhaps the West more broadly, is undergoing a crisis of cultural self-confidence similar to those of the 1930s and 1960s.[8] In the 1930s, the West's economic system and social arrangements seemed inadequate to the challenges posed by advanced industrial development. In the 1960s, the West weathered a rebellion by its youth, who overturned or subverted most of its institutions of education—a process that still reverberates at the end of the century. The West overcame the first threats by defeating one set of opponents in World War II and a second in the Cold War. The West mastered the second challenge by compromise and accommodation, which in some cases paved the way for the present crisis. The dimensions of this crisis are difficult to sketch, but they surely include the rise of criminality, the erosion of traditional means of socialization, and a perceptible decay in popular culture. The replacement of *The Andy Griffith Show* by *Beavis and Butthead* represents a telling symbol of deeper and more distressing trends.

Cultural trends affect national security in at least two ways. First, they have led American leaders to turn inward to address the problems of a society that has lost much of its self-confidence. The 1992 campaign, the first since 1936 that did not feature foreign affairs as a prominent issue, represents an important watershed. The significance of this change, however, has not, thus far, struck a foreign policy establishment that holds earnest seminars on American policy vis-à-vis countries thousands of miles distant, while ten blocks away street thugs have driven most citizens from the streets. The contrast between the formidable military power of the United States and its violent and disorderly cities suggests the hubris of the argument that the United States should pacify Mogadishu and Sarajevo. In the future, then, we can expect Americans to look askance on foreign adventures that aim to do for others what we have failed to do for ourselves. We can also expect politicians to learn from the experience of George Bush: no amount of success overseas will compensate in the future for failure to address problems at home.

The diseases that afflict America have not escaped the notice of others. Americans have discounted the cultural hostility of foreign intellectuals and politicians as a mere apology for their own drive for power. Immune as many Americans (particularly intellectuals) are to the appeal of religious belief, they ignore foreign beliefs as passing impediments to the inevitable development of secular, humanistic, and libertarian societies.[9] Living as they do in the oldest constitutional democracy, Americans assume their package of individual liberties and a legalistic political system will inevitably spread to other countries. Such assumptions are already failing. Not only have they attracted the anger of fundamentalist groups in the Islamic world, but they have also begun to elicit hostile reactions from other societies, including the successful Sinitic states of Asia.

Conceivably, we may have passed the high-water mark for the spread of American culture. Certainly, the United States will find itself at odds with countries that resent American attempts to impose a world order that looks less benign and attractive than Americans believe. In what may be the greatest strategic revolution of all, two concepts that the United States applied to the Soviet Union—deterrence and containment—may be applied to it. Other countries may seek not to contend with the United States for global hegemony, but to box it out of their spheres of interest and influence. Even modest amounts of force, if wielded with determination, will thwart the objectives of a morose and troubled American giant.[10] The recent collapse of American efforts to prevent North Korea's acquisition of nuclear weapons is a case in point.

What Capabilities Do We Need?

The Clinton administration delineated the military forces it believed the United States would require in the coming decade in its Bottom Up Review, published in 1993. Based on a Cold War paradigm of forces required to fight two major regional contingencies, it supported a force structure of ten army and three marine divisions, twelve aircraft carriers, and thirteen active air force wings. Civilians occasionally sneer at generals for preparing to fight the last war: here, their analysis did the same, albeit with an elaborate, analytical superstructure. The Bottom Up Review's chief premise was that the next war, and future conflicts for which the United States should size its military, would be reruns of the 1991 Gulf War. This proposition, dubious enough for the next decade, appears absurd if one looks further ahead. In any case, the projected and conceivable budgets simply do not allow for a force structure of that size, if it is to be adequately paid, trained, and consistently modernized.[11]

The Pentagon did confess that it would fall short by $40 billion of what the Bottom Up Review force required over the next five years; the General Accounting Office estimated the gap at $150 billion, which is probably closer to reality.[12] The 1.4-million-strong force envisioned in the Bottom Up Review will not survive. Given the absence of any great external threat in the next ten to fifteen years, the armed forces will shrink to perhaps a million men and women. Even to recruit and maintain that force (about 40 percent of the Cold War military) will be expensive: older and in many cases married, the modern volunteer demands (and gets) a greater range of social services than draftees of old. Volunteers require salaries that allow families to live decently. Adjusting to the new size means giving up old structures and radically changing ways of doing business. Some of the services are deeply reluctant to do so. The marines, for example, are clinging to a force level of over 170,000—a force a third that of the army and one that will soak up funds needed for the modernization of their equipment. To come down to a more reasonable and useful size (say 100,000) demands painful changes in deployment patterns, organization (currently mandated by law), and manpower policy, changes that require a civilian willingness to contemplate, or enforce, alterations in the basic missions of the services.

Not only will the American military be smaller than at any time since 1940, but it will have to change in two other important ways. First, it will have to reduce its reliance on the permanent forward deployment of combat units, a policy that was sustainable during the Cold War but that will impose insuperable strains on the future force structure. There are advantages to a return of American forces to the United States. Forward deployed forces are often more difficult to move without serious political repercussions than those stationed at home. Moreover, the United States boasts large and sophisticated training areas on its own territory that bases overseas simply cannot match. Second, a smaller military will have to concede that some missions are simply too large for it to handle alone. Indeed, one of the chief strategic choices that the United States faces is that between unilateral and multilateral capabilities.

American defense policy should emerge from answers to the question, "What kind of world does the United States wish to mold?" The answer should be obvious: a world based on an open economic order, friendly to democratic government, one in which no hegemonic power dominates Eurasia and in which no combination or individual power forms that could endanger that order. It will, unfortunately, be easier and hence more likely that American defense policy will result from answers to more modest questions: "What calamities does the United States wish to avert?" and "What goals are worth even a modest fight?" Four sets of capabilities emerge from such an analysis.

First, the United States will have to think hard about *defense proper.* Since World War II American strategists have regarded continental defense with only episodic interest. After a vigorous effort in the area of continental air defense in the 1950s and an attempt to develop ballistic missile defenses in the 1960s, American continental defenses lapsed into somnolence. The Reagan administration's Strategic Defense Initiative failed to attract wide support and came under severe criticism for the stress it supposedly placed on the 1972 Anti-Ballistic Missile Treaty with the Soviet Union. Defense in the narrow sense, however, has a long and honorable American strategic tradition. Three waves of fortification—one from the Federalist period through the War of 1812 and its immediate aftermath, another in the 1840s, and a third in the 1880s—provided the United States with admirable protection for its ports.[13] In the early twentieth century, much of American military planning focused on protection of installations such as the Panama Canal.

Interestingly, the three most serious failures of the American military during World War II—at Pearl Harbor and the debacles in the Philippines and the destruction of Allied merchant shipping along the east and Gulf coasts in 1942—were defensive failures. During the Cold War, the balance of American strategic thinking and military action shifted to the offense, and for good reason: nuclear weapons seemed an overwhelmingly offensive military tool, while political considerations mandated forward strategies in Europe, Asia, and the Middle East.

That has now changed. The proliferation of long-range ballistic (and, in later years, cruise) missiles will make it possible for small and relatively weak powers to strike at North America. Technologies of low-level warfare—everything from car bombs to computer hacking—make it easier to cross oceanic distances that formerly insulated the United States from traditional security concerns. The 1993 bombing of the World Trade Center was, most likely, a sign of things to come. In the nineteenth century the army (and even, to a lesser extent, the marine corps) found itself undertaking defensive or peace-making operations in the western United States and, after the Civil War, in the South, a role to which four thousand troops returned in Los Angeles in May 1992.

Much of the American military will resist conversion to essentially defensive roles. First, its dominant combat arms organizations have grown up as forward-deployed, expeditionary forces; this is their definition of the military profession. Second, defensive missions tend to be intrinsically more complicated and less promising than offensive ones; it is easier to build and operate long-range missiles than to defend against them; easier to launch long-range, special operations than to prevent them. It is, of course, more fun as well. Furthermore, most defensive missions will strain military professionalism. Soldiers do not like riot control and domestic pacification because it invariably brings them into conflict with civilians, and often with civil authority. "The task assumed by the troops is not a pleasant one," as President Ulysses S. Grant put it mildly to Congress in 1875.[14] Regular soldiers left their task of imposing Reconstruction on the South in the 1870s with relief, not least because they knew they were fighting a war they could not win.

A second broad mission of the armed forces will be that of *insurance*. The United States today faces no imminent threats, save the serious, but nonetheless containable, prospects of war on the Korean peninsula and renewed Iraqi adventurism in the Gulf. But it does face a world of uncertainty. Defense planners have attempted to bound such ambiguity by suggesting standards like those of the Aspin Pentagon's Bottom Up Review, which calls for the services to prepare for two, nearly simultaneous, "major regional contingencies." Subsequent examination of this standard underlined that American forces would have logistical difficulty in sustaining one such contingency and that two would exceed U.S. capabilities. But the Bottom Up Review's artificial and short-term standards, even if they represented an achievable target, do not adequately represent the kinds of challenge the United States actually confronts. For the essence of insurance is the preservation of certain *competencies*, upon which the American military could rebuild future forces, as and when they are needed.

Two stand out. First, the United States may, at some juncture, need to deploy substantial land forces overseas, as it did during the Gulf War. In the short term, this is not likely; following a resolution of the division on the Korean peninsula, it will be even less likely. It should be, in general, the task of local allies to defend themselves on the ground, while the United States provides various kinds of support from air, sea, and space. In a pinch, the United States might provide a high-technology, ground expeditionary force and the capability for its higher level command and control.

The heavy portion of the army should preserve and indeed hone its expertise in ground combat and prepare to serve as the decisive nucleus for multinational forces or for a larger American force, constructed initially from the reserves and later from fresh recruits or draftees. This force might not necessarily be smaller than the army of today, but it would be different in at least two respects. It should consist exclusively of regular forces, not relying on reservists for mobilization or deployment. The army's current practice of relying heavily on reserve components to support regular units makes the force less deployable (because of political costs associated with mobilizations). The Gulf War indicated that assignment of reserve combat units to regular ones simply did not work, partly because of a lack of training and partly as a result of the regular military's long-standing mistrust of the reserves. It would be far better to make the reserves a source of relatively small units (say, battalions at most) that could be called up and trained for three months or more before deployment into combat. Rather than thinking of reserves unrealistically as the partner of regular forces, the army should see that they become what they have more traditionally been—a base for long-term mobilization and a link between army and society. This land force would also differ from the current one in its dependence on other states. The Gulf War demonstrated both that allied forces were available, if the United States were assertive enough in demanding them, and underprovided for, in that there had been little practice for such multinational operations outside of NATO.

A second broad area of insurance lies in the realm of nuclear weapons. During the Cold War nuclear strategy occupied center stage in the American policy debate. Today, our nuclear forces are a stepchild of a government eager to see them disappear and a military establishment that has always viewed them with considerable distaste. "The nuclear weapon is obsolete . . . I want to get rid of them all," one air force four-star general commented recently.[15] The navy and army, in particular, were delighted to see these awkward devices removed from their arsenals, for they required specialized handling, posed severe operational problems, and made each service, in different ways, unpopular with local allies. But we will not be able to drive the nuclear genie away so easily. Many small states will take away from the Gulf War the lesson that the best counter to American conventional strength lies in possession of a nuclear arsenal. To deter the use of nuclear weapons (and chemical and biological ones as well) and, if necessary, to preempt the nuclear forces of potential opponents, the United States requires small but always modern nuclear forces. This ultimately requires a low-level testing and development program, particularly for tactical nuclear weapons.

A third mission for the armed forces is *maintenance of world order*. The United States combines, to a degree not found in other countries, military, economic, and cultural power. It can use that power in three ways: to limit, punish, and excise. By *limitation* I mean the denial of certain kinds of capabilities to other countries. The United States, as guarantor of an open commercial order, will wish to prevent others (or substate actors) from blocking or interfering with the free use of sea and air lanes. This role requires, for example, the ability to detect and destroy ships, aircraft, or submarines laying mines in the Straits of Hormuz or the Magellan Straits.

The idea of using military power to *punish* does not normally appeal to Americans. But in the future the United States may not wish to change a political situation on the ground through the direct use of force—say, by occupying and pacifying a country. Rather, it may wish to affect the calculations of troublemakers or simply lay down a marker for future mischief makers. Thus, had the United States used its military power in the former Yugoslavia early in that crisis—say, at the time of the shelling of Dubrovnik in fall 1991—it would have done best not by having placed massive numbers of troops on the ground, but rather by having used its air and naval power to make the Serbian government suffer at home.

During the Cold War the use of military power for punitive purposes acquired a bad name. To hawks, it smacked of timidity and perhaps an enthrallment to academic notions of force as a means of signaling American intentions. To doves, it seemed innately cruel and impossible to reconcile with the concept of just war. To both, it appeared ineffective. Indeed, the experiences of Vietnam bear out the suspicions of hawks and doves alike who foresaw little good in the punitive use of military power. On a more abstract level, nuclear theory called for the use of atomic weapons not for achievement of comprehensible strategic objectives, but for deterrence by sheer frightfulness—the doctrine of mutual assured destruction was the apotheosis of a strategy of punishment.

Here again, however, the Cold War's demise should lead to a reexamination of such assumptions. In the next decades the United States will find itself engaging in what the British called imperial policing: the maintenance of some rough order in unruly parts of the world. Punitive strategies failed during the Cold War because the opponents they targeted lay in the grip of a messianic ideology and because those opponents had access to the resources of the opposing superpower and its major clients. Punitive strategies failed as well because their targets lacked the sophisticated infrastructure of modern states. Peasant societies and economies are less vulnerable to the kind of punishment (chiefly bombing and blockade) that the United States could deliver.

Today, circumstances are different. Our future opponents will not have a superpower patron to rebuild their dams and power plants or to provide comprehensive air defense systems. They will probably be more porous societies than the communist states we opposed in the Cold War—more aware of the world through the mass media—and probably less totalitarian domestically (the debates in the Iranian parliament are worth noting in this regard). They will have more sophisticated economies, which will give them more to lose and open a wider range of targets for American power. No less important, they will know that the key to economic survival lies in engagement with the outside world, even if not in a completely open fashion. Within broad limits, strategies of punishment might work to moderate the behavior of such states—perhaps to curtail efforts to subvert their neighbors or to mistreat ethnic minorities. Moreover, the technologies of precision strike open up new paths for punishment. It is probably feasible, for example, to damage or destroy most of a country's major road and rail networks. To be sure, temporary bridges, rafts, and the like will enable the targeted nation to continue functioning and even to move its armed forces. But the economic dislocation will inflict considerable pain on the society and ultimately put pressure on the government.

Finally, the maintenance of world order will require an ability to *excise* certain capabilities, specifically, weapons of mass destruction. In 1991, when the United States went to war against Iraq, it lacked the intelligence and, in some cases, the specialized weapons and procedures to attack storage sites for Iraqi nuclear and biological weapons and their associated programs. When the war began, American planners had only two Iraqi nuclear targets on their lists: by the time the International Atomic Energy Agency inspectors had finished their work, they had identified *sixteen* main facilities.[16] The U.S. government recognized the counterproliferation mission, as it is called, in the aftermath of the Gulf War. From a purely technical point of view, locating and destroying the ability of countries to use such weapons will prove a difficult task; this is particularly true with respect to biological weapons, which can be manufactured in small laboratories and distributed clandestinely. Should America witness the actual use of such weapons, it will have no choice but to move swiftly—even at high cost—to prevent their repeated use.

The last mission of American armed forces will be *coalition maintenance*. The United States is unique not only in the raw military power it possesses but also in its ability to call on numerous allies for assistance—and, in turn, to answer the claims they often make on our capacities. America's interests lie in providing key elements of support both to its core allies (for example, the British), as well as to occasional partners with whom it may have more ambiguous relations. Indeed, one feature of the new international politics is the greater uncertainties in our relationships with allies. Thus, while American aircraft operated from Italy to survey Bosnian air space, American soldiers in Somalia wondered whether their Italian colleagues had tipped off Somali warlords whom they were attempting to track down.

Abandoning such allies when it is in our interest to remain would be almost as foolish as ignoring conflicts of interest when they occur. The United States needs allies for many reasons: to ensure political support at home and minimize opposition abroad to the use of force, to tap unique skills or local knowledge, to minimize our own weaknesses, and, indeed, to shift some of the burden of policing the world to others. Even with the major decreases in military spending over coming decades, there are some things the United States does so well, or has in such quantity, that other nations will continue to depend on it for support.

Thus, for the time being, the United States can collect intelligence through technical means (particularly from space) in ways beyond those available to others. It can, moreover, process the information acquired and turn it into tactically useful intelligence more quickly than anyone else. At the same time, the sheer size and sophistication of America's logistical infrastructure—its fleets of ships, military transport aircraft, trucks, and the units to handle them—is of an order of magnitude beyond those possessed by any other nation.

What Choices Does the United States Need to Make?

These, then, are the likely purposes of American military power. What choices will the American government have to make if a smaller military is to serve such purposes adequately? During the Cold War, the United States became accustomed to stationing vast forces overseas—a third of a million troops in Europe alone, more than half a million across the world by the mid-1980s. Since the Cold War's end, the United States has kept substantial forces overseas (over 300,000 men and women) and has made increasingly frequent temporary deployments of troops for peacekeeping (in Macedonia), so-called peace making (in Somalia), humanitarian intervention (northern Iraq or Rwanda), or showing-the-flag exercises to reassure friends or build relations with others (e.g., deployment to Kuwait). This trend appears likely to continue as American warships posture off Haiti, the administration promises to send tens of thousands of U.S. troops to Yugoslavia in support of a peace settlement, and diplomats talk loosely of sending a battalion or two to the Golan Heights in support of an Israeli-Syrian peace.

The effects of overstretching U.S. forces may not be fully apparent for some time. Already, however, the strain on service marriages and on morale is clear. When Secretary of Defense William Perry visited Spangdahlem Air Force Base in October 1994, he learned that spousal abuse and alcoholism rates had risen by approximately 10 percent over previous years and child abuse by about 20 percent.[17] Specialized units suffer particularly: for example, airborne warning and control system crews deploy overseas 170 days a year, when the normal limit is 120.[18] The more forces remain tied up in overseas missions incidental to combat, the less time they will have to develop combat skills. Military missions other than war may serve the ends of American foreign policy and provide a sense of purpose to those who undertake them. But such activities exact a price on the organizations that sustain them—including a monetary one. The deployment to Somalia alone cost $2.2 billion from 1991 through 1994, while the emergency move of aid and troops to Rwanda in 1994 gobbled up several hundred million dollars within a couple of months. These costs are separate from less visible drains on the Pentagon budget, such as administration efforts to take $300 million from the defense budget as a contribution to UN peacekeeping efforts.

It is a cliché of American strategic thinking that the United States will henceforth fight as a member of a coalition. But the United States will find itself choosing among three kinds of coalitions—those brought together under the banner of the United Nations, those locked in the formal mechanisms of military cooperation such as NATO, and those constructed ad hoc. During the Gulf War the Bush administration set a precedent, which appears likely to last—the United States used the cover of the United Nations for its military actions overseas. The United States benefited both at home and abroad from the air of legitimacy such authority provided. Should the atmosphere at the United Nations deteriorate—particularly, for example, if China should choose to exercise its veto on the Security Council—the United States may find itself embarrassed by such precedents. The proper course is likely to be one of pragmatic use of the United Nations, if it provides the necessary support, but a periodic reaffirmation (and perhaps even demonstration) of American willingness to act without that endorsement will be important.

NATO remains the most durable and important of formal American coalitions and commitments. In the long run, unless Russia reemerges as a threat to Europe's security, the alliance is bound to deteriorate. As Europe expands, NATO is likely to have more difficulty in agreeing on common foreign and defense policy; the debacle in Bosnia is ample evidence of that difficulty. So, too, is the evidence of persistent disagreements between Germany and some of its western neighbors on NATO's expansion to the east. European difficulties in acting collectively do not diminish America's interest in keeping NATO alive, not just as a wartime command structure, but as a means of harmonizing procedures and familiarizing soldiers from many different nations with one another in times of peace. NATO's most useful work takes place when soldiers, sailors, and airmen agree on standardized means of issuing orders, controlling air traffic, or managing naval operations. From this common basis of practice, NATO military organizations can operate in ad hoc coalitions on the fringes of Europe, even if not under NATO auspices. The Gulf War, in which the United States coordinated the activities of half a dozen air forces by using the procedures and planning tools devised for use in Europe, demonstrated the value of such common experience.

If the path to America's future coalitions is relatively clear, one cannot say so much for its military acquisitions process. The issue here is not so much reforming *how* the Pentagon develops and buys hardware (although the Perry Pentagon deserves credit for trying to streamline a cumbersome process) as in a reconsideration of what it buys. There are three broad trade-offs. The first is between what one might call mega- and micro-systems. The United States has done well in the Cold War with exceedingly large and complex military platforms—aircraft carriers, for example, but also such marvels of modern military technology as the B-2 or the JSTARS surveillance aircraft, or even the M-1 Abrams tank. For a long time in the 1970s, military reformers argued that the United States was ill advised to build larger and more complex systems rather than cheaper ones. They pressed for the purchase of aircraft such as single-engine F-16s or simple diesel-electric submarines rather than the more costly (and capable) F-15s or nuclear-powered submarines.

The military reformers were wrong, at least insofar as hardware was concerned. In the Gulf War, for example, more sophisticated aircraft, such as the F-111 and the F-15, far outperformed the F-16. Ironically, it is possible that the tide has turned in their favor, now that they have been driven from the field. In military affairs, promised transformations often occur well after they have been proclaimed. In this case, the revolution points to smaller systems: cruise missiles that can fly hundreds of kilometers and hit with an accuracy of a few meters, off-road mines that listen for moving vehicles and attack, remotely piloted vehicles that locate targets and bring in artillery fire, cheap glide bombs that pick their own targets or hit predesignated ones. As massive mainframe computers have lost ground to networks of smaller computers engaged in parallel processing, so the future of military technology may turn away from mega-systems toward networks of smaller and cheaper systems, linked together by new information technologies.

This trend toward warfare by micro-system points to another trade-off, that between quality and quantity. As the defense budget falls, the trend will be to concentrate on smaller numbers of high-value platforms. These are not only aesthetically more satisfying and imposing but politically more comprehensible than smaller systems. But the true indices of power in the future may lie in possessing large numbers of cruise missiles and sensors. For, impressive as the performance of individual pieces of equipment may be, the key to their effective use will be their deployment in *quantity*. This will be the case because of all the elements of war that Clausewitz termed friction—the malfunctioning of equipment, inadequate intelligence, and enemy countermeasures. Thus, the January and June 1993 punitive attacks on Baghdad, which used up sixty-nine Tomahawk Land Attack Missiles, ate up $75 million in ordnance, for uncertain, if not negligible, effects.[19] To have real military, and hence, political effect, American generals will need to launch hundreds of strikes repeatedly over time against enemy targets. Not only will scarce defense dollars have to go to maintain adequate stocks of munitions, but the United States will also have to spend large sums of money on manufacturing technologies to drive down the costs of individual rounds. In fact, improving a Tomahawk cruise missile may matter less to its usefulness as an instrument of military power than cutting substantially its $1.2 million price tag.

Large-scale acquisition of the new technologies will be difficult in the face of pressure to maintain large forces and a high operations' tempo. Indeed, the acquisition of new hardware is taking the hardest hits from the Clinton cutbacks. Furthermore, the imperatives of day-to-day operations create pressures contrary to those of sound, long-term strategy. From a long-term point of view the navy might best invest in so-called "arsenal ships"—large, stealthy, semi-submersible vessels densely packed with missiles in vertical launch tubes. Such vessels—which might carry hundreds of missiles, plus reloads—would lurk hundreds of miles from their targets, reprogram their missiles using information transmitted by satellite, and fire on a continuous basis.[20] While an arsenal ship might be handy to have for war, it would be less valuable for showing the flag or administering a blockade. In the same vein, it makes sense to purchase more than the twenty B-2s now on order for the air force and in general to do everything possible to make up for the retirement of older bombers such as the air force's F-111 and B-52 and the navy's A-6. Bombers, however, have little utility for showing the flag and none at all for humanitarian rescues or peace-keeping operations.

The last set of choices confronting the American defense establishment concerns its constituent elements: the armed services. Since the mid-1980s, a cultural consensus has emerged that equates the services with parochial and self-seeking behavior, at odds with the requirements of joint action in war and sound administration in peace. The Goldwater-Nichols Act of 1986, prompted by Congressional dissatisfaction with the Pentagon's internal management, crystallized this disenchantment. The reforms have put increased power in the hands of the chairman and vice chairman of the Joint Chiefs of Staff, together with the Joint Staff, which now comes under the direct control and supervision of the chairman. When Congress in 1994 ordered creation of a commission to examine the services' roles and missions, it complained again about the duplication of effort and the inefficiencies of the competition among the services.

One might infer from contemporary debates that the ideal form for the U.S. military would consist of one kind of soldier wearing one uniform. One country—Canada—actually experimented with such an approach in the mid-1960s. The Canadians, however, discovered that even in their tiny military there was a natural break among land, sea, and air services. Morale suffered from such apparently minor matters as discarding traditional uniforms, a decision reversed twenty years later in 1985. (The U.S. Navy relearned this in 1977, when it reinstated the cherished bellbottom trousers and white sailor's caps taken away in 1971 by a chief of naval operations zealous for efficiency.) Soldiers, sailors, and airmen inhabit different worlds and have different cultures: whereas army captains are chiefly leaders and managers, captains in the air force (at least those who fly combat aircraft) are individual warriors.[21] Or consider the difference between sailors—who routinely deploy for six months at a time and who on ship spend seven days a week, twenty-four hours a day, in an operational environment—with the soldier who puts in a long day but usually spends evenings and weekends as a civilian.

The differentiation in service cultures is inevitable, bred as they are by the physical environments in which soldiers, sailors, and airmen operate. They are also desirable. There may be no compelling operational requirement for a distinct marine corps (armies have conducted amphibious operations— provided sufficient training), but the marines' élan and professionalism, combined with the peculiar organizational forms they have evolved, make them a unique asset. Even when they do duplicate army missions, they do those missions differently, and often better. Interservice competition and differentiation is, in fact, a good, not a bad, thing. We take it for granted in business that customers get better services with competing franchises than from monopolies: we do not call the existence of several national newspapers, for example, a deplorable failure of rationalization. We do not regard the existence of bicameral legislatures as an indication of inefficient government. In the same fashion, it is beneficial to have the services compete for such missions as counterinsurgency or theater ballistic missile defense.

Moreover, much of the so-called duplication does not represent unnecessary effort. If the air force controlled all combat aircraft, the U.S. military would probably have a similar number of aircraft at sea on carriers, albeit supported by an organization less familiar with the environment. At a time when most corporations are attempting to decentralize and reduce hierarchy, the impetus for jointness may create a more monolithic *and* unwieldy organization. Furthermore, because of the technological flux characterizing military developments, it makes sense to let competition, and not a chimerical master plan, shape the choices available to those charged with guiding national defense.

This does not mean that the current array of services is inevitable or desirable. There may be a case for increasing the services, for example, by creating one devoted solely to space and long-range missile operations. It is surely desirable to shape the competition among the services, which after all do not produce their own revenues. But it is the services that have the longest view in the defense establishment. Goldwater-Nichols gave more power to theater commanders (the so-called CINCs), including a voice in making budget decisions. By the nature of their tasks, however, theater commanders, and to some extent even the chairman, have to address immediate operational concerns and problems. They will worry about having enough airlift to send soldiers to a trouble spot tomorrow; a service chief of staff has to worry about equipping the force ten years hence.

One supposedly obsolete element of the current defense structure is the continued existence of service secretaries—civilian heads of the different departments. Too often these posts go to campaign contributors or to figureheads who provide the administration with a reward for assorted constituencies. For their part, the uniformed services know how to lull their nominal civilian superiors with endless rounds of ceremonial speeches and enjoyable excursions—driving tanks, flying aircraft, or conning a submarine.

Yet the secretaries are potentially the most important figures for asserting civilian control over the military. They control (in theory, at any rate) the service personnel and promotional systems. They can, and sometimes do, know the general officers better than a busy secretary of defense or his deputy possibly could. If they do their job well, they can turn military tourism into an intimate knowledge of the working conditions, spirit, and needs of both offi- cer and enlisted ranks within their service. The business world has learned the value of lateral entry—bringing in executives from other corporations to run their activities. The armed services, perhaps of necessity, promote from within. The civilian secretary can, if he or she has been carefully selected, bring a fresh, institutionally disinterested view to bear, which generals or ad- mirals with thirty years of service simply cannot provide. Most civilian sec- retaries have not usually fit such a description but occasionally some have. John Lehman, secretary of the navy during the Reagan years, and Donald Rice, secretary of the air force during the last administration, though very dif- ferent in their approach, provided clear direction and leadership to their re- spective services.

What Kind of Civil-Military Relations Does the United States Require?

The United States needs careful selection of service secretaries, now more than ever, because civil-military relations in America have undergone a long- term deterioration. There have been a number of warning signs: the failure of Chief of Naval Operations Admiral Frank Kelso to retire, despite the re- quest of his superior, Secretary of the Navy John Dalton, that he do so, or the instruction by General Barry McCaffrey, commander U.S. Southern Com- mand, that his subordinates report to him and not (as law requires) to the ambassadors in their respective countries.[22] The Clinton administration has managed to show a singular lack of understanding of the military and even, on occasion, contempt for it, while meekly submitting to insubordinate be- havior by all too many senior officers. But the problem goes deeper than the troubles of a flawed administration. The deterioration in U.S. civil-military relations was evident in the willingness of Chairman of the Joint Chiefs of Staff Colin Powell to oppose publicly government policy in former Yugoslavia and in the generally hostile attitude of military staffs to press and civilian pol- icy makers during the Gulf crisis.[23] The extent of this troubling state of affairs has appeared in the writings of thoughtful officers such as Colonel Charles Dunlap, Jr.—author of a disturbing (and prizewinning) black fantasy "The Origins of the American Military Coup of 2012"—and the military historian Richard Kohn.[24]

What are the sources of the distemper? The first is the trauma of Vietnam. Only 40 percent of draft-age men served at all during that war; of this group, only a quarter (that is, 10 percent of all draft-age men) went to Vietnam, and only a small minority of those served in combat (between 10 and 30 percent, depending on one's definitions). The artful public reconciliation of the Reagan years, replete with parades and the Vietnam War Memorial, together with the passing of time has smoothed over the overt sharp edges of that conflict. But scars that will not fade lie deep in the organizational culture of the American military. For American servicemen—even those who did not serve during Vietnam, a group, after all, that now commands the combat battalions and skippers the ships—Vietnam is an ur-memory. The U.S. military was, from the Civil War through the early 1960s, a popular institution; in the 1960s it encountered violent antipathy from the most educated part of the population—an antipathy that has scarcely abated. Believing as they do that the United States has never lost a war, American officers still feel a sense of humiliation at the failure of their predecessors to defeat an impoverished country with barely a tenth of our population. The majority believe that this failure stemmed from civilian interference in the war's conduct and from the failure of politicians to assign a clear mission to the military. The American military are well aware that the Vietnam experience corroded the morale, discipline, and professional expertise of their forces. It took at least a decade to repair that damage. The debacles of Lebanon in the early 1980s and Somalia a decade later, though smaller in scale, have only confirmed such beliefs.

On the other side, politicians, particularly those of the Vietnam generation who evaded service (probably the majority in both parties of that age cohort), are often shy of exerting civilian control of a kind familiar to Lincoln or even Roosevelt. Accepting, as many do, the military's assessment of the Vietnam War—an evaluation of the war's history with little merit—they fear the penalties of putting popular myths in harm's way under any save benign circumstances. For both soldiers and politicians, the Gulf War is the ideal paradigm: the conduct of a war for nominally limited and concrete (although in reality ambiguous) objectives, with overwhelming force, against an enemy, completely isolated, who, indeed, practically invited attack.[25]

There is a further factor. The tools of force themselves have become increasingly complex and difficult to understand. The American government, and in some ways the military itself, barely understood the enormous advantage that it had over Iraq in the Persian Gulf. In the old days one could, in some fashion, count military items and have a rough sense of the balance of power. Battleships, tanks, and heavy bombers were comprehensible units of account in the development of national power. Today, however, one missile looks much like another despite enormous difference in capabilities, while combat often takes place invisibly in the jamming of radars or the cloaking of aircraft, ships, and tanks by exotic materials and design. As fewer politicians bring military experience to bear, civilian dependence on military staffs will increase.

This will not lead to a coup, surely, nor even necessarily to wrenching confrontations like that between MacArthur and Truman. But it will lead to mutual miscomprehension and the distance between soldiers and statesmen that makes for foreign policy disasters and bitter recriminations. One can imagine an increasingly politicized officer corps, leading members of which identify themselves with politicians, if not with political parties. The evolution of warfare itself will complicate the process. One of the few burgeoning areas of military thought and activity is "information warfare"—the conduct of conflict through manipulation (not merely the interception or exclusion) of information. Tools of information warfare will include spurious satellite broadcasts, disruption of financial systems, forging of electronic messages, and corruption of databases. It is the kind of activity that mischievous teenagers and greedy computer wizards have already engaged in over the past decade.

Military organizations have always disposed of great power. But, by and large, such capabilities have had little direct relevance to the conduct of normal political, social, and economic life; one does not make coups with heavy bombers, and it makes little difference to societies if some individuals have learned how to operate long-range launchers with efficiency. The new techniques of information warfare, however, will increase the role played by the American military in a number of everyday transactions. In this respect, the attempt by a government agency to set standards for data encryption is merely a portent of things to come. It was not only the FBI that wanted the Clipper Chip standard enforced, but also the National Security Agency, the signal intelligence bureau of the United States, headed by a three-star general or admiral. At lower levels, other kinds of frictions will occur. Elite commando units worry about their members—trained in the black arts of breaking and entering, not to mention other, far nastier criminal skills—going bad. It has happened rarely, in part due to careful screening and training. But as the military breeds more information experts, however, one wonders how long such screening will be effective. The temptations of computer hacking are greater and safer than, say, assassination for pay.

None of this should suggest that the United States has the potential for a rogue military. In many ways this is the most acutely self-aware armed force the country has ever had and one that, in part, worries considerably about its relationship with the broader society. Its leaders are, as the Gulf War demonstrated, more politically astute and sensitive to the imperatives of foreign policy than their predecessors. The difficulty is largely on the other side, in the absence of a civilian class familiar with military matters and comfortable with soldiers, sailors, or marines. As the generation that served in the military yields place to those who have not, and who probably do not know anyone who has, the unfortunate gap grows.

One of the chief legacies of the Cold War was a narrowing of debates about national defense to an obsession with weapon systems (should we buy cheap single-engine fighters or more costly twin-engine fighters?) or simply the bottom line of the defense budget. This cramping of debate resulted from the existence of an altogether desirable consensus about the essential parameters for defense. All responsible people agreed that the United States should have a large military, that the nation should forward deploy those forces, that they should be embedded in NATO, and so on. That consensus helped win the Cold War. But it has resulted in the atrophy of our capacity for a debate of the kind that occurred at the turn of the century, when the United States became a great power, or in the late 1940s, when the United States accepted its status as a superpower. In the absence of forcing events, we may find it hard to engage in such comprehensive self-scrutiny. It is conceivable that we shall pay no large penalty in the short term. The longer view, however, may be a different matter. Francis Fukuyama's famous verdict that we have reached the end of history, defined as the rise of a world of essentially pacific liberal democratic states, may be right, and all this concern about defense an atavism, a survival of an older and bloodier age. The greater wisdom, however, may rest with Winston Churchill:

> Certain it is that while men are gathering knowledge and power with ever-increasing and measureless speed, their virtues and their wisdom have not shown any notable improvement as the centuries have rolled. The brain of a modern man does not differ in essentials from that of the human beings who fought and loved here millions of years ago. The nature of man has remained hitherto practically unchanged. Under sufficient stress—starvation, terror, warlike passion, or even cold intellectual frenzy, the modern man we know so well will do the most terrible deeds. . . . We have the spectacle of the powers and weapons of man far outstripping the march of his intelligence; we have the march of his intelligence proceeding far more rapidly than the development of his nobility. We may find ourselves in the presence of the strength of civilization without its mercy.[26]

In the wreckage of Saddam Hussein's nuclear program, in the dimly glimpsed transactions of Russian plutonium merchants, in the anonymous ferocity of those who bomb buildings in New York and Argentina, one catches flashes of what "the strength of civilization without its mercy" looks like. That being the case, the United States must break the habits of the Cold War and meet the challenges of a possibly less dangerous, but almost certainly more turbulent, age.

Chapter 4

Crack-up: The Unraveling of America's Military

Robert W. Gaskin

As Saddam Hussein's army rumbled into Kuwait on 2 August 1990, President George Bush unveiled his new national security strategy that called for a fundamental reexamination of America's role in the world. Recognizing that the United States could no longer justify continued defense spending at Cold War levels, Bush argued that regional, rather than global, threats should become the central focus of U.S. security; he proposed a sweeping 25 percent reduction in America's military strength.[1] General Colin Powell, chairman of the Joint Chiefs of Staff, characterized the reduced force structure as the "Base Force," while Secretary of Defense Richard Cheney defended the proposed cuts as prudent and necessary.

The initial reductions started in 1991 when the Bush administration began to slice army divisions, air force wings, and ships from the military structure. Under the Bush plan, the American military would decrease to 1.6 million active-duty service personnel by the mid-1990s.[2] But Bush was not around to implement his plans for decreases in defense; his successor, Bill Clinton, was elected in 1992, and the new president believed even this reduced level of defense spending was too high. Clinton stated his position clearly while campaigning late in the election; he announced his intention to cut defense spending by an additional $68 billion from the Bush five-year defense proposal.[3] In fact, he planned to cut it much more.

Shortly after Clinton's inauguration, the administration's spending priorities emerged. In March 1993, newly installed Secretary of Defense Les Aspin unveiled the new defense budget. Clinton's proposed budget cut defense far more deeply than Bush's plans, actually doubling his 1992 proposals to a $127 billion reduction over five years.[4] There was no mistaking the fact that Clinton had come to cut the deficit and get the American economy back on track. It was equally obvious from where most of the administration's budget reductions would come—defense. As for the severity of such cuts, Aspin rebuffed the criticism; he insisted that the new budget could maintain a credible force structure. In September 1993, he unveiled the Pentagon's Bottom Up Review, which, he argued, should guide a restructuring of the American military over the remainder of the decade. More important, the Bottom Up Review revealed, in specific detail, Defense Department plans to reshape American forces to conform to the administration's smaller six-year plan.

Since manpower cuts yield quick savings, the Pentagon focused on substantial personnel reductions. Under Aspin's plan, the armed forces would continue to shrink, going from the 2.1-million-strong force that fought Desert Storm, past the Bush Base Force of 1.6 million, to an active duty structure of 1.4 million. Finally, in 1999, after a decade of cuts, defense reductions would end. In the new plan, defense outlays as a percentage of gross domestic product would have declined from a high in the mid-1980s of 6.3 percent to 2.8 percent, the lowest percentage since before World War II. Buying power would also decrease sharply over the period; already in 1995, defense dollars buy 35 percent less than they did a decade earlier.[5] By 1999, the Pentagon's buying power would likely have fallen by another 17 percent.

Critics of administration plans, including the newly elected Republican Congress, troubled by such trends, have insisted that the defense budget is inadequate and forecast serious future problems unless defense receives a higher level of support. On the other hand, critics of defense spending maintain that the Pentagon no longer needs the large defense budgets it enjoyed during the Cold War and that even the Clinton defense budget might be too high. Both sides may be missing the real problem, which is not *whether* the Pentagon needs more or less money, but rather how it spends the funds that it receives. By spring 1995, two years after Clinton unveiled his proposals for restructuring America's defenses, a series of disturbing trends had emerged that suggest serious problems in the not-too-distant future. This chapter examines the collective dangers that each trend poses for American military forces. It is not a pretty picture.

❦

Slamming the Brakes on Modernization

Many defense experts believe that there is no longer sufficient funding in the administration's long-range procurement budget to replace current inventories of weapons. In fact, budget authority for procurement has plummeted from $132 billion (1995 dollars) at the height of the Reagan buildup to a 1995 low of $43.3 billion, a reduction of more than 67 percent. Compared to other defense accounts, the drop is even more glaring; for example, the accounts for military personnel and operations and maintenance have only dropped by 24 percent and 10 percent, respectively.[6] Yet, the Pentagon remains unmoved by the trends because the current strategy is to live off the fat of the Reagan procurement years. To illustrate how drastic the cuts are, the Pentagon bought only 127 aircraft and six ships in 1994 compared to 511 aircraft and twenty ships in 1990, five years ago.[7]

Aspin's replacement, William Perry, has admitted to Congress that the current procurement holiday cannot last forever; he has argued that his goal is to recapitalize the force structure fifteen years from now.[8] And indeed, the backlog of prior procurement authority is huge, topping $218 billion at the end of the 1993 fiscal year.[9] Accordingly, Perry suggests that the Pentagon needs to increase procurement accounts only by a modest 20 percent between 1996 and 1999. Martin Marietta Chairman Norman Augustine also agrees that it is possible to live off the high Reagan defense investment for a short period but warns that such an approach is not a wise policy for maintaining a highly capable force structure. He points out that the only firms that adopt such practices are those that are going out of business.[10]

The Defense Department's confidence rests largely on a shaky set of assumptions. For example, the Pentagon has repeatedly argued that it anticipates significant savings from procurement reforms and wholesale infrastructure reductions. Unfortunately, it now appears that such savings will neither be sufficient nor materialize fast enough to make up for projected shortfalls in long-range procurement accounts. Second, the Pentagon has significantly underestimated the cost increases in its advanced weapons systems; historically, program increases of upwards of 40 percent have been common.

To make things worse, the Pentagon's budget mathematics are doubtful. On 16 March 1994, Dr. Robert Reischauer, director of the Congressional Budget Office, testified that a possible $20 billion shortfall in the administration's five-year plan was incorrect; he argued that the gap was much smaller.[11] But six months later, on 20 September 1994, Deputy Secretary of Defense John Deutch admitted to the Senate Armed Services Committee that the Pentagon, in fact, now estimated a $40 billion shortfall in the five-year plan.[12] In

July 1994, the General Accounting Office released a report highly critical of the Defense Department's overoptimistic defense estimates; it suggested that the Pentagon had overprogrammed the 1995–99 defense plan by a total in excess of $150 billion.[13] The first significant manifestation of these budget problems came on 18 August 1994, when Deutch issued a memorandum directing the services to consider termination or significant delay in most major weapons programs. The memo targeted the army's Comanche helicopter, the air force's F-22 fighter, the marines' V-22 Osprey tiltrotor, and the tri-service trainer.[14] The message was clear—consider less costly alternatives because your modernization plans are out of touch with budget realities.

Defense experts such as Jeffrey Ranney believe that deferring modernization is not the answer. In fact, he warns it will make the long-term situation even worse. According to Ranney, the Pentagon needs substantially more money in its annual procurement accounts to recapitalize the force than the Clinton administration plans to spend over the next five years. He makes his point on the recapitalization deficit by taking the annual equivalent of procurement funds needed to replace or maintain the current force and dividing current replacement value by expected operational lives of the end items in the force. This is not exactly simple, "back-of-the-envelope" analysis, but it provides an idea of the magnitude of long-range problems. For example, the Pentagon must spend $68 billion *annually* to purchase the 593 aircraft and helicopters needed to replace the Bottom Up Review's fleet of 17,132 aerial vehicles assigned to the four services.[15] The longer one postpones this long-term investment, the larger will be the procurement "bow wave" and block-obsolescent problems. In fact, many defense experts are not as pessimistic as Ranney; they argue that most weapons systems will last longer than he estimates, but they do agree that deferring modernization to fund current operations and maintenance has serious implications for the future. There is a critical balance between current and future accounts, and the Pentagon cannot sacrifice one to fund the other without mortgaging its future.

There is another factor that will have a negative impact on the Pentagon's optimistic procurement projections—techflation, a word that refers to the constant increases in the costs of weapons systems. The chairman of Martin Marietta has calculated growth in the cost of weapons through the course of the twentieth century; the techflation growth factor is approximately 3.4 percentage points above the rate of inflation, and when compounded over time, it will have an enormous impact on modernization.[16] Somewhat tongue in cheek, he has suggested that if the Pentagon cannot contain the current growth in weapons costs by the year 2054, it will be able to afford one aircraft.[17]

The Pentagon's understandable desire to inject the most modern, most potent—and thus most expensive—technology into each new generation of weapons has driven techflation. Unfortunately, since most of this leading-edge technology is new and unproven, development risks are high. Acquisition experts refer to the process as "building a bicycle while riding it." Many mistakes, corrections, and course reversals occur throughout the process, and those changes drive costs ever higher; eventually, the spiraling costs result in fewer systems purchased because the weapons cost so much. The pattern occurred throughout the Cold War, most notably with aircraft purchases. During the 1950s, the Pentagon bought 2,700 fighter aircraft a year; a decade later, as jet aircraft became increasingly sophisticated, it could afford only 700—one quarter of the yearly buy of the previous decade. During the 1970s, aircraft buys dropped to approximately 300 per year. Under Presidents Reagan and Bush, the figure remained constant (around 300 per year), but only because defense spending effectively doubled.[18]

With the demise of the Cold War, the Defense Department must rethink its weapons development paradigm that demands rapid development and production of increasingly sophisticated weaponry. Perhaps the threat justified the frenzied pace of modernization and development during the Cold War, since America's strategy was to win future wars by playing the quality card. But today the U.S. military has considerable breathing room. Yet the Pentagon is *still* replacing Cold War weapons in the same fashion that it originally procured them, that is, by high production runs tied to uncertain Congressional appropriations, which continue for a few years and then abruptly terminate. The substantive difference is that far fewer weapons programs are under way today than during the U.S.-Soviet competition. The results of this approach, however, are enormous production overcapacities in defense industries—overcapacities that not only make weapons unnecessarily expensive but actually subsidize a host of inefficient practices. When B-1B production ended, there were no follow-on upgrades or modernization programs matched to the aircraft's life cycle; everything just stopped. The same approach occurred with the C-5B at Lockheed and the F-15C and the F-15E at McDonnell Douglas. The Lockheed F-16 will soon meet a similar fate. Once production runs are complete, everything evaporates. Even the prospect of foreign military sales offers only a temporary palliative.

The air force is now gearing up to replace its F-15 with the Northrop F-22, using the same production schemes that produced the F-15 twenty years ago. According to retired General Michael P. C. Carns, the former air force vice chief of staff, this procurement paradigm—with its large capacity, high overhead, numerous workforce, and expensive tool and die setups—is exactly the wrong approach to procurement of current weaponry. Carns argues that the Pentagon needs a radically new paradigm based on "lean production" techniques now sweeping private industry. He would focus production on tailored facilities that produce small annual buys while keeping a "living," highly adaptable, and efficient production line open for years. To accomplish this, Carns would flatten air force major procurements, such as of the F-22, C-17, and so forth, for decades rather than years. He would have the air force buy in organizational quantities per year—squadron(s) per year, for example, while incorporating improvements such as new technology block by block into follow-on aircraft. In addition, he would implement new design programs that would extend the service life of aircraft by decades rather than years.[19]

As for the F-15, the air force would have to extend modestly its service life to make up for lower F-22 production rates, but even here technology offers an opportunity to improve the basic model as its service life extends. For example, in September 1994, McDonnell Douglas indicated that it could double the F-15E's range to nearly 900 miles by modifying its wing design, and at an affordable price. But is a new approach to defense manufacturing, based on lean manufacturing, really possible? Lockheed thinks so. Since 1991, that company has searched for ways to trim costs and improve manufacturing processes. It has consolidated test laboratories and support functions while outsourcing small-part manufacture, thus significantly lowering overhead. As a result, Lockheed reportedly offered to sell the air force its top-of-the-line F-16 Block 50D for $20 million, a significant discount from current costs of $23 million.[20]

Others have proposed different solutions to the Pentagon's procurement difficulties, most of which will not work, since they fail to address the real problems. The General Accounting Office, for example, suggested that the air force could safely delay the F-22 for eight years, and even Deutch thinks a four-year delay necessary. Both are probably right; however, delay does not address the basic problems with either the procurement process or the budget gap; it only delays the inevitable. Another Deutch idea reportedly is to produce approximately one hundred F-22s in order to have a special "silver bullet" force of stealthy fighters.[21] Unfortunately, such an approach would make the F-22 so expensive that it would inevitably turn into a tempting target for Congressional budget cutters and doom that aircraft to the fate of the B-2. In addition, the basic issue would still remain; what would replace the F-15?

Undoubtedly, by incorporating many of Carns's ideas, the Pentagon could realize substantial procurement savings, but even such a radical departure from current practices would not be enough—the gap is too big. According to Carns, the modernization investment gap will remain until the Pentagon finds a way to balance annual defense costs, such as operations and maintenance (O&M), against investments in a viable and capable force in the future. Today, that balance is entirely lacking; instead, the Pentagon bends over backwards to keep the current force viable while placing ten pounds of future modernization in a five-pound bag.[22]

Infrastructure Overload

When military bases open, a hose is attached from the Pentagon to the nearby community, a valve is opened, and millions of federal dollars flow into the local community on a constant basis. This creates jobs and businesses, people move in to share the wealth, communities sprout around the base, and the local economy "greens up" courtesy of the U.S. taxpayer. No sane politician wants to stop the money flow, no matter how much the Pentagon can save by closing the base. In fact, from a political perspective, bases are a perfect example of undiluted benefits accruing to communities paid for by the dispersed contributions of millions of taxpayers.[22] In theory, it is a perfect setup.

Unfortunately, for many local communities, reality has a bad habit of quashing theory and disrupting federally produced, false prosperity. After all, the Pentagon has a mission and a budget to execute that mission; when money gets tight, the Pentagon, like all businesses, must cut excess overhead. That means excess bases should close, but in the current political world the operative word is *should*. In the past decade Congress has thrown every legislative obstacle it could to obstruct Defense Department efforts to close obsolete or unneeded military bases. There is nothing new in this phenomenon, however. For over thirty-four years the Pentagon has fought Congress on this issue.

On 30 March 1961, Robert McNamara, then secretary of defense, announced that he intended to close thirty-seven bases in the continental United States. Congress, surprised and angered by his move, initiated hearings, a move clearly designed to intimidate the new secretary of defense and his department. Undaunted, McNamara announced continued closings over the next several years: thirty-three bases more in 1963; sixty-three bases in April 1964; and ninety-five more only six months later in November 1964.[23] Congress's first attempt to block the Pentagon's ability to close bases came in 1965, when Congress passed H.R. 8439, which contained a number of minor legal obstacles to base closings. Wisely, President Lyndon Johnson vetoed the legislation; he declared: "The president cannot sign into law a bill that substantially inhibits him from performing his duty. . . . The times do not permit it. The Constitution prohibits it."[24] Congress retreated and passed a weaker bill that required the Pentagon to delay closings for a thirty-day period after reporting to the Armed Services Committees the reasons for closing bases with a total of more than 250 military and civilian jobs.

The real battle began in 1973 when the Nixon and Ford administrations tried to close excess bases following the Vietnam War. In April 1973, Secretary of Defense Elliot Richardson announced 274 closure and alignment actions; not surprisingly, Congress reacted heatedly. It held hearings again, but no serious threat to the Pentagon's closing process emerged. But when the Pentagon announced a further 147 bases targeted for realignment or closure in 1976, Congress passed short-term legislation establishing a modest beachhead for blocking such closure efforts.

The next year, Congress passed, and President Jimmy Carter signed, the Military Construction Authorization Act of 1978. The legislation created an armada of legal obstacles and delays sufficient to make it virtually impossible for the Pentagon to shut down any military installation. Defense experts have always been highly critical of Carter's decision to reverse Johnson's stand a decade earlier. As expected, the law was lethal to the Pentagon's flexibility to close excess installations; between 1977 and 1988 Congress vetoed *all* attempts by the Department of Defense to close or realign major military installations.[25]

The inability to shed excess properties caused serious financial problems for the Department of Defense, which began downsizing in 1985. Though the Pentagon reduced its personnel numbers substantially, the bases that housed them remained open due to Congressional mandate. Congress finally confronted its own irresponsibility in 1988 by creating the first Base Realignment and Closing Commission (BRAC). Proponents sold the initiative on Capital Hill as a device to allow Congress to cash in on what many believed would be the "peace dividend" while insulating its members from the political fallout of an angry electorate. The commission's successes rested on the fact that it was completely nonpartisan. Neither Congress, the secretary of defense, nor the president could tinker with the commission's recommendation. It was either all or nothing.

The results of the first BRAC in 1988 were modest, but it represented a hopeful sign. Admittedly it identified only twelve major bases and a number of smaller installations for closure, but the model appeared to work. Congress built on that success and passed legislation in 1990 that authorized three more BRAC rounds in 1991, 1993, and 1995—all nonelection years. But then the world changed. In less than two years the Berlin Wall fell, Eastern Europe threw off its shackles, and the Soviet Union vaporized. By summer 1991, without warning, the Cold War had ended. Congress, to its horror, realized that it had conveniently created a process that would finally allow the Pentagon to close hundreds of obsolete military installations across the country.

Since the convening of the first BRAC in 1988, the process has targeted over sixty-seven major bases for closure, with many others substantially reduced by realignment. On 1 March 1995, the final BRAC will convene, and two weeks later, on 15 March, the Defense Department will submit a new list of proposed base closings for the final BRAC round. Pentagon officials have long warned that this round will represent the "mother of all base closings," dwarfing all previous proposals. The problem is that the previous three base-closing rounds have closed the easy bases: there are few easy choices remaining. Yet the BRAC must make choices if the Pentagon is to reduce its bloated infrastructure.

The Pentagon's larger problem is that as BRAC '95 concludes, so too will its flexibility to shed excess installations. As the Defense Department continues its downsizing, possibly dropping below the Bottom Up Review's force of 1.4 million, the need to rationalize infrastructure will be more pressing; yet the tools are not in place. Johnson was right when he vetoed Congress's attempt to tie the Defense Department's hands in 1965. Perhaps the new Republican leadership will have the moral courage to reexamine the 1978 law that effectively prevents the Pentagon from closing any of its bases. If the will is lacking, then Congress should reauthorize three follow-on BRAC rounds for further reductions in excess installations. However, if Congress does nothing, as most defense experts expect, the drain on smaller operations and maintenance accounts will get worse with each passing year.

Organizational Reform

Something quite extraordinary is going on at 1100 Wilson Boulevard in Arlington, Virginia. There, in Suite 1200F, a distinguished group of civilians is attempting to reshape America's post–Cold War military forces. To understand why this is happening, it is necessary to revisit the Reagan era.

The mid-1980s were a time of military scandal. News organizations jostled one another to expose the latest example of Pentagon "waste," and the Pentagon provided ample fodder. Media stories highlighted $74,000 ladders, $400 claw hammers, and $7,000 coffee pots and soured the American public's attitude toward military spending.[26] Not surprisingly, Congress screamed for reform, and defense spending levels began a long decline that has yet to bottom out. At approximately the same time, reform of another sort was taking place. Many in Congress believed that the power of the individual services was a significant impediment to efficient operation of the U.S. military. The resulting legislation empowered the chairman of the joint chiefs to adopt more rational management practices. The legislation also contained a provision requiring the chairman to report to the secretary of defense every three years on recommendations for changes in the roles and missions of the services. The main focus of this requirement was on improving efficiency by cutting duplication, redundancy, and waste.

Admiral William Crowe completed the first roles and missions report in September 1989. It was a report that many thought fundamentally flawed.

General Michael J. Dugan, then serving as the deputy chief of staff for plans and operations in the air force, complained to the joint staff that the report was too long and failed to provide a rationale for change. He argued that the complex matrix of service functions "did little to pave the way for needed changes" and added that the matrix could even be dangerous in the hands of Congressional staffers, because it tended to oversimplify crucial issues.[27]

For whatever reasons, Crowe never delivered his report to the secretary of defense. Instead, he finalized the report hours before he retired and dumped it on the desk of the incoming chairman, General Colin Powell. Powell's new duties soon focused his attention on other issues. Finally on 2 November 1989 he forwarded the report to the secretary of defense with a covering letter that praised Crowe's efforts but underlined his own concerns with much of the report. The new chairman pointed out that the report was not a consensus document, unlike the Key West Agreement of 1948.[28] Cheney replied three months later, agreeing that Crowe's ideas required study in greater detail.[29] The exchange was not unusual, since the Bush administration was relatively new and Cheney wanted the advice of his staff on a document with far-reaching implications. But Saddam's invasion of Kuwait interrupted review efforts six months later. One year later, the Soviet Union collapsed and the Cold War ended. Eventually the report died a quiet death as the Pentagon turned its attention to a post–Cold War "Base Force." For those who participated in the first effort since 1948 to streamline roles and missions, the report's demise was a clear indication that change would not come easily.

As the date for the chairman's second report neared in spring 1992, many in Congress realized that the reporting provisions in the Goldwater-Nichols Act of 1986 allowed the Pentagon to avoid public scrutiny of the issue. Since the chairman's report was only to the secretary of defense, the entire process remained internal to the Pentagon. Congress then inserted provisions into the 1993 Defense Authorization Bill requiring the chairman to forward his triennial report to Congress. The legislation also forced the secretary of defense to submit his views to Congress on the chairman's report.[30] The issue would go public for the first time in half a century. Senator Sam Nunn, chairman of the Senate Armed Services Committee, raised the stakes with a speech on the Senate floor in July 1992. He charged that Key West had failed to solve wasteful redundancy and duplication in the services and called for a thorough review of service roles and missions.[31] The pressure on Powell and the joint staff to produce a substantive report further increased when presidential candidate Bill Clinton endorsed Nunn's speech in Los Angeles the next month.

Then the 1992 presidential election was over: Clinton turned to health care instead of military reform; Nunn never repeated his speech on roles and missions; Dr. John Hamre, Nunn's expert on the issue, became the Pentagon's comptroller; and Powell remained alone to resolve this crucial issue. Lacking political support from Clinton, who has remained silent on the issue since his August 1992 speech, and with a secretary of defense who had not expressed strong views on the subject, Powell did the best he could. The general's report did identify important opportunities for achieving management reforms and recommended positive changes in the assignment of command responsibilities. Nevertheless, it shied away from recommendations that would have reduced or made significant changes in redundant service functions. The General Accounting Office declared that a major cause of Powell's failure was his report's shallow analysis, which refused to support the sweeping reforms favored by Nunn.[32]

When Pentagon briefers laid out the chairman's recommendations before the House and Senate Armed Services Committees early in 1993, the legislators were clearly disappointed. Congress then went to work to fix the problem. If the generals and admirals could not reform, then Congress would turn the problem over to outsiders: the Fiscal Year 1994 Defense Authorization Bill contained legislation creating an independent Roles and Missions Commission, whose charter was to establish a list of recommendations for the secretary of defense that delineated major reforms in the roles and missions of the services.[33]

Congress's frustration is justified. The current Pentagon regulation that allocates service functions—roles and missions—is dated September 1987. Yet despite considerable efforts by Crowe and Powell, not a single comma in that regulation has changed in over eight years. Given the stakes involved, and the long history of interservice battles, the continuing gridlock on roles and missions is not surprising. The legislation by which Congress unified the armed forces in 1947 lashed the four services together as a team under direction of a civilian secretary of defense. In reality, they have continued to operate as four separate fiefdoms that have feuded with each other for the biggest share of the defense budget while training for war under totally separate doctrines. Each service justified its weapons "wish list" on the roles and missions outlined in the Functions Director, or DoD Regulation 5100.1. But that directive completely fails to address the question of why the services insist on replicating each other's capabilities.

One reason lies in ingrained preferences for operating as independently as possible, within each service's independent "bubble," with an array of forces whose capabilities are, in many instances, redundant to those of other services. The navy does not trust the air force to build and deploy satellites that meet its needs, and vice versa. The air force failed to take navy and marine refueling needs into consideration when it designed and procured tankers for

Strategic Air Command, while the marines still do not want to integrate their air and land forces under air and land component commanders.

Desert Storm represented a departure from this mind-set, but its conduct does not necessarily reflect the model for future conflicts. The marines and navy still smart from the fact that they had to operate under a joint force air commander. Even the highly successful integrated air campaign clashed with army doctrine for employing rotary-winged aviation; as a result, army helicopters purposely sat out the air war, when they could have been of considerable use in reducing the Iraqi Army's combat capabilities. The unfortunate result of a predisposition to fight as independent services is that each maximizes independent war-fighting capabilities by fielding a host of costly duplications and redundancies.

Mistrust is also a major factor. The more the services depend on vital support from each other, the more they are likely to develop organic capabilities that address that anxiety. For example, the army had developed and is already fielding the Advanced Tactical Missile System (ATACMS) to strike directly at targets deep in enemy rear areas, despite the fact that the air force and navy field hundreds of fighters and bombers to execute that mission. In another instance, the army fields a vast armada of attack helicopters to provide close air support to its ground forces. Meanwhile, the air force partially justifies its force of A-10s and F-16s for the same mission. There is a reason for the duplication; only army helicopters remain under direct army control, thus assuring their availability.

On the other hand, the marines have insisted on their own air force ever since the navy abandoned them on Guadalcanal in 1942. To the marines, the navy remains thoroughly untrustworthy. As a result they operate one reserve and three active air wings, each assigned to support a marine division. Moreover, the justification for a separate marine air force rests in law rather than military necessity; since the Korean War, Title 10 has specifically stated that there would never be fewer than three marine air wings. In fact, the marines are the only service fortunate enough to have their force structure protected by law.

It is questionable whether the Roles and Missions Commission established by Congress can, in fact, unravel the Gordian knot, or even make substantial changes. First, the commission's recommendations are not automatic; the secretary of defense must act on them. When the secretary forwards the commission's recommendations to the Joint Chiefs of Staff for their views, no service will take elimination or consolidation of forces or missions lying down. Second, even if the secretary of defense agrees with the commission's recommendations, members of Congress will most likely move to prevent their service constituencies from harm. Third, those in Congress who have championed this issue, Senator Nunn and Representative Dellums, are now in the minority. The only Republican on either Armed Services Committee who has taken a strong stand on this issue is Sen. John Warner of Virginia, and he has been silent of late. Therefore, there will be little significant pressure on the commission for producing real change, for eliminating redundant service forces and capabilities. And finally, the size of the commission's agenda is staggering. Clearly, the list is too large, and the issues too complex, for resolution in the time allotted to the commission. To be successful, it must resolve at minimum an average of four or five issues per month—a tall order; to move at such a clip, the required analysis risks being as shallow and unsupportive of sweeping change as was the Pentagon's 1993 report.

If the Congress or the Pentagon proves incapable of eliminating at least some of the services' redundant missions and capabilities, the American military will enter the twenty-first century with a World War II organizational framework, since the current division of service functions occurred at the end of that conflict. Worse, the Department of Defense will fail to address one of the most important challenges it faces: namely, to reorganize itself during the next few decades to take advantage of the enormous capabilities provided by modern technology. It is clear that we are on the edge of a revolution in military technology and doctrine that will change how we calculate power and military effectiveness. Such changes, in turn, are crucial to providing the basic calculus for funding decisions in future decades. Only by restructuring the roles and missions can we hope to fight and win future conflicts.[34] Our future adversaries will not be so encumbered with the baggage of a half-century of interservice conflict and rivalry. This is not a budget issue, as many have assumed. It is really about spending wisely the money that Congress allocates. But more important, it is about whether this country fields a force that can win, and win fast, in the future.

Strategy Force Mismatch

On 1 September 1993, the Pentagon unveiled its $1.3 trillion future year defense program, the Bottom Up Review. The newly appointed secretary of defense, Les Aspin, initiated this project in March 1993 to "provide the direction for shifting America's focus away from a strategy designed to meet a global Soviet threat to one oriented toward the new dangers of the post–Cold War era."[35] The Bottom Up Review also attempted to solve the major problem that had bedeviled the Pentagon since the liberation of Eastern Europe and the collapse of the Soviet Union in 1989: namely, with the end of the Cold War, Americans' major security threat disappeared. The Bottom Up Review hypothesized a new set of "dangers," or threats: aggression by regional powers, the proliferation of weapons of mass destruction, the failure of democratic reform in Russia, and the need to sustain a strong American economy essential to underwriting future defense needs.[36] In fact, most of the Bottom Up Review dealt with dangers presented by regional aggression; more specifically, it focused on the ability to fight and win two major regional conflicts occurring simultaneously.

Accordingly, the Bottom Up Review emphasizes a smaller force mix than the Bush administration's Base Force structure, which itself represented a 25 percent reduction in the force that fought the Gulf War in 1991. (See Table 4 – 1.) The requirement to fight two simultaneous major regional wars, perhaps in the Gulf and on the Korean peninsula, with even the Bush administration's Base Force would be a tall order. For example, the last Joint Military Net Assessment performed by the joint staff in 1992 stated, "A second major regional crisis affecting U.S. interests—while still involved in Southwest Asia—would require extraordinary measures." More specifically, it stated that the Base Force was capable of handling—with low risk—"only one major contingency at a time."[37] In addition, the report concluded that the response to a second major regional conflict would "significantly disrupt the [U.S.] economy," due to a huge and sudden drain on national resources and industrial production.[38] Remember, these conclusions referred to a force much larger than the Bottom Up Review's force.

Table 4–1.

	Base Force	**BUR Force**
Ground Forces		
Active army divisions	14	10
Reserve army divisions	6+	5+
Marine divisions	3	3
Maritime Forces		
Major warships	443	346
Aircraft carriers	13	12
Navy air wings	13	11
Marine air wings	3	3
Tactical Air Forces		
Active fighter wings	16	13
Reserve fighter wings	12	7

A more recent study done by the Electronic Industries Association (EIA) and released in October 1994 casts further doubts on the Pentagon's ability to fight two simultaneous major contingencies. "Fulfilling a [two major regional contingency] strategy just isn't in the cards," noted Ed Waesche, chairman of the EIA task force.[39] His pessimistic assessment appeared in the association's thirtieth annual ten-year defense forecast, which has considerable credibility due to its successful track record of forecasting national security issues. According to the report, there is a 15 percent gap between the Bottom Up Review requirements and the funding required to support the force.[40] In light of the report's ominous conclusions, there are serious questions about the Bottom Up Review's optimistic assumptions. Can the United States, in fact, fight and win two near-simultaneous major regional crises? And other than funding shortfalls, are there other, more serious problems?

Many defense analysts believe that strategic lift represents the Bottom Up Review's major limiting factor. According to the Pentagon's Defense Planning Guidance for the fiscal years 1996–2001, "constraints on strategic airlift and sealift will limit the rate at which the United States can project force to the MRCs [major regional conflicts]."[41] Vice Admiral Paul D. Butcher admitted to George Wilson of the *Army Times* that the lift constraints were so bad that the United States could never repeat Desert Storm. Even in that conflict the United States was so short of lift that it had to borrow half the sealift for our forces from other nations.[42] General Joseph P. Hoar, commander U.S. Central Command, testified in March 1993, "Airlift in this country is broken right now. I'm not even sure it's workable for one major regional contingency."[43] General Ronald Fogleman, the new air force chief of staff and at the time commander Air Mobility Command, echoed Hoar's assessment, "I can't provide lift for two major regional contingencies. I can do it for one ... although even here, there are some fairly heroic assumptions that are made with regard to the activation of the civil reserve air fleet."[44]

Other cracks in the Pentagon's airlift assumptions appeared last fall. An update of the 1992 Mobility Requirements Study concluded that airlift enhancements, critical to the Bottom Up Review's strategy, would not be in place until years later than originally estimated. Specifically, the report stated that since the airlift fleet will be approximately thirty C-17s short at the turn of the century, the Pentagon's ability to fight two major regional conflicts will remain sharply limited until 2006 at best.[45] The fact is the Pentagon has no long-term strategy for upgrading airlifters in Air Mobility Command whose average age is now twenty-five years and growing. Air Mobility Command will have to phase out its core airlifter, the C-141, years earlier than planned because of premature aging, due partly to delays in purchasing and fielding the C-17. In December 1994, a remarkable 25 percent of the entire airlift fleet was either in overhaul or out of commission.[46]

Logistic bottlenecks represent a further limiting factor. In summer 1994 the General Accounting Office delved into problems presented by the cuts in European bases. It found that without three key staging areas—Lajos in the Azores, Rhein-Main in Germany, and Torrejon in Spain—airlift operations would slow significantly. Specifically, the report warned that since Rhein-Main and Torrejon alone supported 58 percent of the airlift missions for the Gulf War, the United States could not fight a similar conflict in the Middle East without these bases.[47] But the air force turned Torrejon over to Spain in 1992 and placed it on standby status. In addition, air force presence on Rhein-Main has significantly declined since the Gulf War, although it does retain much of the infrastructure on standby. Still, the bottom line is clear—when the U.S. military completes its drawdowns, America will have less than 50 percent of the overseas bases it enjoyed during the Cold War. Moreover, many key bases for moving supplies to the Middle East and Europe will no longer be available. This state of affairs will have an enormous impact on the rapid deployment and support of any force that needs to move to the Gulf or Europe to fight a major regional conflict.

The Bottom Up Review is probably correct that airpower will have to join any conflict early with as much high-tech weaponry as possible to make up for reductions in overall fighter strength. For example, the Bottom Up Review stresses that the armed forces need a number of "enhancements" to win two near-simultaneous major regional conflicts; specifically, it stresses the leading role that precision weaponry—one of the most important enhancements—must play.[48] But sufficient amounts of such weaponry may not be available for the foreseeable future. General Merrill McPeak, formerly air force chief of staff, warned Congress in March 1994 that until the air force can make significant enhancements to its bomber fleet, it cannot meet the two-major-regional-conflicts goal.[49] Such improvements will not occur until near the end of this century at the earliest. Even then, some of the Pentagon's precision weaponry may not make it into production. The Pentagon canceled Northrop-Grumman's problem-plagued TSSAM stealth cruise missile last December due to poor performance and a spiraling price tag. Even basic precision munition accounts are short, according to air force leaders. General Michael Loh, commander of Air Combat Command, testified to Congress last year that his forces will be critically short of precision munitions such as the 2,000-pound GBU-24. He warned that should the United States fight two major regional conflicts, the air force would have to depend heavily on unguided weapons.[50]

In reality, the Pentagon will continue into the next century with a force that consists largely of platforms that drop dumb bombs. Ninety-three percent of navy and air force fighters cannot at the present time employ precision weapons. Of twenty air force wings planned under the Bottom Up Review, only six will have the capacity of dropping precision weapons.[51] The Defense Science Board's Task Force on Tactical Air Warfare issued a scathing report in November 1993 highly critical of the low priority placed on precision weapons by the Pentagon; it also warned not only that the current unwillingness to extend precision capabilities was short-sighted but also that it would prove costly in money and lives in the next war.[52] The Defense Science Board also pointed to significant shortfalls in the future for precision weaponry. Specifically, production in Paveway III laser-guided bombs, ultimately planned for the F-117, is a paltry 240 per year. As a result, less than half of the Bottom Up Review's planned number of these weapons will be available by the end of the decade.[53]

While the United States sent only a quarter of its tactical fighters to the Gulf, almost all of its high-tech weaponry went. Ninety-three percent of aircraft capable of employing laser-guided bombs, 92 percent of aerial tankers, and over 60 percent of laser-guided weapons in air force inventories deployed to that single contingency.[54] If the Pentagon were suddenly tasked to fight two simultaneous regional wars, the force for each contingency would be far less capable than the Desert Storm forces of 1990–91, since there are now fewer resources available, and the U.S. military would have to divide those systems between the two conflicts.

Most senior officers have serious concerns about the smaller force size. General Gary Luck, commander of U.S. forces in Korea, recently stated that he believed that he would need nearly 400,000 troops to defeat a North Korean invasion.[55] Since this total represents slightly less than the entire active army envisioned by the Bottom Up Review, elementary math suggests that if Luck is right, there would be virtually nothing to fight a second major regional conflict. Marines might help, but they are not equipped as is the army for sustained combat operations ashore and would suffer substantial casualties as a result. Army reserves will take time to equip and train and might not be available in timely fashion for either contingency.

Thus, what emerges from any examination of the Bottom Up Review's assumptions is that the risk is much higher than most realize, even in the most favorable cases. How much risk is debatable. Secretary of Defense William Perry and Chairman John Shalikashvili have testified before Congress that the risks are only moderate. But others suggest differently. Rear Admiral Francis Lacroix, the Joint Staff deputy director for force structure, testified in

March 1994 that the Bottom Up Review structure "puts troops at high risk," though he never satisfied a panel of frustrated Congressmen as to exactly what he meant by "high risk."[56]

The real problem with the Bottom Up Review is that it fails the "truth in labeling" test. It does *not* provide a force tailored to fight and win two simultaneous regional wars; rather, its major focus seems to be on deterrence and intimidation instead of war. The operative word is *presence*. The Pentagon's problem is that presence does not come cheaply; in fact, it is expensive. So to make ends meet in the harsh budget climate of 1994 the Pentagon lopped off chunks of the nation's real military capabilities in support of a naval strategy whose central tenet is continuous forward deployment. This is especially curious, given the fact that naval presence plays a relatively minor role in the strategy supporting the Bottom Up Review. For example, while the Bottom Up Review devotes eight and one-half pages to discussing the parameters of two major regional conflicts, it gives only five paragraphs to naval presence at the report's end.

Any future discussion on the Pentagon's maritime priorities needs to focus on what makes presence so valuable and how planners in the Defense Department have arrived at such conclusions. Answers to this issue may depend on how one defines presence. The navy prefers to define it in the narrowest of terms, that is, continuous deployment of large-deck carrier battle groups at possible crisis points in the Persian Gulf, Indian Ocean, Mediterranean, and Western Pacific. The navy defends these deployments by claiming two important benefits. First, by their presence, they indicate an American commitment that deters and intimidates. Second, if deterrence fails, they represent a force ready for war. The problem with both arguments is that they do not hold up under scrutiny. The nature of deterrence, for example, is far different than during the Cold War, when a carrier battle group represented a significant warning to the Kremlin. Now, U.S. Adriatic naval deployments hardly entice more than yawns from Serb troops in Bosnia. Second, while the power of a modern carrier battle group is impressive, it is hardly enough to address more than minor contingencies. For real combat power, land-based army and air forces are crucial, a fact even the navy acknowledges.

Statistics from the Gulf War provide an insight into understanding how little carrier battle groups could contribute to regional wars. During the first two weeks of the air campaign in the Gulf War, the average number of daily strike sorties per deck from six carriers was approximately eighteen. The average went higher later in the war when the carriers moved further into the Gulf, but even then it only reached twenty-four sorties per deck per day for the six carriers.[57] In other words, at peak efficiency, the navy's six carriers mounted the equivalent of a single air force fighter wing flying a standard two sorties per day. Much has been made of the navy's Tomahawk (TLAM) missile. To put the public relations in perspective, thirty-six air force F-117s attacked more targets on the war's first day than all six carriers and TLAMs combined. Moreover, air force B-52s delivered more than twice the ordnance that all six carriers did over the course of the war.[58]

The navy's problem is that many of its aircraft can contribute nothing to the war on the ground; many are there simply to defend the fleet. As a result, five times as many aircraft as those based on land must support each attack aircraft. With this support-ratio problem, the navy provided only 8 percent of the strike sorties during the war, despite the fact that it had 20 percent of the combat aircraft. The air force had 46 percent of theater combat aircraft, yet it provided 68 percent of all strike sorties.[59] Even some naval officers marvel at the navy's overemphasis on carrier forces that seemingly deliver so little. Retired Captain Steve Ramsdale, former director of aviation history at the Navy Historical Center, visited all six carriers during the course of the conflict in that position. He confided the following during a recent interview: "[Schwarzkopf] was aware that the navy was contributing 140 sorties per day to the war effort. Well, I'll tell you what, six carriers divided into 140 sorties is less than twenty-five per day. And you can't commit the kind of resources that we have committed as a nation to seaborne power and get that kind of return and still find it acceptable. I am surprised that the navy has managed to skate around that one ever since."[60]

The above is not meant to suggest that we do not need carriers. We do, but with very different capabilities. In some respects, like the air force, the navy has been its own worst enemy. Its procurement decisions in the 1980s have been less than wise; its replacement for the A-6 attack aircraft, the F/A 18, has less range, fewer capabilities for the attack mission, and only one crewmember. The navy has even less ability to deliver precision-guided munitions than the air force, while many of its aircraft are single mission, so if there is no enemy air opposition (such as in the Gulf, for example), the premier air defense fighter, the F-14, can only bore holes in the sky. Finally, carrier air wings are still configured to confront the high-tech air capabilities of the Soviets (which put a high premium on defending the fleet) rather than to putting bombs on the targets that would arise in a major regional contingency.

The marines also play a considerable role in the Pentagon's presence strategy. With a smaller marine corps, however, that mission is exacting an increasing toll on troops and equipment. At a recent symposium, Brigadier General Michael Ryan expressed worry about the strain. "We need to get our hands around the [operations' tempo]," he declared. "We have twelve of twenty-four infantry battalions deployed, and twelve of thirty helicopter squadrons deployed in excess of six months annually."[61] The marine corps totaled 200,000 active-duty marines as recently as the late 1980s with approximately 24,000 deployed. The marines have dropped to 174,000, yet have increased the number of troops deployed to 27,000. As a result, the marine corps has stretched itself to the breaking point, largely in fulfillment of the presence mission.

Yet, the senior marine leadership remains committed to the corps' forward presence in places like Okinawa and Japan and on amphibious-ready groups deployed continuously in the Atlantic and Pacific. The ostensible "requirement" for such commitments provides the justification for a marine corps of somewhere between 159,000 and 174,000. The Pentagon's problem is that the "presence" budget is driving a gigantic hole through the Bottom Up Review force. The argument against presence posits that in today's world it is quite possible to get the same *effect* as maritime presence by displaying determination on CNN or in a speech at the United Nations. Perhaps the C-130s lifting off from Fort Bragg with the Haitian invasion force provided enough "presence" to convince General Cedras that the game was up, though they were still hundreds of miles away.

But the real justification for the marine corps lies in its ability to perform a difficult and complex mission (one in which the army has no recent experience): namely, the ability to provide significant intervention capabilities from the sea. Presence in the current day is no longer enough; if presence cannot translate into hard military capabilities it is of little use. The crucial intervention mission, however, is being held hostage by the navy's support for twelve carrier battle groups that the defense budget cannot support. Thus, the marines are scheduled to spend much of their limited procurement budget on an aircraft, the F/A 18, that augments naval air for the carrier battle group rather than providing the crucial support for amphibious forces. Without procurement of sufficient amphibious vessels and support structure over the coming decade, the marines will steadily lose the capabilities that in fact justify *any* spending on the carrier battle group. Thus, the marines are being dragged away from the weapons and support they need for their essential mission by the navy's demands for a carrier force structure the nation can no longer afford as well as by the corps' own historical memories of the 1st Marine Division's abandonment on Guadalcanal in 1942.

Analysts at Lockheed Corporation have recently finished a two-year study that examines the relative costs of alternative force structures. Its central finding is that if the defense budget declines to approximately $220 billion in the next several years, as is likely, then the Bottom Up Review force is not affordable. Consequently, the Pentagon will have to make choices. If, for example, it wishes to provide a navy of twelve carriers and 346 ships, then it must give up eight air force fighter wings and three army divisions. On the other hand, if it decides to retain the army and air force at Bottom Up Review levels, then it will have to slash the navy's force structure to nine carriers and 296 ships. And even here, $220 billion will not support the ten active army divisions, so the army will have to drop to eight active divisions.[62] In reviewing these options, sooner or later the Pentagon must question the credibility of the navy's presence arguments or the army's maintenance of an armor-heavy force in the continental United States that has lift only sufficient to go to Mexico or Canada. If it does not question such a force structure and make hard choices, it will wreck its long-term capabilities.

The navy bases the need for twelve large-deck carriers on the requirement to keep three forward-deployed continuously. Given the choices outlined by Lockheed, it may be possible to achieve presence in another fashion while reducing the number of large-deck carriers. For example, if a way could be found to eliminate one of the three current carrier's forward-deployed stations, then the force could be brought down to nine carriers and fewer than 300 ships. Savings may then be available to pay for army, air force, and marine capabilities and the support structure needed to fight the Bottom Up Review strategy. There may be a way. The air force recently completed a classified study on overseas presence that recommends substituting marine amphibious carriers as an alternative to the navy's Nimitz-class carriers in the presence role.[63] Such an approach would also allow substantial increases in the actual ability to intervene over the beaches, should presence fail. The navy has rejected such arguments by pointing out that marine amphibious carriers do not possess the capabilities of navy large-deck carriers, which is true. But the argument is not about capabilities—it is about presence.

Others, including naval aviation experts, agree with the thrust of such suggestions. James L. George, graduate of the Naval Academy, five-time winner of the Arleigh Burke Essay Contest in *Proceedings*, and author of six books on naval strategy, is one of them. His most recent book, *The U.S. Navy in the 90s, Alternatives for Action*, argues that large marine carriers, LHAs and LHDs, offer real alternatives, not only in the presence role, but in projecting power. Moreover, he believes that if the marine carriers possessed ski-jumps and arresting gear, they could employ aircraft with more range and payload than the present class of vertical-lift jets in marine aviation.[64]

While the Clinton administration attempts to maintain the Bottom Up Review force for the present, it cannot do so for the long term, given its own forecasts for defense spending. Currently, the administration embraces a two-major-regional-conflict strategy and claims to have the force necessary to execute that strategy. In the opinion of most defense experts and industry analysts, it does not. Given the overprogramming (or underfunding) emphasized by the General Accounting Office, along with accompanying modern-ization shortfalls, the administration must make hard choices soon between combat capabilities or forces designed primarily to provide presence. The lat-ter is a recipe for disaster.

Raiding the Defense Budget

One of the most disturbing trends in the current defense climate is the growing willingness to raid the defense budget for programs that contribute little to national security. In an era of declining defense budgets, this trend carries excessive costs. Every penny robbed from defense for trendy programs or pork is a penny robbed from readiness and training, military pay, or weapons systems procurement and modernization. In the fiscal year (FY) 1990 defense budget, $3.1 billion went for nondefense programs. By 1994, that amount had skyrocketed to approximately $12.7 billion, while the FY 1995 budget provides more of the same: approximately $12 billion in nondefense spending.[65]

Clearly the Pentagon budget has become a cash cow for special interests (i.e., pork) or for federal agencies competing for fewer federal dollars. If pres-ent trends continue, we will see even more waste and diversion from the ser-vices' legitimate needs. For example, defense funds have been, and are continuing to be, used for World Cup Soccer ($15 million) and the Summer Olympics ($7 million), to provide medical research on Lyme disease ($850,000), breast cancer ($215 million), and prostate cancer ($6 million), to study land use on Indian reservations, and to support universities and research centers working on nonmilitary projects.[66]

The Clinton administration, on the other hand, has willingly used the defense budget to fund other federal agencies. Whether assigning to the Pen-tagon duties traditionally performed by civilian agencies or transferring de-fense dollars directly to such agencies, the administration has bled away funds from an already severely constrained defense budget. The 1995 Defense Au-thorization Bill has allocations for $25 million for the Department of Justice, $50 million for the Small Business Administration, $43 million for the Farm-ers Home Administration, and an estimated $300 million distributed among the Commerce, Energy, and Transportation departments, NASA, and the National Science Foundation. In addition, the costs of environmental cleanup have grown from $1.6 billion in FY 1990 to almost $6 billion in FY 1995, while foreign assistance programs have grown from virtually nothing in FY 1990 to over $200 million in the FY 1995 defense budget.[67]

In their own right, many such projects are worthy of federal funding, but there is absolutely no reason that they should receive funding from the Pentagon at the expense of priority defense-related projects. What makes these programs hard to kill is the lack of financial accountability in the defense budgetary process. The Office of the Secretary of Defense, the military services, and the defense agencies do not maintain much of the relevant cost data concerning their participation in non–defense-related activities. Furthermore, the data they do possess exist in a variety of formats dispersed throughout a complex budget report, which complicates any analysis.[68] Table 4 – 2 represents a list of some of the nondefense spending items included in the defense budgets between 1990 and 1995.

While such items make up the largest share of diverted funds in the Pentagon budget, there is a growing problem of military construction pork—projects not requested by the armed services but added by lawmakers. From FY 1990 through FY 1994, Congress earmarked $4.4 billion for unrequested military construction projects in the defense budget.[69] This equates to $880 million every year in needless projects to support local constituencies rather than military needs. In the fiscal 1995 military construction appropriations process, the House added $731 million in members' projects, the Senate added another $718 million, while the 1995 military construction conference (between the houses) increased the total to $987 million in unrequested projects. To put it another way, Congress takes $1 billion per year from essential military programs to fund pork-barrel projects the Pentagon does not want and does not need. And it happens every year. A list of just some of these projects appears in Table 4 – 3.

The practice of loading the defense budget with nondefense items or unneeded military construction projects is extremely dangerous, since the funding for these programs comes for the most part from the operations and maintenance account in the defense budget, the source of funding for the

---

Table 4–2. FY 1990–1995 Nondefense Spending in DoD Budget

Civilian sporting events	$53,904,000
Memorial Day and July 4 celebrations	$3,023,000
Museums	$21,700,000
Hawaiian volcano observatory	$500,000
Transfer to National Park Service	$25,000,000
Transfer to Department of Energy	$30,000,000

Source: Congressional Research Service.

Table 4–3. FY 1995 Military Construction Add-ons

Physical fitness center addition, Redstone Arsenal	$2,600,000
Student pilot dormitory, Luke Air Force Base	$4,900,000
Passenger processing terminal, Dover Air Force Base	$5,900,000
Child care center, Kanehoe Bay	$4,900,000
Combat pistol qualification range, Fort Custer	$ 400,000

Source: FY 95 Senate Defense Authorization Bill.

readiness of U.S. armed forces. The money spent in the last two years on non-defense items alone could have supported the payroll for 200,000 troops for a year, replaced the Aegis cruiser fleet, funded more than the entire F-117 fighter force, or procured 120 F-16 fighters and spares.[70] Clearly, such opportunity costs are substantial. Moreover, this problem transcends obvious readiness and modernization issues. It deceives the American taxpayer and falsely labels the nature of the defense budget. Simply put, it is bad business. The American people expect to pay for military muscle—not fat—so that the Pentagon can concentrate on its real mission: to provide for the common defense, not to enhance domestic comfort.

Readiness

"When the admirals declare that morale in the fleet is good, I wonder who they're talking to. People at the deck-plate level of the navy are tired and frustrated," a navy commander recently declared.[71] He was one of a growing number of officers and enlisted personnel in all of the services who believe that the operational readiness of U.S. armed forces is being ground down by relentless deployments that take their toll on people, equipment, *and* training.

Readiness, by its implicit definition, is independent of the number or types of units in the military establishment. It consists of two basic indicators: whether existing units have enough people and equipment, and whether training and maintenance levels are adequate to establish operational competence. The troops' working definition of readiness fits into General Colin Powell's "four pillars" of military capability. In the late 1980s, Powell argued that force size, modernization, sustainability, and readiness constituted the four pillars of military power. Readiness in his definition lies in the ability to operate effectively in the opening days of war; "sustainability" involves broader questions of national mobilization for a campaign of months' or perhaps years' duration.

By the short-term definition, the readiness pillar is cracking. The personnel strength of U.S. forces has shrunk by 384,000 since 1990, but deployments to Rwanda, Haiti, Kuwait, and the Balkans have increased the burden on each service.[72] The sun never sets on America's globally deployed military forces. On any given day, about half the navy's 390 ships are deployed, a back-breaking commitment for both men and machines. In the air force, AWACS radar plane crews find themselves deployed from home bases approximately 200 days per year. The average EF-111 electronic warfare crew spent nearly 155 days away from home this year. In fact, each of the services finds itself spread to more countries with fewer personnel than during the Cold War. This has led to a terrible "wearing down of the force." In July 1994, a blue-ribbon readiness task force, headed by former Army Chief of Staff Edward (Shy) Meyer, warned the secretary of defense that U.S. forces were "running too hard—getting too little rest between deployments."[73]

On 15 November 1994 Representative Floyd Spence, ranking Republican on the Armed Services Committee and its next chairman, challenged the Pentagon's assertions that readiness was better today than in 1990, before the onset of Operation Desert Shield/Storm. "The volume of evidence from the field is as clear as it is unavoidable—U.S. military units are caught in the early stages of a downward readiness spiral that shows no prospect of easing in the foreseeable future."[74] Unquestionably, the most explosive of Spence's charges was that three of the army's twelve combat divisions were no longer combat ready, because of the administration's decision to use military forces in such nontraditional missions as helping refugees in Rwanda and stabilizing civil strife in Haiti. In addition, an unplanned major deployment of forces to Kuwait in October further drained the Pentagon's operations and maintenance budget. These unplanned operations ripped an estimated $2 billion from the operating accounts, since Congress refused to fund an account for such operations in the annual budget.[75] The day after the release of Spence's letter, Secretary of Defense Perry admitted that the congressman was correct and that it would take until 1995 to restore the units to combat readiness.[76]

The November 1994 elections made clear a national dissatisfaction with current defense policies. Defense cuts had gone too far, at least in the public mind as well as that of the new Republican leadership. One of the central tenets of the Republican Contract with America focused on reversing cuts in the defense sector. In what some call a preemptive attack, Clinton issued a surprise announcement on 1 December 1994 stating his intention to seek an additional $25 billion over the next six years. To many in Congress, the administration's announcement tacitly acknowledged that underfunding and an unwillingness to make hard choices had inflicted serious damage on the Defense Department. The problem with Clinton's proposal is that the lion's share of his proposed increases come after the turn of the century: $6 billion in 2000 and $9 billion in 2001. Today's problems will only get worse in the interim.

Meanwhile, the strains from worldwide high-tempo operations continue to mount: spousal abuse has risen 25 percent since 1990, while suicides have increased to more than 230 last year.[77] On the equipment side, maintenance backlogs are increasing, and vital stockpiles of spare parts, both at unit and depot levels, have declined. Soldiers in mechanized outfits note that unit parts allowances have shrunk and that on average it takes far longer for the army's supply system to respond to requisitions for spares.

All over the globe, American airmen, sailors, and pilots enforce no-fly lines and naval embargoes, while in other places their comrades take part in humanitarian and peacekeeping exercises. These unprogrammed activities have ravaged the Pentagon's operations and maintenance accounts; and because Congress has refused the Pentagon the money to execute these new duties, the Pentagon has had to come, hat in hand to Congress, to get cash transfusions to prevent its forces from clanking to a halt. This past September, Perry astonished lawmakers when he told them that unless the army received quick relief, the 1st and 4th Infantry Divisions would exhaust their spare part inventories, the return of equipment from Europe would end, and scheduled training at the army's National Training Center would cease.[78] Estimated costs for peacekeeping operations in 1993 were nearly $1.2 billion; Congress reluctantly provided $400 million to backfill the drain, not nearly sufficient to cover the shortfall. The situation actually worsened in the fiscal 1995 defense budget. Again, the Pentagon sought a modest $300 million for peacekeeping, but Congress instead funded a $1.2 billion appropriation to pay back debts to the United Nations.[79]

One measure of readiness is training. Units that do not train cannot fight and win; yet the current climate of high operations' tempo has had a thoroughly negative effect on training. Frustrated navy and air force fighter pilots receive insufficient cockpit time to maintain proficiency. VFA-81, a navy F-18 squadron, deployed to the Balkans on the *Saratoga* in 1994, but according to the squadron commander, pilot training was barely adequate prior to deployment. According to an internal Pentagon report, "VFA-81 did not maintain C-1 (fully combat ready) during deployment, in part because of a funding shortfall . . .[t]he squadron was funded at 25.5 flying hours per pilot per month . . . compared to a C-1 requirement for 32.8 hours."[80]

Today's readiness crisis is a self-inflicted wound. According to one recent study, readiness is a metaphysical swamp in which lost Pentagon officials are floundering without benefit of a map or compass.[81] The data needed to measure current readiness are not available; consequently there are no analytic means to predict tomorrow's readiness. Unquestionably, it is costing more to operate today's larger, heavier, more complex equipment. In 1982, the Defense Science Board lamented a trend toward ever-bigger equipment and dubbed this worrisome trend "the technological bloat factor."[82] "The correlation between cost, weight and size growth is uncanny," it warned.[83]

Another factor straining the operational readiness of America's fighting equipment might be described as "the heavy burden of weightless electrons." Virtually all of America's latest high-technology weapons feature an increasing density of electronic sensors, computers, and display and fire-control components. Although these systems are more reliable, the evolution toward a "remove and replace" maintenance and repair concept has increased costs in two ways. First, a greater share of the repair burden has shifted from operating units to distant depots and, second, the variety and quantity of spare parts flowing through the maintenance system have necessarily increased as a direct result of the shift.

"Economically, remove and replace technologies greatly increase overhead costs when one accounts for the proliferating variety of individually accountable items and the cost of maintaining a more closely regulated pipeline," concluded a recent evaluation of F-18 fighters.[84] The F-18 is perhaps the most reliable high-tech aircraft fielded by the navy to date. Indeed, the navy is an excellent example of the rising cost of a smaller military. As Table 4 – 4 indicates, today's fleet is substantially smaller than the 1980 navy.

Table 4–4.

	1980	1994
Inventory		
Ships	479	390
Airplanes	5,355	4,327
Operating Tempo		
Steaming days/ship/QTR	56.6	50.5
Nondeployed ship	28.6	29.0
Flying hours/plane/month	24.2	24.4
Costs		
Then-year $	$42.7B	$86.7B
In fiscal 1995 $	$81.2B	84.9B

Note also that the operating level in terms of *budgeted* steaming days and flying hours has remained relatively stable (the figures here do not include unexpected contingencies, which can increase time at sea and for which supplemental appropriations pay). Yet, while the fleet is approximately 20 percent smaller, and the budgeted operating tempo has remained relatively stable, the costs of buying and operating the force have risen measurably.[85]

Similar trends exist in the army and air force. The latter, for example, has shrunk by one third from a force of more than 9,000 aircraft in 1980 to 6,000 aircraft in 1994, but in constant 1995 dollars, the average cost per flying hour has increased from $6,000 to $10,000.[86] The active-duty army has shrunk from a force of 175 maneuver battalions in 1980 to slightly more than 100 maneuver battalions in 1994, but the operations and maintenance budget has remained virtually unchanged at approximately $21 billion in FY 1995 dollars.[87]

With the forces shrinking, where are the operations and maintenance funds going? At a symposium on the future of naval aviation, Rear Admiral John Lockard admitted, "We have a difficult time understanding the total ownership cost of our equipment."[88] Nevertheless, one startling conclusion emerges: "Contrary to the promises of lower life-cycle costs, equipment developed in the 1970s and 1980s is more expensive to operate. The shift to 'Black Box/Remove & Replace' maintenance technologies, while substituting replacement for repairs at point of activity, actually increased total support costs. . . . Not only are operating costs *higher*, future costs are more difficult to predict."[89]

The increasing age of the equipment now in service is a major reason future costs are more unpredictable. The F-18 fighter, for example, has been a most reliable aircraft, at least during its first 1,200 service hours. However, when F-18s were "opened up" at that point in their service life for corrosion inspection, unexpected maintenance problems appeared. Worse, a fix in one area often resulted in serious problems with other components and subsystems. "Chasing problems downstream" is the term used by experienced F-18 maintenance personnel to describe the problem of cascading breakdowns in older F-18s.[90]

The implications for the readiness rates of tomorrow's force structure are considerable. Planned modernization rates will not reverse the increasing age of U.S. major weapons systems. In the year 2011, for example, the army's reconnaissance and attack helicopter force will be about twelve years old, on average, even with planned acquisition of the Comanche scout/attack helicopter. This force will be older than when the Apache armed helicopter entered service in the early 1980s.[91] Even with production of an upgraded version of the F-18, the "E/F" model, the average age of navy combat jets will skyrocket from approximately nine years in 1995 to thirteen years by 2005.[92] Moreover, there will be many more aircraft with over 1,200 hours, with every likelihood of the greater maintenance problems experienced thus far on older, high-time aircraft. Assuming the air force acquires its planned force of 442 F-22s, the new fighters will not arrive at a rate sufficient to reverse the increasing age of the service's fighter/attack fleet.

By 2011, the average air force tactical combat jet will be twenty-two years old—higher than any time during the Cold War.[93] Similar trends apply to navy ships, army tanks and infantry fighting vehicles, and marine corps medium-lift helicopters. The increasing age of America's military hardware, coupled with the higher costs of maintaining geriatric equipment, is on a collision course with pressures to cut the operations and maintenance budget. The administration's Future Years Defense Plan, for example, projects a decrease from about $93 billion in constant FY 1995 dollars to $81 billion in FY 1999 for the operations and maintenance budget.[94] This $12 billion cut represents a dark cloud on the fiscal horizon; material readiness, already hurting, could suffer further deterioration. For example, in July 1994 the army National Guard grounded virtually all of its helicopters for want of money to fly, while there were approximately 186 "bare firewalls" (engine compartments without engines) in the navy's fleet of 976 F-18 fighters.[95] Pentagon staffers have dismissed such problems as isolated pockets of readiness shortcomings, but the trends are ominous.

If equipment readiness remains difficult to assess and predict, training readiness represents an even more intractable problem. According to a recent internal review with a number of retired general officers, "[u]nit training readiness measurement and reporting is subjective, inadequate . . . inconsistent between the services and in need of more detailed information."[96] The reported numbers may simply not be reliable. For example, flying hours are a standard benchmark of pilot proficiency, but not all hours are important for honing combat skills. The shootdown of two army helicopters by two air force F-15 pilots over the northern Iraq no-fly zone in April 1994 while an AWACS watched the episode on its screens is a case in point. In the subsequent investigation, the lead pilot admitted firing a missile at what he believed was an Iraqi Russian-built Hind helicopter, but he also admitted that his predeployment training lacked "quite a bit."[97] In the month prior, he had flown approximately ten flights ferrying F-15s from Germany to Turkey. They were utterly routine flights, "boring holes through the sky," in aviator jargon. As the pilot noted, "Autopilot on, one landing to a full stop, but we still have to log those as combat training sorties, because we don't get enough sorties to stay mission ready."[98] Furthermore, his testimony revealed that composite training sorties with AWACS were rare. And, as it turned out, the AWACS crew on duty over the no-fly zone had never flown together. "The shootdown was a training readiness mistake," an advisor to the recent Defense Department study of training readiness admitted.[99]

But "the system" reported none of these deficiencies. Indeed, the F-15 pilot's confession reveals a readiness reporting problem known as the "coefficient of fiction."[100] Inadequacies at the unit level do not necessarily reach up the chain of command. The greater the density of false or misleading reports percolating to the top, the higher the "coefficient of fiction." What is not reported is not a problem. In this regard, the Pentagon's training management system is virtually blind. The training officer in an air wing or ground division can itemize the type and amount of training necessary to maintain a high level of training readiness. He can determine with fair precision the associated costs of that training as well. The operations and maintenance account provides funds for both equipment and training readiness but makes no distinction between these two activities. For want of any breakdown between operations and maintenance, a training readiness task force could only conclude: "We do not know what our current level of training readiness costs."[101] Furthermore, it is virtually impossible to assess the relationship between budget inputs and training readiness outputs.

The absence of understandable data for decision makers could not come at a worse time. Training requirements are increasing, not decreasing. The services need to train their personnel not only for their mainstream war-fighting tasks but also for a wide range of additional missions: peace keeping, disaster relief, civil unrest, counterdrug, and the like. "If carried to the extreme, the tasking of too many new missions concurrent with severe reductions in resources could threaten future training readiness," warned a task force report on training readiness.[102] However, training comes out of operations and maintenance funds that are not tightly earmarked for training. In fact, the operations and maintenance account has recently paid for cold weather gear, teenage child care, furniture, and batteries to operate radios and night vision goggles.[103] To prevent, or at least discourage, the diversion of funds needed for training, subcategories in the operations and maintenance account must be made visible.[104]

Conclusion

In the early morning hours of a rainy, miserable day in July 1950, a battalion of the 24th Infantry Division, under command of Lt. Col. Brad Smith, made first contact with the invading spearhead of the North Korean army north of Osan, South Korea. The Americans were thoroughly confident, embarked as they were on just "a police action." After all, had not the might of America's military wrecked Nazi Germany and Imperial Japan in less than four years of war? But the troops in "Task Force Smith" were in effect poorly trained garrison troops from Japan despite their job description as combat infantrymen. As a result of the drastic decline of U.S. defense budgets since World War II, they had received relatively little combat training, their weapons were the leftovers from the last war, and their artillery support possessed only *six* rounds of antitank ammunition, the entire supply available in the Pacific Theater. Finally, Task Force Smith possessed bazookas, the rockets of which bounced off T-34 armor at fifteen yards.[105] The results were disastrous: "Task Force Smith, designed to be an arrogant display [MacArthur's words] of strength to bluff the enemy into halting his advance, had delayed [the North Koreans] exactly seven hours [before its extinction]."[106] The harsh reality is that current trends suggest that what happened to Task Force Smith could occur sometime in the future to U.S. forces and perhaps to an even greater extent.

In early November 1994, the American people turned the House of Representatives and the Senate over to the Republicans, who explicitly argued for the need to address the defense deficit. If the Republicans follow through on the "Contract with America" promise for an "accurate and comprehensive review of U.S. defense needs," then perhaps the armed forces may avoid another Task Force Smith, but only if Congress *acts* to reverse the negative trends that affect our military forces. At present, the U.S. defense establishment has reached a crucial crossroads. To avoid the crack-up that is so clearly approaching, the president *and* Congress must make tough choices. The Pentagon will have to break some "iron rice bowls."

If the United States is indeed planning to fight two, nearly simultaneous, major regional conflicts, then it must maintain adequate air, sea, and land-based power, not cut from the core combat capabilities of the services as is being done currently. The ideal solution is for Congress and the administration to agree on a budget that supports an ability to fight and win at least one major regional conflict—something that we will soon not be able to do if present trends continue.

Congress must also stop raiding the defense budget for pork projects to satisfy the folks back home. The incoming Republicans have proposed to rebuild the firewall between defense and discretionary spending so that it will become more difficult to raid Pentagon accounts for projects that have nothing to do with national security. This sounds like a sensible course. In March 1995, the Pentagon will likely forward to the Base Closure and Realignment Commission a large list of bases it wants to close. Once the commission, the Congress, and the president have agreed on what bases must close (by fall

1995), the process must proceed as intended. Bases need to close. Given that approximately 60 percent of the Pentagon's budget goes for fixed costs, there is an urgent need to cut the support costs for unneeded installations. But the base closing process needs to continue beyond 1995. Congress should revisit the overly restrictive 1978 legislation that prevents the Pentagon from closing excess bases. Failing this, Congress, at a minimum, must authorize at least three follow-on BRAC rounds.

Those charged with national defense, civilian as well as military, must also restore some sense of balance between spending for today and spending for the future. The Pentagon must keep reasonable modernization programs on track. Weapons age and wear out; they will need replacement by newer, more capable systems before that happens. At present, there is no modernization crisis because the Pentagon is still living off the legacy of the Reagan buildup. Soon, however, the Pentagon must restructure current accounts to modernize a force that is aging rapidly. There will not be a shortage of candidates for the budget knife. The Roles and Missions Commission, for example, will hopefully recommend a host of money-saving changes that may also enhance combat power.

Finally, the administration and Congress must come to terms with the fact that the Pentagon, given current funding and force levels, cannot respond to every humanitarian and peacekeeping crisis without eventually seriously compromising its ability to fight. The Republicans claim to recognize the dangers of the current situation more clearly than the administration. Aside from the rhetoric, one thing is clear; American military forces are approaching burnout. Unless things turn around, the future specter of American forces retreating in ragged defeat on a foreign battlefield is entirely possible. For those who scoff at such a notion, a visit to a small hilltop just south of Suwon, South Korea, might provide a sobering second thought. There, perched on the crest amidst the trees, is a monument to Task Force Smith and its futile stand in the face of overwhelming odds. We need no more such reminders.

Chapter 5

The Clinton Defense Strategy

Andrew F. Krepinevich

B ill Clinton, the first post–Cold War president of the United States, assumed office at a time when the nation confronted a strategic *and* a military revolution. These massive shifts in the landscape of national security have dramatically increased the level of uncertainty surrounding the formulation of defense policy and strategy in Washington. Whatever the ambiguities, the collapse of the Soviet Union also finds the United States, as the world's sole superpower, more secure than at any time since the 1930s.

This chapter examines the Clinton defense strategy by addressing two principal questions. First, does the administration's defense program meet the demands of a less dangerous (at least in the short term) but more uncertain strategic environment? Put another way, does it minimize the risks to the United States, given projected resources available for national defense? Second, irrespective of the Clinton defense program's desirability, is it affordable? In other words, can the United States sustain it over the long term with the resources currently available?

Planning Under Conditions of Uncertainty

One would expect that American strategic planning would emphasize the addressing of the most formidable, or most likely, risks and challenges to national security. What are these challenges?

The Geopolitical Revolution

The near-term strategic challenges confronting the United States are minor compared to those of the Cold War. Then, the threat of great-power confrontation was omnipresent. The Soviet Union and its allies presented a clear and present danger to America's security as well as that of its allies. This danger no longer exists, and the United States finds itself in a threat "trough." Both the Bush administration's Regional Strategy and the present administration's Strategy of Engagement and Enlargement have revived regional threats like Iran, Iraq, and North Korea as major near-term dangers to U.S. security. Still, even these threats are minor compared to future strategic challenges that could arise if the United States and its allies were unable to build an enduring and stable international order or if they failed to arrest the proliferation of weapons of mass destruction and advanced military technologies throughout Third World states. Unfortunately, history is hardly encouraging on this score. Vigorous competition among great powers has been the rule, not the exception, since men first recorded history. History also suggests that once a military technology appears, military organizations that want it and can afford it, will obtain it.

In short, positioning the United States to meet such long-term challenges would likely require considerable attention, ingenuity, and resources on the part of any American administration. The failure to create a relatively stable international order will return the international system to great-power rivalries, rivalries that, in this century alone, have produced two world wars and a cold war, a period of conflict that has spanned virtually the entire century. Moreover, failure to stem the diffusion of advanced military technologies could lead to the emergence of military forces in the Third World substantially different from, and far more capable than, the Iraqi forces that the Western coalition encountered during the Gulf War. In short, the greatest challenges to U.S. security lie at least a decade or more into the future. But decisions that the United States makes now with respect to its defense strategy and investment of resources to support that strategy will strongly influence the means available to counter or confront future dangers in the twenty-first century. Prudence dictates a national strategy that accords high priority to extending the "threat trough" as far into the future as possible and that also seeks to devote as much as possible to the research and development required to prolong U.S. technological superiority into the next century.

As for the near term, the greatest likely danger to American interests lies in the form of a major regional conflict (or MRC in the Pentagon's parlance). A major regional conflict would involve aggression by a regional antagonist, such as Iraq or Iran in the Middle East or North Korea in Asia. Finally, the most likely situations in which the United States will commit its own forces in the near term are those best described as "peace" operations, or what the U.S. military refers to as "operations other than war."

The Military Revolution

While there has been considerable discussion of how the geopolitical revolution might influence defense requirements, defense experts have said little as to the prospective influence of a military revolution on such requirements. Over the next several decades, military systems and operations and the force structures of the Cold War will confront new, far more capable means and methods of warfare and possibly new, or considerably modified, military organizations. This "military revolution" will not be unique; the West has undergone a series of ongoing military revolutions since the fourteenth century.[1] But the current revolution appears to have the promise of exerting a profound influence on the character of conflict and the determinants of military effectiveness.

By radically changing the nature of the military competition, whether in peace or war, military revolutions have often dramatically devalued dominant elements of military power, including both weapons systems and doctrine. One recalls the rapid rise of the carrier and submarine and the relatively sharp decline of the battleship in the period from 1930 to 1940, as well as the concomitant rise of an entirely new military system and concept of operations: the long-range bomber and strategic bombardment. Military revolutions also often witness unexpected, and seemingly rapid, declines in dominant military organizations that refuse to adapt to changing competitive environments. Perhaps the classic example in this century is the French Army, which, although victorious in World War I, failed to cope with the rapid transformation in land warfare made possible by dramatic advances in mechanization that resulted in the German *Blitzkrieg* in spring 1940. In summary, military revolutions occur when the applications of new technologies to military systems combine with innovative operations, concepts, and organizational adaptation to alter fundamentally the character of conflict. They produce dramatic increases in the combat potential and military effectiveness of armed forces.

Those nations that emerge from such revolutionary periods with dominant or competitive military capabilities are those whose military organizations accept the need for change and innovation and remain flexible and adaptive enough to innovate in the face of institutional barriers. Seen in this light, Desert Storm was more a harbinger of things to come than a confirmation that a revolution in warfare had occurred. First, the American military has only begun to exploit the potential of the emerging areas of technology to transform its military doctrine and organizations. Second, it has yet to identify those military systems that can best exploit such technologies and develop operational concepts for managing their introduction into the force structure. Third, there exists no clear doctrine, nor operational concept, to exploit these new systems.

In short, the military revolution reinforces the strategic incentives provided by the geopolitical revolution. Both encourage placing substantially greater emphasis on developing access to military *potential* over the long term as opposed to maintaining it in the near term. Such an approach would, however, be substantially different from the one followed by American strategic planners throughout the forty years of the Cold War.[2]

Although the current administration released its National Security Strategy in July 1994, the guiding force behind its defense strategy and associated force posture lies in the so-called Bottom Up Review released almost a year earlier, on 1 September 1993. Then-Secretary of Defense Les Aspin initiated the Bottom Up Review in March 1993. Aspin intended the review to be a comprehensive "examination of the nation's defense strategy, force structure, modernization, infrastructure, and foundations."[3]

The Pentagon conducted the review purportedly from "the bottom up" because of the dramatic changes that occurred in the international security environment as a result of the Soviet Union's collapse and the Cold War's demise. These changes required a fundamental reexamination of U.S. defense "concepts, plans, and programs from the ground up."[4] According to the administration, the review provides the United States with a blueprint for transitioning from a defense posture aimed primarily against the Soviet threat to one oriented toward challenges of an emerging post–Cold War strategic environment. Although the Bottom Up Review's architect, Aspin, has resigned, Clinton remains committed to the review's defense program, as does Aspin's successor, former Deputy Defense Secretary William Perry.[5]

The Bottom Up Review's examination of the post–Cold War world identifies four major sources of danger to American security: regional conflict; proliferation of weapons of mass destruction; the failure of former communist states (primarily Russia, and perhaps even China) to transition successfully to democracy; and an inability to maintain a strong economic base, the foundation of any defense. But regional threats are the primary "driver" of the review's force requirements and budget needs. Depending upon how the administration's proliferation initiatives evolve, the second danger, from the proliferation of weapons of mass destruction, may also have considerable influence over its recommended force structure and budget priorities. The last two strategic rationales, efforts to encourage democratization and support for the U.S. economic base, should exert negligible influence on the military's force structure and defense budgets.[6]

Regional Dangers

The Bottom Up Review and the administration's National Security Strategy of Engagement and Enlargement advocate a force posture capable of dealing with aggression by countries such as North Korea, Iran, and Iraq. More specifically, a "central factor" in the analysis is the judgment that the United States must maintain forces "capable, in concert with its allies, of fighting and winning two major regional conflicts that occur nearly simultaneously."[7] The U.S. armed forces should be capable not only of achieving quick and decisive victory but also of supporting the "stationing and deploying [of] . . . military forces overseas in peacetime" as "an essential element in dealing with new regional dangers and [in] pursuing new opportunities."[8] Furthermore, U.S. forces will have to engage in a range of lesser contingencies, including peacekeeping, peace-making, and humanitarian assistance operations.

The Nuclear Danger

The Bottom Up Review accords a high priority to American nonproliferation, cooperative threat reduction, and counterproliferation efforts. Nonproliferation, as cited in the review, involves effort "to prevent the spread of weapons of mass destruction to additional countries through the strengthening of existing controls on the export of [weapons of mass destruction] technologies and materials, and the improvement and expansion of international mechanisms and agreements for limiting and eliminating nuclear, biological, and chemical weapons."[9]

Cooperative threat reduction includes working with the former Soviet republics that possess weapons of mass destruction to support the elimination of such weapons and to prevent the spread of nuclear weapons, their components, and related technologies and expertise within and beyond the borders of the former Soviet Union.[10] In response to the review's findings, the Defense Department announced a counterproliferation initiative in December 1993. The initiative aims to develop a strategy for responding to the threat of nuclear proliferation. According to the Department of Defense, counterproliferation involves efforts to deter, prevent, or defend against the use of such weapons if American nonproliferation endeavors fail.

The Clinton Response

The Bottom Up Review calls for a significant reduction in the so-called Base Force structure developed by the Bush administration to transition away from the Cold War's defense posture. However, as in the case of the Base Force, dangers to regional security have driven the review's force structure requirements. The Bottom Up Review's planners also had to respond to the administration's substantially greater emphasis on involving U.S. forces in peace-keeping operations. In short, the review proposed to cover a broader set of requirements with lower budgets and a smaller force structure than called for by Bush's Base Force. Viewed from this perspective, it is perhaps inevitable that the Bottom Up Review would generate considerable controversy.

The Defense Department adopted its two-major-regional-contingencies strategy, dubbed "win-win," reportedly after a close examination of a force posture that called for U.S. forces to win one major regional war while conducting a holding operation in a second such conflict. The planners characterized such an approach as a "win-hold-win"; that is, once U.S. forces had triumphed in the first conflict, they would reinforce U.S. troops holding the enemy in the second. The Pentagon adopted the "win-win" option because it claimed that it would be relatively inexpensive to add the additional capability to move from "win-hold-win" to "win-win."[11] The shift to "win-win" also produced an eleventh-hour addition of two carriers to the force structure, fifteen "enhanced" national guard brigades, and $5 billion in "force enhancements" in the form of improved strategic mobility, army firepower lethality, and long-range bomber precision-strike support.[12] (See Table 5–1.)

Funding the Clinton Defense Posture

The Defense Department's budgets have declined since FY 1985, when the Reagan buildup, the largest in the nation's peacetime history, reached its apogee. The weakening of public support for defense spending accelerated following the Soviet Union's collapse in 1991. Clinton won the presidential election in November 1992 primarily on a platform that emphasized a domestic agenda as well as reductions in the federal deficit. In fulfilling his campaign pledge of deficit reduction, the new president signed Congress's Omnibus Budget Reconciliation Act in August 1993. The act placed tight spending "caps" on discretionary spending, which primarily comprises domestic and defense spending. The caps, which run from FY 1994 to FY 1998, actually reduce discretionary spending in real (inflation-adjusted) dollars.[13]

Accepting the American people's opposition to higher taxes, Clinton recognized that support of his ambitious domestic agenda and progress on reducing deficits demanded a substantial "peace dividend" from the defense account. The latest Clinton plan will reduce defense by some $100 billion below the level estimated in the last Bush plan. Even with these cuts, however, the federal government will allocate nearly $1.3 trillion for national defense over the five-year period from 1995 to 1999. (See Table 5–2.)

Table 5–1. Force Posture Options

	Base Force	One MRC Requirement	Win-Hold-Win	Two MRC Requirement
Army				
Active divisions	12	8	10	10
Reserve divisions	6	6	6	—
Reserve brigades	—	—	—	15
Navy				
Carrier battle groups	13	8	10	12
Marine Corps				
Active divisions	2⅓	—	—	—
Active brigades	—	5	5	5
Reserve divisions	1	1	1	1
Air Force				
Active wings	15	10	13	13
Reserve wings	11	6	7	7

Source: The Joint Staff, *1992 Joint Military Net Assessment* (Washington, D.C.: The Joint Staff, August 21, 1992), p. 3-3 and Aspin, *Bottom-Up Review*, p. 30.

The Clinton National Security Strategy

Several weeks after announcing the Bottom Up Review, the administration declared a policy of "enlargement," under which the United States would attempt to expand and strengthen democracy around the world.[14] But, in the wake of the administration's erratic policies with respect to peace operations in Somalia and Bosnia, it declared certain tests for future U.S. involvement in such operations.[15] Subsequently, the administration developed Presidential Decision Directive 25 that set more restrictive guidelines for the use of American military forces in peace operations than the president had advocated during the 1992 election campaign. In July 1994, eighteen months after inauguration, Clinton released his *National Security Strategy of Engagement and Enlargement*. This document codified the defense priorities established in the Bottom Up Review and the "tests" for intervention laid down in Direc-

Table 5–2. Bush Baseline Versus Clinton Department of Defense Future Years Defense Program (*Billions of Dollars in Budget Authority*)

	FY 95	FY 96	FY 97	FY 98	FY 99	FY 95–99
Baseline	258.5	261.5	266.8	271.1	274.1	1,332.0
Clinton budget	252.2	243.4	240.2	246.7	253.0	1,235.5
Reduction	6.3	18.1	26.6	24.4	21.1	96.5

Source: FY 1995 DOD Budget: Congressional Staff Briefing, February 1994. In addition, Department of Energy activities and other defense-related programs will likely require some $65 billion in budget authority (BA) during this period.

tive 25. Nevertheless, these pronouncements do not appear to provide clear strategic guidance upon which the Pentagon can base its planning priorities. For example, although Clinton made developing U.S. capabilities for conducting multinational peace operations a high defense planning priority, such operations failed to receive a high priority in the Bottom Up Review.

At the moment, the administration and the Department of Defense confront a series of critical questions. What takes precedence: short-term military capability or long-term military potential in a period of increasingly constrained defense resources; the greatest dangers, or the most likely? The United States does not have (nor did it ever have) sufficient resources to cover every possible risk. Put another way, the United States has a limited budget with which to purchase "insurance" against security risks. Spending those resources effectively requires the administration to set priorities with an eye toward minimizing the overall level of risk with the limited resources available. Does Clinton's defense strategy constitute a good "insurance policy" against the risks of a new and uncertain security environment?

Assessing the Clinton Defense Strategy

The Bottom Up Review's recommended force posture derives primarily from its evaluation of four broad classes of potential military operations, or contingencies: major regional conflicts; smaller-scale conflicts such as peacekeeping or intervention operations; overseas presence; and deterrence from attacks with weapons of mass destruction.[16] The Bottom Up Review deferred consideration of the last mission pending a review of U.S. nuclear forces (and, one would presume, the initial findings of the Defense Counterproliferation Initiative).[17] The president's *National Security Strategy* offers a brief outline of

U.S. strategy to combat the spread and use of weapons of mass destruction and missiles.[18]

The Two-Major-Regional-Contingencies Requirement

The Bottom Up Review places its principal emphasis on maintaining U.S. military capabilities over the near-term future to deter or defeat possible regional aggressors. Specifically, the review's recommendations are that the United States "maintain sufficient military power to be able to win two major regional conflicts that occur nearly simultaneously."[19] The review's contingencies posit U.S. forces combating a resurgent Iraq or North Korea (although the Pentagon did not intend these contingencies to be predictive; that is, there are other plausible regional conflicts, such as with Iran).

The Pentagon's planning criteria for waging two major regional contingencies nearly simultaneously represents a holdover from the Bush administration's defense policies, rather than the product of new thinking on the part of the administration.[20] In fact, some have labeled the Bottom Up Review's structure as a slightly more modest version of Bush's Base Force.[21] Reflecting the expanded scope of the Clinton strategy and declining resources for defense, the review explicitly acknowledges that, while the proposed force structure should be able to meet two major regional contingencies, it cannot do so *and* provide forces for significant peace-keeping and peace-making operations such as in Somalia, northern and southern Iraq, Haiti, and prospectively, Bosnia or the Golan Heights.

Why Emphasize Major Regional Conflict in the Near Term?

There are several reasons—strategic and organizational—why requirements based on major regional contingencies are driving the planning process for the post–Cold War defense posture. First, major regional conflicts constitute the immediate danger to U.S. security. These conflicts also are the most "familiar" to the American military in terms of preparations for war. Such contingencies also "fit" Cold War defense planning, which had at its center a clearly defined enemy and near-term requirements (the immediate threat was so great that according it primary emphasis was justified). Not surprisingly, in the absence of clear and forceful administration guidance to the contrary, planning remains largely oriented on preparing for the most demanding and familiar near-term threats.

Moreover, major regional contingencies represent, in a sense, the most "comfortable" security challenges. The American military knows how to defeat a military threat like Iraq. Indeed, Desert Storm allowed the U.S. to fight a war for which it had trained for two generations, only instead of combating the Soviets in a major European conflict, the coalition confronted a similar, but smaller, force whose equipment and training were significantly inferior to those of the Soviets and, as a final bonus, in open desert terrain.[22] The relevance of the Gulf War to the future wars in which U.S. military forces will find themselves involved is at best doubtful. Therefore, basing the posture and focus of U.S. military forces on such a paradigm is equally open to question.

Indeed, the Bottom Up Review's prototype aggressor for the two regional contingencies that shape its force structure is an "Iraq on steroids," that is, an aggressor whose forces and operational approach are roughly similar to those employed by Baghdad before the Gulf War. The potential aggressor, however, by Pentagon estimates would have more capable forces than Iraq in 1990 (e.g., better tanks, armored fighting vehicles, combat aircraft). Its assessment also assumes that a future aggressor could possess ballistic missiles, weapons of mass destruction, and diesel submarines. Astonishingly, the review refuses to address U.S. operational concepts and force requirements for defeating or neutralizing the military forces of such an opponent in any detail.

Second, the relatively brief tenure in the Pentagon of both key senior civilian and military leaders encourages a short-term perspective. Only two defense secretaries and one chairman have served much more than five years in office. The same is true for senior Defense Department and National Security Council staff officials, as well as for the service chiefs and the military's regional and functional commanders in chief. It is only human nature for such leaders, with limited periods in office, to worry about potential catastrophes on their "watch." Since that "watch" covers only the near-term future, it is not surprising that the Bottom Up Review focuses primarily on preserving American military capabilities for the near term.

Why a Two-Major-Regional-Contingencies Requirement?

The Defense Department's concentration on two major regional conflicts rests on its assertion that "regional aggressors represent a danger that must be deterred and, if necessary, defeated by the military capability of the United States and its allies." But why two regional conflicts? The review provides two reasons to justify its assumption. First, it suggests that if the United States were "drawn into a war in response to the armed aggression of one hostile nation, another could well be tempted to attack its neighbors—especially if it were convinced the United States and its allies did not possess the requisite military capability or will to oppose it." Second, the review argues that "a future adversary might one day confront us with a larger-than-expected threat, and then turn out, through doctrinal or technological innovation, to be more capable than we expect."[23] In light of their dominant influence in the Bottom Up Review and the resource constraints that limit the "insurance" the American budget can afford, these planning assumptions deserve careful examination.

Why two major regional contingencies? Why not plan for one major regional contingency? Or three? Or four? The Bottom Up Review cites at least three major regional threats—North Korea, Iran, and Iraq. One might also consider Libya, Cuba, and perhaps Syria or even a Greater Serbia as constituting significant regional threats. In part, the Pentagon appears to have arrived at the planning requirement for two regional conflicts by examining the trade-offs between the cost of maintaining military capabilities to address two contingencies (which would include the opportunity cost of diverting these resources from other programs) and the probability that the United States would confront such a contingency and suffer unacceptable losses as a consequence. Given these considerations, the review planners evidently determined that the two-major-regional-contingencies requirement was the maximum "insurance" the United States could afford, given the administration's priorities, and that prospects of facing more than two major contingencies were sufficiently remote as to constitute an acceptable risk.

Naturally, the two-regional-conflicts posture has opportunity costs. It "crowds out" investments in both preparing for the most likely conflicts U.S. forces will confront and maintaining access to military potential (e.g., through modernization and research and development) over the long term, where the greatest risks to American security lie. Thus, one should pose the questions: Why not a *one*-major-regional-conflict requirement in lieu of a requirement for two? What is the likelihood that the United States, once engaged in a major regional conflict, would confront another case of regional aggression nearly simultaneously?

No one can predict with precision the probability that the United States would confront such a possibility. History, however, provides a pattern. Since the United States emerged as an active global power after 1945, it has engaged in three major regional conflicts: Korea, Vietnam, and the Gulf War. In all three instances, the United States committed the bulk of its conventional combat power. In two instances, during Korea and Vietnam, the United States had its combat forces deployed for more than three years. During these same two conflicts, the prospective second "hostile nation" was not Iran, Libya, or North Korea, but its superpower rival, the Soviet Union, whose ability to exploit U.S. engagements, either directly or through proxies and clients, dwarfed any possible adversary in the current world or any that the U.S. can anticipate over the next decade. Yet in none of these instances did the United States confront a second major regional conflict. Moreover, it is doubtful that a second major regional contingency would occur on short notice.

A Hedge Against Innovative Regional Aggressors?

The two-contingencies planning requirement also represents a hedge against an adversary that might confront the United States with more sophisticated capabilities than expected through doctrinal or technological innovation. It does seem reasonable to hedge against this kind of contingency. The review's conflict scenarios envision an innovative adversary. However, its force posture derives from planning scenarios that measure the effectiveness of U.S. forces against adversaries that are similar in doctrine and force structure to the Iraqi armed forces of the Gulf War. (See Table 5–3.)

The two scenarios employed—one envisioning an attack by Iraq against Kuwait and Saudi Arabia, the other an attack by North Korea against South Korea—orient the future forces to refighting the last war more effectively, rather than preparing for dissimilar challenges that they might well face if the United States is unable to avoid the next war. The Bottom Up Review scenarios assume that an aggressor's military operations would rest on "an armor-heavy, combined arms offensive against the out-numbered forces of a neighboring state."[24] This description is more appropriate to the kind of attack U.S. forces planned on combating during the Cold War. It does not examine the possibility that a regional aggressor might combine new technologies with innovative and imaginative military doctrines.

Table 5–3. Comparison of 1990 Iraqi and BUR Aggressor Force Levels

Category	1990 Iraqi Forces	BUR Aggressor Force
Tanks	5,000	2,000 – 4,000
Armored fighting vehicles	5,000	3,000 – 5,000
Artillery pieces	3,000	2,000 – 3,000
Combat aircraft	700	500 – 1,000
Naval craft	60	100 – 200
Ballistic missiles	600	100 – 1,000

Source: Department of Defense, *Conduct of the Persian Gulf War* (Washington, D.C.: Government Printing Office, April, 1992), pp. 9, 11, 97; The International Institute for Strategic Studies, *The Military Balance*, 1990 – 1991 (London: Brassey's, 1990), pp. 90 – 91, 105 – 106; and Aspin, *Bottom-Up Review*, p. 13.

If a regional power were in fact more formidable than U.S. military planners anticipate, it is more likely that its capabilities would result from technological and operational innovation than from increased numbers of tanks, artillery, and aircraft. It is difficult to accept the belief that a U.S. force structure optimized for the Cold War will also be optimal as a hedge against an innovative regional power. Furthermore, it is hard to see how such a threat will emerge in the near term. Integrating new technologies, military systems, and innovative military doctrines takes a great deal of time, even in the most adaptive military organizations.[25] Why, then, does the Bottom Up Review recommend that the United States maintain an expensive force structure for the present, designed for the last war, as a hedge against a very different kind of threat, one unlikely to appear until the mid-term future, at the earliest?

The Bottom Up Review's planning scenarios are reminiscent of America's recent experience in the Persian Gulf. It is difficult to accept, for example, that even in the near term "an armor-heavy" offensive would characterize a war in Korea.[26] Given that the terrain is highly unfavorable for armored operations and that North Korea may well possess nuclear weapons, the review's planning suffers from the belief that "one scenario fits all" contingencies, sometimes referred to as the "canonical scenario."[27]

Moreover, the review offers little discussion regarding how U.S. forces might approach an aggressor that had acquired nuclear weapons. Nor do U.S. planners give consideration to the prospect that potentially hostile powers in the Third World might learn from Iraq's disastrous showing in the Gulf and that they would consequently take very different approaches from Iraq's in structuring and operating their military. It seems likely that regional powers hostile to the United States would emphasize those weapons that worked for Iraq during the war—ballistic missiles and mines, for example—and combine such weapons systems with selective employment of relatively advanced military systems (e.g., cruise missiles —perhaps even stealth—and precision-guided munitions).[28]

Finally, the Bottom Up Review declares that the United States must size and structure its forces "to preserve the flexibility and the capability to act unilaterally, should we choose to do so."[29] But what is the risk that the United States will find itself engaged in two major regional wars without support from long-standing allies? Put another way, is it not reasonable to assume that the United States can count on significant allied support in major regional conflicts?

Again, while one cannot predict the future, history suggests an affirmative answer. During the Korean War and the Gulf War, U.S. forces received significant support from NATO and other members of the United Nations. Even in Vietnam, two South Korean army divisions as well as ANZUS (Australian and New Zealander) troops, among others, supported the U.S. military effort. Where the United States has acted unilaterally, it has done so in relatively small contingencies, such as the invasions of Grenada in 1983 and Panama in 1989. It seems unlikely that the American people would sanction involvement in two major conflicts if the nation's principal allies refused support for either contingency. Given these considerations, the review planners appear to be "over-purchasing" insurance by mandating a U.S. capability to wage two wars unilaterally. The Pentagon must provide the burden of proof for maintaining a force structure capable of "decisive victory in two nearly simultaneous major regional conflicts." It has yet to do so.

Peace Enforcement and Intervention Operations

If future major regional conflicts do not resemble Desert Storm, and if the *greatest* dangers to U.S. security lie in the out years, the most likely challenges American forces will confront already exist in the form of religious and ethnic conflicts, international terrorism, and drug trafficking. They involve U.S. military forces in peacekeeping, peace making, and humanitarian operations. Such operations typically call for the use of the American military in conflict environments that, for them, substantially differ from the mid- to high-intensity conventional (or "traditional") conflicts for which they have prepared over the last half century. The last several years have seen U.S. forces conducting nontraditional operations in northern Iraq, Macedonia, Somalia, Rwanda, and Haiti. Given Clinton's policy pronouncements as well as the current international situation, the Bottom Up Review observes that "there are likely to be many occasions when we are asked to intervene with military force overseas."[30]

Acknowledging that the Defense Department must provide "forces and military support for other types of operations, such as peace-keeping, humanitarian assistance and to counter international drug trafficking," the review concludes that "such operations call for small numbers of specialized forces or assets, [and] they are not likely to be major determinants of general purpose force structure."[31] Many experts, however, have raised concerns as to the nature of potential opponents, the notional "building block" that the U.S. military would employ in such operations, as well as the "tests" laid out in Clinton's national security strategy to determine whether the United States would commit its armed forces to peacekeeping operations.

❧

The Nature of the Threat

The Bottom Up Review failed to conduct a scenario-based analysis of nontraditional operations as it did of major conventional operations. Rather, it assumed that the threat comprised "a mix of regular and irregular forces possessing mostly light weapons, supplemented by moderately sophisticated systems, such as antitank and antiship guided missiles, surface-to-air missiles, land and sea mines, T-54 and T-72 class tanks, armored personnel carriers, and towed artillery and mortars." In addition, it suggested that "adversary forces might also possess a limited number of mostly older combat aircraft (e.g., MiG-21s, 23s), a few smaller surface ships (e.g., patrol craft), and perhaps a few submarines."[32]

The threat posed in the review approximates the *relatively* conventional forces faced by the United States during its interventions in Vietnam (particularly in the Vietnamization period from 1969 to 1973), in post–Desert Storm Iraq (Operation Provide Comfort) and, arguably, Panama. Prospectively, one might imagine such a threat in an intervention against Greater Serbia. Such a threat is, perhaps, the most conventional kind of military force one might expect in such a contingency. Conversely, the review's threat profile completely failed to address the relatively *unconventional* threats encountered by U.S. forces during most of the Vietnam intervention (1962–71), in Beirut in the early 1980s, in Somalia, in Haiti, or, prospectively, what they might encounter in Bosnia. And, given overwhelming U.S. superiority in traditional, or conventional, aspects of military power, America's adversaries will have great incentive to adopt unconventional approaches. It appears the review fashioned its threat profiles for limited-war contingencies more on the basis of the operational and social preference of the U.S. military than on the technological, logistical, or doctrinal dimensions of potential opponents.[33]

The Bottom Up Review Response

With the exception of some intervention operations (e.g., Grenada, Panama), the military environments in most potential Third World conflicts dramatically differ from those found in conventional war. Not surprisingly, the military requirements for nontraditional operations, in terms of force structure, equipment, doctrine, and training, also differ from the conventional operations conducted during Desert Storm.

As the U.S. military has discovered in a variety of nontraditional situations, from Vietnam to Beirut and Mogadishu, advantages in technology, military systems, and logistics will not necessarily prevent imaginative exploitation of the operational and social dimensions of the military situation by our opponents. By dispersing forces and adopting a strategy of protracted war and by exhibiting a disregard for casualties (military and civilian), the enemy can pose severe problems for U.S. forces, which have long emphasized a preference for relying on technology and materiel to avoid casualties. As Aspin admitted, "[I]n the end, peace operations are a job [sic] that gets done on the ground, which means it's a job for the army."[34]

Aspin also acknowledged that peace missions require different training and equipment as well as a different "mix" of forces than those necessary for waging conventional war.[35] However, the Pentagon's training for unconventional operations seems likely to suffer from the same shortcomings that such training did in the early 1960s prior to the U.S. entry into the Vietnam War.[36] At the present time, training U.S. forces for peacekeeping is entirely additional to "their primary training for fighting and winning wars."[37] According to present priorities, intensive training in peace operations would begin only after units received orders for deployment to a specific peace operation.[38] This is, perhaps, an inevitable consequence of the heavy demands made on limited resources by the training requirements necessary to prepare for two major regional conflicts.

Limited, unconventional operations also require different equipment from that employed in conventional operations. Tomahawk Land-Attack Missiles and F-117 fighter aircraft would be substantially less effective in Haiti (or, prospectively, in Bosnia) than they were against Iraq during the Gulf War. While the authors of the review acknowledge this reality, the U.S. military will certainly confront the temptation of applying technological solutions where they do not fit, due to their focus, training, culture, and preferences. The force package that the review concludes is "prudent" for major interventions or peace enforcement operations is as follows:

- one air assault or airborne division

- one light infantry division

- one marine expeditionary brigade (MEB)

- one or two carrier battle groups

- one or two composite air force wings

- special operations forces

- civil affairs units

- airlift and sealift forces

- combat support and service support units[39]

Such a force package is not dissimilar to the forces that the United States initially dispatched to Vietnam in 1965.[40] The point here is not that the United States will find itself bogged down in future Vietnams; rather, it is that U.S. planners cannot assume that force packages that are a subset of forces designed for major conventional conflicts are optimal or even effective in unconventional situations. Nontraditional operations also tend to be protracted. They also require a rotation base to sustain U.S. forces beyond immediate commitments. Such a rotation base inevitably will increase force commitment totals by a factor of at least two. Given this fact, the review's conclusion that its proposed force structure cannot meet planning requirements for two major regional conflicts and provide forces for nontraditional contingencies is right on the money.

Finally, one needs to address the administration's "tests" that will supposedly guide U.S. involvement in peace operations. In the wake of the casualties suffered during the Mogadishu raid in October 1993, the administration developed a list of tests that policy makers must consider prior to committing American forces to multilateral peace operations. The administration then incorporated these factors into its *National Security Strategy of Engagement and Enlargement* and into Presidential Decision Directive 25. The factors include:

- Are the costs and risks commensurate with the stakes?

- Have nonmilitary means been given sufficient consideration?

- Is the use of force carefully matched to U.S. political objectives?

- Is there reasonable assurance of support from the American population and their elected representatives?

- Is there an exit strategy?

- Will U.S. action bring lasting improvements?[41]

The administration provided additional "tests" for the contingency that U.S. forces might support a UN peace operation.[42]

No single "test" is a "showstopper"—that is to say, the administration's criteria make clear that the decision to commit U.S. forces will rest "on the cumulative weight of the above factors, with no single factor necessarily being an absolute determinant." Thus, it is possible to "pass the test" without getting a perfect score. Still, this begs the issue of how useful such tests might be as guidelines for intervention. In the wake of Vietnam, U.S. administrations, Republican and Democrat alike, have prescribed "tests" for American intervention as a means of avoiding future military debacles.

Although the Clinton tests aim to address specific forms of military intervention, they are remarkably similar to the "Weinberger Doctrine" established during the Reagan administration by Secretary of Defense Caspar Weinberger. To "pass" the Weinberger tests, a U.S. vital interest had to be at stake; the administration had to define clear political and military objectives; the resources committed had to be sufficient; policy makers had to review the match between objectives and resources continuously; congressional and public support must exist; and all other alternatives to the use of force—political, diplomatic, and economic—had to be exhausted.[43] Most policy makers would agree that such tests are useful tools to address or assess whether or not to commit U.S. forces to combat. There is, however, one problem in employing such tests: they are not particularly effective in predicting whether prospective U.S. military operations will succeed or fail.

For example, during the Reagan-Bush years, Weinberger's tests went unheeded at times, with mixed results. U.S. forces deployed to Beirut as part of an international force that withdrew ignominiously after the terrorist bombing of the marine barracks. But U.S. forces conducted successful interventions in Grenada in 1983 and Panama in 1990—countries not necessarily of vital interest to the United States—without any clear indication of congressional or popular support. As for the Gulf War, it is easy in the aftermath of the Coalition's crushing victory to forget that the Senate's vote for war was close and that Americans were more divided than in 1965 when the United States intervened in Vietnam. In short, military interventions are notoriously unpredictable. Even the best plans seldom survive contact with the enemy; the only certainty is that events will surprise us (sometimes even pleasantly, as in the Gulf).

Colin Powell has established a singular test: apply overwhelming force against the enemy to achieve a rapid, decisive victory. Admittedly, the doctrine of overwhelming force worked well in the Gulf. It did not work so well in Vietnam or Beirut, where enormous U.S. advantages in firepower and mobility did not translate into overall military effectiveness against an enemy operating as guerrillas and terrorists. Nor is it likely to work as well in the Somalias and Bosnias of the emerging strategic environment. Such low-intensity conflicts are not amenable to quick solutions based primarily on military power. Indeed, the lower one descends along the spectrum of conflict, the less relevant military power becomes to the political, economic, and social dimensions of war. Perhaps this is why Powell remained so reluctant to employ U.S. forces in such operations during his tenure as chairman. Implicit in Powell's tests is the ability to accomplish U.S. objectives quickly. This, of course, is more easily achieved in conventional military operations like Grenada, Panama, and Desert Storm than in low-intensity environments like Vietnam,

Beirut, Somalia, Bosnia, and Haiti. But these are precisely the kinds of conflicts that the Clinton administration has confronted.

Because low-intensity conflicts are protracted in nature, "litmus tests" or
social science paradigms are not necessarily of great utility. Not only do objectives change, as occurred in Vietnam, Beirut, and Somalia (the feared
"mission creep"), but resource requirements also change, sometimes dramatically. Furthermore, a "wild card" already exists in operations that would rely
on allied support, since allies can always decide to go home on short notice—
a factor that could alter the ends/means test calculus substantially.

That Clinton failed to follow his own criteria in altering the mission of
U.S. forces in Somalia, or in deploying them to Haiti, does not in itself indicate that the operations will fail (although that is what happened in Somalia). If one attempted to predict the future, the history of the last forty years
suggests that the prospects for success are greatest when U.S. forces deploy
for brief periods and where there is a legitimate regime capable of assuming
control when the U.S. intervention occurs.[44] In summary, the Clinton "tests"
are not a substitute for a comprehensive strategy for using U.S. military
power—a strategy that American leaders would clearly have to elaborate to
the American people and that would win the support of their elected representatives.

Forward Presence

The Bottom Up Review accords significant weight to the maintenance
of an American military presence overseas in its sizing of post–Cold War
forces. In part, this approach involves the continued forward basing of sizable
air and ground forces in Western Europe and Northeast Asia. The review argues that the United States should retain roughly 100,000 troops in Europe
and some 98,000 or so troops in East Asia, primarily in South Korea and
Japan. Furthermore, the United States currently has, and evidently will retain over the foreseeable future, some 20,000 troops in the Middle East.[45]
These forces would also support U.S. involvement in any major regional contingency.

In the case of naval forces, the review argues that the United States must
give special consideration to their use in the forward presence mission in addition to their maritime commitment to supporting U.S. forces in two major
regional conflicts. Specifically, the review states that U.S. "overseas presence
needs can impose requirements for naval forces, especially aircraft carriers,
that exceed those needed to win two major regional commitments." The carriers' "flexibility" and "their ability to operate effectively with relative independence from shore bases, makes them well suited to overseas presence

operations."[46] The review recommended twelve carriers—a force structure that permits the United States to maintain carrier battle groups full time in the three geographic regions covered during the Cold War, and carrier forces in another two regions eight months each year. In short, twelve carriers buy twenty-eight carrier months of forward presence. This averages less than three months of forward presence per carrier because of the time required for overhaul, transit times between home port and forward locations, personnel considerations, and other related factors.

There is an obvious trade-off involved; the more carriers in the fleet, the shorter the gaps in carrier forward presence. For example, according to the review, if one were to accept a four-month gap in one of the three major geographic regions where the navy has had a full-time carrier deployment throughout the Cold War, the United States could operate with ten carriers instead of twelve (given that ten carriers would provide twenty-four carrier months of forward presence).[47]

Evaluating Carrier Requirements for Forward Presence

With respect to employing carriers in the forward presence mission, one needs to know how important forward presence is in accomplishing America's strategic objectives and whether carrier battle groups represent the optimal force for such a mission. The Bottom Up Review states that maritime presence forces demonstrate both to "friends and potential adversaries that the United States has global interests and the ability to bring military power quickly to bear anywhere in the world." Furthermore, U.S. maritime forces "have the operational mobility and political flexibility to reposition to potential trouble spots by unilateral U.S. decision." Such operations would include crisis resolution, evacuation of American nationals in danger, rendering humanitarian assistance, and strike operations "against countries supporting terrorism or defying U.N. resolutions."[48]

Yet questions remain. Are forward presence operations *with carriers* essential if the United States is to demonstrate its global interests and ability to bring power quickly to bear at any point? Carriers are expensive, both to construct and to operate. Furthermore, since carriers operate with other ships whose principal mission is the carrier's protection, the cost of the carrier must also include the cost of its escorts and aircraft. On average, it costs over $1.7 billion a year to equip, operate, and support a single carrier battle group.[49] The Congressional Budget Office has estimated that the Pentagon could save $15 billion over five years if it were to lower the number of carriers from twelve to ten.[50]

The review does not establish that carriers are unique in their ability to resolve crises, evacuate U.S. nationals in danger, or render humanitarian assistance. For example, in 1988, maritime forward presence operations included deploying an amphibious squadron off Haiti, a marine antiterrorist force to Panama, and a marine amphibious ready group off the coast of Burma during periods of civil unrest in those countries. Carriers did not take part in any of these operations. Moreover, U.S. forces successfully conducted the 1990 Somalian and Liberian evacuations *without* carrier involvement.[51] While carriers have deployed off Somalia during the Provide Hope operation, one carrier air wing commander observed following the October 1993 battle in which army rangers sustained heavy casualties that, despite the carriers' mission to protect servicemen in Mogadishu, carrier aircraft "might be the last thing . . . used" in dealing with such a crisis.[52]

With respect to strike operations, the carriers' relatively low speed resulted in their being left out of the Panamanian invasion in December 1989. In 1986, two carriers had to have major assistance from air force F-111s based in Britain to execute a limited raid against Libya. The long-range retaliatory strike against the Iraqi intelligence headquarters in Baghdad in 1993 was executed, not by a carrier, but by USS *Peterson*, a destroyer, and USS *Chancellorsville*, a cruiser, launching Tomahawk cruise missiles.[53]

These cases suggest the dramatic changes in military capabilities that have occurred since carriers established a dominant position in the navy during World War II. As advances in technology led the major maritime powers to move from the battleship to the carrier, even greater advances in technology in the past decade have provided U.S. policymakers with a range of options for the forward presence mission. Satellites provide a global reconnaissance capability. As land-based aircraft and cruise missiles have extended their range, payload, and accuracy, those situations in which carrier aircraft are the only means of conducting effective strikes have diminished greatly. In the future, will the leaders of a hostile state (such as Libya was in 1986) worry more about carrier battle groups whose movement they can track with relative certainty or strikes from submarine-launched cruise missiles or from long-range stealth aircraft?

Carriers will remain an important element in forward presence operations, although they no longer exercise a monopoly. Their ability to operate independently of on-shore bases, for example, provides important flexibility to U.S. planners. However, given tight constraints on resources, Clinton's defense program as outlined in the Bottom Up Review is not persuasive in its advocacy of the need for continuous presence of carrier battle groups in the Pacific Ocean, the Indian Ocean, and the Mediterranean Sea.

Nonproliferation and Counterproliferation

With the Soviet Union's collapse, U.S. attention in nuclear matters has shifted dramatically: it needs much less attention on the need to maintain the "balance of terror" with a Russia in economic and political disintegration. Reflecting a dramatic drop in tensions between the United States and Russia, START II, signed by Bush and Boris Yeltsin in January 1993, called for sharp reductions in the nuclear arsenals of both powers. The two nations have committed themselves to reducing their strategic arsenals to no more than 3,500 nuclear warheads by 2003. Although this will leave both powers with more nuclear warheads than any other state, it also represents a sharp drop in their nuclear arsenals.

Consequently, U.S. defense strategy has now focused more on the problem of blocking, slowing, or countering the spread of weapons of mass destruction, particularly nuclear weapons. The administration has accorded great emphasis on arms control agreements and regimes to support its nonproliferation efforts. It hopes to extend the Non-Proliferation Treaty, up for renewal in 1995, indefinitely and to strengthen the Nuclear Suppliers Group and the International Atomic Energy Agency. It also intends to press for a broadening of membership in the Missile Technology Control Regime, the prompt ratification of the Chemical Weapons Convention, and the toughening of compliance measures in the Biological Weapons Convention.[54]

Despite such efforts, some states will still acquire weapons of mass destruction as well as missile delivery systems. As a hedge against such an event, the administration intends that U.S. forces "be prepared to deter, prevent, and defend against their use."[55] The administration has not restricted its potential military options for retaliation. Rather, it apparently advocates adding the options of missile defense and preemptive strikes against powers acquiring weapons of mass destruction to the retaliation option.[56] The key issue here may be the administration's ability to fund a vigorous effort in this area while maintaining the Bottom Up Review's force posture. During the Gulf War, the ability of U.S. forces to disable Iraq's nuclear weapons program, seek out its ballistic missiles (the famed "Scud-hunting" operations), defend against ballistic missile attacks, and perform accurate battle damage assessment of the results had much room for improvement.[57]

The Price Tag: An Ends/Means Disconnect?

It is an old military adage that "amateurs discuss operations, while professionals discuss logistics." With respect to the present defense posture, one might say that "amateurs discuss strategy, while professionals discuss budgets." The fact is, no matter how enamored one might be of the Clinton defense program, the Pentagon cannot sustain its forces without sufficient resources. Indeed, the essence of strategy is the optimal employment of limited resources to achieve one's objectives. Does the Clinton program carry too hefty a price tag? Can the Pentagon execute the program given the resources available? Answering such questions requires an examination of both the near-term and long-term affordability of the administration's defense assumptions.

Near-Term Prospects (the Next Five Years)

Projected funding levels for defense over the next five years fall short of what the Pentagon requires to support the current force structure and modernization plans. Just how much of a mismatch exists, however, is unclear. Clinton's five-year funding target for the Bottom Up Review contained an "extremely tight fit" between strategy and resources.[58] The administration had hoped to cover potential funding shortfalls through savings derived from a variety of sources, including Vice President Gore's National Performance Review, the ongoing closure of military bases, reform of the acquisition system, and the review's examination of strategic programs.[59] However, such hopes failed to materialize, at least to the extent hoped. Independent analyses initially placed projected funding shortfalls as high as $50 billion more.[60] In July 1994 the General Accounting Office estimated that the five-year funding shortfall could reach $150 billion, or perhaps even higher.[61] The following month Deputy Secretary of Defense John Deutch instructed the services to review their major acquisitions programs; he implied that each was subject to delay or cancellation.[62] Deutch's memo has the potential to undermine the program decisions reached in the Bottom Up Review, particularly "force enhancements" necessary to support the two major regional contingencies. By September 1994, the Defense Department admitted to a funding shortage over its five-year program of some $40 billion, or $49 billion over the 1996–2001 six-year period.[63]

In December the administration announced plans to redress the $49 billion funding mismatch. First, the Pentagon would receive $25 billion in additional funding, primarily to improve near-term readiness. The services would recover the remaining shortfall of $24 billion by cuts in acquisition ($8 billion) and by other, as yet unspecified, savings. In acknowledging the administration's plans, Deutch admitted that the administration was sacrificing future military capabilities to maintain current force structure and short-term readiness.[64]

It is not clear that these measures will, in fact, close the plans/funding mismatch. As noted above, the administration's estimate rests at the low end of a range of estimates that run as high as $150 billion. If the mismatch proves greater than current estimates, force structure reduction is a possible solution to funding difficulties. According to Powell, eight active army divisions (and six reserve division equivalents), eight carrier battle groups, the same marine forces required for two major regional contingencies, and sixteen air force fighter wings would provide the United States with a force posture capable of fighting one major conflict (with some "leftover" capability, presumably for peace operations).[65]

It is unlikely that the Defense Department will realize major savings over the next few years in other areas. The so-called Nuclear Posture Review resulted in modest cuts to U.S. nuclear forces, which, in any event, comprise only a small portion of the defense budget.[66] With respect to savings from cuts in infrastructure, the Bottom Up Review concedes that while the savings may be "significant," the Pentagon would not realize them until the late 1990s.[67] Indeed, the process of closing bases typically exacts significant up-front costs, rather than savings.

Long-Term Prospects

If the Defense Department could somehow cover the Bottom Up Review's funding shortfall over the near term, would prospects be brighter in the out years? Although the administration has not yet provided detailed projections of future defense funding levels, calculations using the administration's own data suggest an emphatic "no"—not if the Bottom Up Review's 1.45-million-person force structure is to remain combat ready and is modernized at currently projected rates. According to a Congressional Budget Office analysis, the review's estimates may suffer from a long-term funding shortfall of some $12–25 billion *per year* once the review's force posture is in place.[68] The lower estimates assume that the costs of new weapons systems do not grow above current estimates, while the higher shortfall estimates assume a continuation of historic cost trends.

Bad Choices

While the Bottom Up Review's force structure is clearly not affordable over the long term, it might possibly "limp along" over the next several years. Given recent administration actions outlined above, this seems to be the preferred course of action. The Pentagon can afford to underfund procurement in the short term because it is moving toward a smaller force structure and because it procured large quantities of new equipment in the 1980s. However, unless additional cuts in procurement converge with further cuts in the size of the force structure, they will only compound procurement shortfalls the Pentagon will confront in the out years. Alternatively, the administration could make deeper cuts in current research and development costs to cover near-term underfunding problems. Such an approach would have less of an immediate impact on U.S. military capabilities. But the long-term consequences would be even more detrimental than cuts in procurement. Moreover, research and development funding is already programmed to suffer a 25 percent cut over the next five years.

If the administration were to make deeper reductions in defense investment accounts (procurement and research and development) to protect the Bottom Up Review's 1.45-million-person force structure and a high combat readiness, the American military would begin to feel the negative effects of such reductions before the end of the current fiscal year Defense Plan, since some weapon systems can reach the forces by the late 1990s only if ordered over the next couple of years. Conversely, if the administration protected procurement and research and development accounts, the Pentagon would have to make deeper cuts in the operations and maintenance account—the only other major Pentagon account. The likely result of such an approach would be an increasingly "hollow" force of 1.45 million.

If the administration wants to avoid the results inherent in trying to support and sustain too large a defense structure with too few resources, it has two options. First, it could provide the increased funding necessary to implement defense programs the president has embraced. But the president's domestic priorities as well as the new Congress's emphasis on deficit reduction and tax cuts make significant increases in projected defense budgets highly unlikely. Second, the administration could direct the Pentagon to recast its strategy and the associated force structure to come in line with available resources. This approach would almost certainly mean dropping the current force posture. It might increase the United States' near-term security risks. On the other hand, it at least promises that the Defense Department could increase the priorities given to dealing with the greatest and most likely threats to national security. Moreover, the United States would be more secure in the long term by spending marginally fewer dollars on the right priorities than more dollars on the wrong priorities.

The refusal to acknowledge the existence of a plans/funding mismatch and the attempt to execute the review's recommended defense program with currently programmed defense budgets will result in the maintenance of near-term military capabilities at the expense of future military potential. The results will be a United States that finds itself in the out years with insufficient military capabilities, demands for another military buildup, and an acute funding crunch.

Conclusions

The current National Strategy of Engagement and Enlargement is more ambitious than the Bush administration's Regional Defense Strategy. Yet, Clinton has adopted the centerpiece of the Bush strategy while supporting a substantially larger role for the U.S. military in peace operations. Since his inauguration, the president has lowered slightly the ambitious role he foresaw for U.S. forces in such operations. However, in the wake of the military occupation of Haiti and the president's commitment to provide substantial American forces for Bosnia (should a peace be negotiated), it is not clear whether he intends to bind his policy by his own "tests" for commitment of U.S. troops.

Moreover, given funding problems, the decision to maintain the Bottom Up Review's force structure is curious. The secretary of defense acknowledges that the United States is not likely to fight an adversary of the type envisioned in the review over the near term. Yet, the deputy secretary of defense admits that, in trying to maintain a force structure oriented to meet such near-term threats, the Pentagon risks sacrificing the modernization of its forces required to confront potentially greater dangers in the long run.

In the absence of clear strategic guidance, the Pentagon has proceeded as bureaucracies do in an uncertain environment: it has attempted to "fit" the new situation to already existing planning and resource allocations. The result is a defense program that addresses the most *familiar* threats, as opposed to the *greatest or most likely* ones. It also is a defense program that the United States cannot afford—indeed, which becomes progressively *less* affordable over time given resource constraints—a force structure primarily organized to fight the last war more effectively.

What challenges (or dangers) should claim top priority? Considering the strategic and military revolutions now under way, several crucial areas deserve greater emphasis than the Clinton program is currently providing. First, the administration should tailor defense programs to forestall a resurrection of the great-power rivalries that have characterized the twentieth century. This would involve providing higher priority to the preservation of the long-term *potential* of U.S. forces, as opposed to near-term *capabilities*. Such an approach implies placing greater emphasis on research and development, operational and organizational experimentation, innovation, and selective modernization, all areas that would serve to preserve the military potential of the United States. It also implies providing relatively less priority to the preservation of the current force structure.

Second, the Pentagon might accord increased emphasis to shaping the defense budget and forces to respond to the threat of nuclear weapons and proliferation as well as the diffusion of advanced military technologies. It might place greater emphasis on identifying ways to dissuade, discourage, deter, or defend against hostile regimes or organizations that intend to acquire, or who do acquire, nuclear or advanced conventional systems. A major component of such an effort would involve resolving the uncertainties between nonproliferation and counterproliferation strategies and encouraging innovation and experimentation among the military services.

Third, the Pentagon should accord a higher priority to the most likely challenges to security. The administration needs to resolve the competition between preparation for combat operations and peace operations. As Somalia, Bosnia, and Haiti suggest, peace operations require significantly different doctrines, force structures, equipment, and training than do the major regional contingencies. The Bottom Up Review admits that it cannot provide forces for "sizable peace enforcement or intervention operations" and also meet the requirement to fight two major regional contingencies. In cases where priorities compete, the administration must decide which will take precedence.

Orienting America's defense program to meet the greatest and most likely challenges to its security means that something must give. The Pentagon will have to accept increases in the level of risk to national security in some areas in order to minimize potentially greater risks in other areas. This is not a new concept. Establishing a defense posture with limited resources has always involved the acceptance of some degree of risk.

Unless the president can make a better case for the Bottom Up Review's defense program, he would be prudent to adopt a one-major-regional-contingency strategy while reviewing forward presence requirements. This approach offers several advantages. First, it would bring the force structure more in line with projected resources. Second, it would free resources to address the greatest and most likely challenges to U.S. security. Third, by reducing stress on other portions of the defense budget (i.e., the personnel, procurement, and operations and maintenance accounts) the new approach would facilitate the fielding of modern, capable, and ready forces that the president has pledged to maintain, forces that address the principal near-term threat to American security in a period of relative safety. Fourth, it would provide the Pentagon greater flexibility in promoting operational and organizational innovation, experimentation, and adaptation. This will be necessary if the new capabilities emerging from the military revolution are to develop in an optimal and fiscally responsible manner that reflects the challenges and opportunities of a new era.

Chapter 6

The Second Nuclear Age: Insecurity, Proliferation, and the Control of Arms

Colin S. Gray

T he precipitate collapse of the Soviet Union did not—alas—signal the decline and fall of many strategic fallacies. Indeed, the current interwar period, otherwise known as the post–Cold War era, is permissive of fallacies on a heroic scale. With the Damoclean sword of nuclear weapons removed strategically, though not physically, for the present, all things seem possible to many, no matter how ill founded in experience or common sense. Nevertheless, history, even "history as such," has not come to an end.[1] Neither has nuclear-age history.

The 1990s, and perhaps only the 1990s, comprise a second nuclear age. This period is distinct from that of 1945–89, when nuclear issues, anxieties, and theories necessarily had their principal focus on the possibility of Soviet-American nuclear war. Notwithstanding discontinuities between the first and second nuclear ages, popular errors persist in approaches to nuclear weapons, the control of arms, and the enduring character of world politics. Those imprudent during the first nuclear age have not suddenly acquired wisdom in a new and different political context.

The subtitle of this chapter refers to the control of arms rather than to arms control. *Arms control* refers to the formal or tacit negotiation of constraints upon either the number and kinds of national armaments (structural arms control) or permitted behavior within armaments frameworks (operational arms control). The *control of arms*, in contrast, refers to those factors that actually constrain the accumulation, modernization, or employment of arms (e.g., deterrence, combat, cost, and doctrine). Those reared on the promise, and fears, of arms-control theory usually believe that the alternative to arms control is a lack of control of arms. Such a belief is, in fact, without foundation. From an Anglo-American perspective, arms control in the twentieth century has been an all but trivial pursuit. Nevertheless, Western actions have limited the strategic effect of enemy arms time after time.[2] For example, a combination of external as well as domestic factors controlled the strategic effect of Soviet armaments throughout the Cold War.

Enervating confusion and underappreciated contradictions pervade the current debate on nuclear proliferation. Nuclear proliferation has always been an issue of relatively small importance; for many years during the Cold War, nuclear perils so overshadowed the issue that it escaped the theoretical overkill that was the fate of more pressing strategic policy areas. Although worries about nuclear proliferation persisted as a small but steady cottage industry in the 1960s, 1970s, and 1980s, its study was never a coherent part of national security policy; nor did it become a part of mainstream strategic studies.[3] The institutions of the U.S. government perpetuated the neglect. It was not that senior officials and other defense professionals failed to worry about the spread of nuclear weapons; rather, there were more immediate, apparently more serious, and arguably more tractable nuclear issues that preempted their attention.

Consequently, nuclear proliferation continues to stand apart from the theory and practice of arms control. Arms-control experience in the twentieth century is vast, but the application of that experience to current efforts to slow the spread of nuclear weapons is difficult to locate in the popular or professional literature—or, for that matter, in statements of public policy. This noticeable isolation of nuclear proliferation has allowed strategically unprofessional analyses to attain preeminence. On the one hand, there are the smugly certain contributions from the rarefied realm of international relations theory. Fred Iklé has sharply and accurately noted the following on one theorist's arguments: "Measured in a few millennia of human history, what is genuinely stable, alas, is the pernicious lethality of plutonium; the apparent stability of mutual nuclear deterrence can disappear as the result of one coup d'état, one sudden civil war, one human mistake."[4] On the other hand, advocates of an essentially technical approach to security have reveled in the high technicity of nuclear fuel cycles and the like.[5] What has been missing is a steady strategic gaze on the subject of nuclear proliferation.

❧

On Nuclear Ages and Nuclear Fact

The Cold War comprised a distinctive, "first" nuclear age. It follows that the 1990s comprise a distinct, "second" nuclear age, an age that assuredly will give birth to a "third" age characterized, indeed driven, by renewed great-power rivalries. Thus, one can view the nuclear age as both singular and plural. It is commonplace, but nonetheless important, to register the permanence of nuclear weapons in matters of security. However fashionable ideas about disarmament, arms control, and the military promise of conventional armaments may be, the nuclear shadow will remain as an actual or prospective presence both in and around conflicts until man's time on earth ends. Because of their temporarily unmatched superiority in conventional military power, as well as for familiar reasons of strategic ethnocentricity,[6] many Americans have embraced variants of what amounts to a postnuclear syndrome. An America, at present, alone on the leading edge of a "transformation of war" that favors those who command and employ real-time information may find itself less and less in need of *nuclear* muscle.[7] Most of the world, however, is not capable of waging information-age, conventional war to any considerable effect. There are, however, a number of answers to the strategic challenges posed by the conventional potency of the U.S. military, one of which is clearly the possession and ability to use nuclear weapons. As Eliot Cohen has suggested about the lessons of the Gulf War, the war "has made it clear that no country can match the United States in a conventional conflict. To a hostile general staff, nuclear weapons look increasingly attractive as a means of deterring either the Yankees or (more likely) their local clients, who provide the bases from which American military power operates."[8]

The pull of the secondary, if not the trivial, troubles the whole subject of nuclear proliferation. A brute techno-empiricism always threatens to overwhelm the discussion. By analogy, many are more comfortable studying and discussing ships than they are considering what ships mean for naval, much less maritime, strategy. Bomb design, reactor technology, and procedures for safeguard inspections are more interesting to most experts on nuclear proliferation than are the political and strategic assumptions and arguments that provide meaning to technical detail.[9] To establish an appropriate foundation for meaningful debate, four basic points require recognition.

First, *nuclear weapons are a permanent fact in the strategic equation.* Nuclear ages will succeed one another in different configurations of the balance of power, but the vista and benefits of nuclear threats or use have joined death and taxes as certainties for the future. The very character of modern scientific research, the demonstration of theory on 16 July 1945 at Alamogordo, and the rather later generations of physics and nuclear textbooks have opened the secrets of the atomic age to all. It was easier for the Eastern Roman Empire in the fifth century A.D. to deny barbarians state-of-the-art weapons,[10] and it would have been easier for the gunpowder-oriental polities of the eleventh and twelfth centuries to retard proliferation of gunpowder technology,[11] than it would currently be for nuclear states to limit their own numbers.[12] States may choose not to invest in nuclear weapons, but the ability of the possessor states to deny access to key knowledge or materials will not play a critical, dissuasive role in the future.

Unlike gunpowder weapons in the late medieval period, nuclear weapons will never become "conventional" as the regular weapon of choice. Nonetheless, the gunpowder precedent holds in that "the nuclear revolution" is truly global.[13] Nuclear weapons are not cheap to acquire,[14] but many members of the United Nations are already in a position to acquire a strategically useful military capability. Many, probably most, polities will elect not to join the ranks of nuclear-weapons states over the course of the next half century. Nevertheless, such a move will remain open to them. The fact remains that the nuclear age, like the gunpowder age, is open to exploitation by those polities that perceive their national interests as requiring nuclear support.

Second, *complete nuclear disarmament, whether regional or global, is as impracticable as it would be undesirable for international security.* Given the growing accessibility of nuclear capability, nuclear disarmament can only be as robust as the political motives for its sustenance. Since treaties and agreements register interests, calculations of political interest drive nuclear armament or disarmament. Polities whose leaders believe that their nations might have to wage war for vital interests and possibly survival are polities that have strong motivation to proceed down the path of nuclear acquisition or nuclear armament. A regional or global regime of nuclear disarmament could survive only as long as the permissive political conditions that resulted in its birth. That logic is scarcely startling or novel; it is a general truth about agreements between states *and* a particular truth about arms control. If nuclear capability is accessible, there is much to be said in favor of local, regional, and global retention as a regular part of the security landscape. The alternative would be to encourage the secret or hasty introduction—or reintroduction—of nuclear weapons into conflicts.

Third, lest there be any misunderstanding on this fundamental point, *it is in the interest of the United States, possessing nuclear weapons, that there should be as few nuclear weapons states in the world as possible.* In June 1962, then-Secretary of Defense Robert S. McNamara forcefully and ungraciously expressed the American attitude to what then was called the "Nth country" nuclear problem. He was ungracious and tactless because he was talking in a NATO forum explicitly about the nuclear aspirations of other NATO members. Mc-Namara argued that "limited nuclear capabilities, operating independently, are dangerous, expensive, prone to obsolescence, and lacking in credibility as a deterrent."[15] Duly translated for different times, strategic contexts, and proliferant polities (e.g., no longer France vis-à-vis the USSR), McNamara's statement captures the spirit of the persisting American view of the nuclear programs of other polities.

The implications of nuclear-weapons status, explicit or unannounced, vary widely with political identity. By themselves nuclear weapons are not the problem; rather, the problem lies in the acquisition of nuclear weapons by polities whose motives are more ambitious than their own protection. Yet again, this is a general truth about arms control. An evenhanded approach to weaponry attracts a naive moralism (e.g., it is "unjust" that nuclear states should conspire to deny like armament to others); such an understanding is blind both to the nature of world politics and the realities of U.S. national interests.

The acquisition of nuclear weapons by other countries has different security implications for the United States and is by no means always an unmitigated disaster. Indeed, there are cases of unannounced nuclear states, which support the argument that nuclear proliferation in some circumstances can contribute to regional stability (i.e., to date, Israel in the Middle East and Pakistan in South Asia).[16] As a general rule, however, diffusion of nuclear weapons will be bad news for the only, if reluctant and wavering, superpower and guardian of world order. For a polity whose "long suit" in the 1990s is the reach and lethality of its conventional striking power, nuclear proliferation threatens to place a terminal constraint on American freedom of action.

Fourth, *opposition to the further proliferation of nuclear weapons is a major interest, but generally not a vital interest, of the United States.* An elementary difficulty in public debate is that few are sufficiently careful in the use of the concept of national interest. Any analysis of national interest requires the competent and honest to identify gradations of concern. Here I choose to identify *survival* interests, *vital* interests, *major* interests, and *other* interests. Survival interests are those for which the polity must fight if it is to survive; vital interests most often require military force for their defense; major interests most typically do not warrant active military support; while other interests will not merit military action. With this four-way split in mind, cases of nuclear proliferation should rank in U.S. policy only in the category of *major* interests, save on the rarest of occasions. In practice, however, principle and strategic theory always must descend to specific application. Some countries matter more to the United States than others, and some countries' actual or hypothetical weapons programs also matter more.

The United States has good reason to care about nuclear proliferation, but nuclear proliferation itself should trigger an American policy response as a *vital* interest only if other features of the proliferant state's policy point compellingly to a rogue character (i.e., the likelihood of unpredictable, erratic, and dangerous behavior). Much of the muscular American antiproliferation advocacy of recent years has completely failed to meet reasonable cost-benefit standards. The simple fact is that the cost to the United States of stopping nuclear proliferation may very well be a major war. And in most cases, the United States should not, and will not, go to war to prevent other polities from exercising the same nuclear option that the United States itself exercised in the 1940s.

That being said, there will occasionally be states that are candidates for nuclear-preventive, military discipline. In addition, the United States can and should apply a wide range of active, quasi-military measures (arguably short of "war") to retard the pace of progress toward usable nuclear arsenals. Nonetheless, the principal thrust of this fourth point suggests that overt military opposition (in peacetime) to nuclear weapons programs will rarely be in the net national interest of the United States. One can conceive, design, and—with some political-moral courage—implement an active, but short of military, counterproliferation policy. But neither the global community, nor the United States specifically, has so much at stake that one could justify the price of war in most cases to retard, halt, or roll back nuclear proliferation.[17]

Nuclear Fallacies

On the grounds that before reaching good ideas, it is first necessary to identify and clear away poor ideas, it would be useful if theorists and experts could spare this second nuclear age avoidable and erroneous assumptions. To that end, this chapter will discuss those fallacies whose unmerited popularity, even authority, inhibits sensible policy making.

Fallacy 1: There is a single general problem of nuclear proliferation toward which the United States can vector a single general policy.

In practice, there are at least as many problems with nuclear proliferation as there are would-be proliferants. There is no simple—or perhaps elegant—essentialist truth about nuclear proliferation. Just as the causes of wars have proven to be sufficiently distinctive as to thwart even the most rigorous and massive assaults of political scientists (based on misreadings of the historical record),[18] so a close examination of nuclear proliferation reveals diverse sets of problems for antiproliferation policy makers. Nuclear proliferation, in common with war, is the product of richly individual sets of circumstances.[19] There is no golden key to open the way to all-embracing solutions.[20] Indeed, to seek such a key, or philosophers' stone, is akin to seeking a single, all-case solution to war via, for example, a common language, world government, general and complete disarmament, peace education, and so forth. Nuclear proliferation comprises many problems, which require the application of many solutions and palliatives.

Fallacy 2: Nuclear proliferation is stoppable.

Nuclear weapons are here to stay. To recognize the harsh fact that some polities will judge formal or unadmitted (but known, for deterrence) nuclear-weapons status to be a major asset for national security is not to succumb to a "fatalist fallacy" along the lines argued by Richard Betts.[21] There is at least one important sense in which fatalism is realistic and prudent. Namely, it is sensible to be fatalistic in a general way about the persistence of nuclear weapons as a factor in world politics. Perhaps the more fundamental fallacy is that which points to a neat, simple binary universe. *Either* we endeavor to stop nuclear proliferation, *or* we seek to manage it. The latter would be the wiser of the two choices were the range of policy alternatives confined to two, which it is not. In common with most general truths about strategic matters, however, the policy problems for specific cases must always remain unique.

Nuclear weapons are here to stay, and statecraft must accommodate that fact. Nonetheless, particular countries may well step back from a nuclear-weapons path (e.g., Sweden, Brazil, Argentina, South Korea) or even actually denuclearize (i.e., South Africa), while the consistent pressure of the counterproliferation instruments of grand strategy can harass some potential candidates for nuclear weapons by impeding or lengthening their path to acquisition (e.g., Iraq).

Nuclear proliferation is not a problem, or a set of problems, that can be open to solution; the diffusion of nuclear weapons is not, in general, stoppable. Nevertheless, in principle any particular case of a would-be proliferant yields specific opportunities for the arrest, retardation, or even elimination (pro tem, at least) of the nuclear-weapons program at issue. In order to minimize the possibility of unproductive debate on false alternatives, one must restate the parameters within which policy discussions should take place.

- The nuclear age is here to stay—it cannot be repealed.

- As motives for possession of nuclear weapons must vary from case to case, there will be opportunities for the international non-, or anti-, or counterproliferation pressure to exercise influence over the pace of achievement, and possibly even the goal, of nuclear-weapons acquisition by some states.

- Even if the United States and the international community can retard or perhaps even stop all proliferation, they cannot reliably retard or stop it indefinitely. In the long term the pertinent problem will always be the strength of the political will of certain polities to acquire those weapons.

Fallacy 3: The answer, or answers, to the problem(s) posed by nuclear proliferation lie in the imposition of what amounts to a technological or administrative peace.

This third nuclear fallacy is a corollary of the broader fallacy that "weapons make war; abolish weapons and we will abolish war."[22] If the menace were nuclear technology, including civilian nuclear technology, then a technological solution would be workable. Not surprisingly, however, the historical record suggests that countries have not stumbled unconsciously onto nuclear weapons capabilities as a result of mere technological competence. Again, for the broad analogy, history provides no clear lessons that demonstrate convincingly that one can trace the causes of, or even triggers for, war to weapons or to competitions in armaments.[23]

In theory, suitable policies of denial enforced by an antiproliferation regime of like-minded polities and international institutions can technologically inhibit nuclear proliferation. But, in practice, the "playing field" today and in the future tilts in favor of would-be proliferants who possess sufficient financial, technological, and economic resources. Scientific and engineering knowledge, skilled scientists and engineers, and accessible paths to acquire both fissile material and the nonnuclear materials required for weapons production are all available for hire, purchase, or national development.

The bottom line is that the international community and the United States cannot deny a nuclear arsenal to a polity with the necessary will and financial resources; it is just not possible. However, in some cases the international framework might persuade a would-be proliferant that its security interests lie in eschewing nuclear weapons (overt or not admitted, but less than thoroughly covert). Alternatively, the United States and the international community might so harass a would-be proliferant with determined measures that the cost of its nuclear-weapons program becomes prohibitively expensive.[24] As a further possibility, with Iraq in mind for the 1990s, for example, antiproliferation policy could delay the pace of achievement of nuclear capability. Nevertheless, the fallacy of a technological peace points unerringly toward a higher-level font of error, the fallacy of new opportunities for arms control.

Fallacy 4: Rejuvenated by its triumphs in, or over, erstwhile East-West strategic relations, arms control now has new opportunities to save the human race in the field of nuclear nonproliferation.

It has become fashionable to note that the end of the Cold War has moved nuclear proliferation to center stage in the drama of arms control. As one commentator has claimed, "The end of the Cold War has opened the way to greater international collaboration to prevent nuclear proliferation and led to a merger of nuclear arms control and nonproliferation activities."[25] It is rather less fashionable to note that authors of the sins and errors of past arms-control efforts are reproducing their efforts faithfully. As a British strategic theorist in the 1920s wrote modestly of his own endeavors, "there is nothing new in this. It has all been said by Clausewitz, by Foch, and by Henderson, and by many others, for here what is new is not true, what is true is not new."[26]

Many of the academic experts who failed to understand the central problem with strategic arms control in the Cold War are now perpetuating misunderstanding by applying fallacious theories to the leading successor issue, nuclear proliferation. The subject is different, but many of the authors and their intellectual errors remain the same.

Kathleen Bailey has stated clearly the central problem with arms control in general, as well as with new opportunities for arms control in the 1990s. She explicitly draws on the case of Iraq. "The key conclusion drawn from the Iraqi case is that the nuclear nonproliferation regime cannot prevent a determined proliferant, even when that nation is a participant in the regime."[27] Bailey does not relate her persuasive judgment to the history of arms control, as she could have done. Her observation that the nonproliferation regime cannot handle a truly determined proliferant points to the latest case of a structural phenomenon. Specifically, arms control, in common with collective security, cannot handle the hard cases.[28] The Nuclear Non-Proliferation Treaty and its associated International Atomic Energy Agency work adequately in those cases where states have little motivation for developing nuclear weapons or for cheating on solemn, legal undertakings.

It would matter little for international peace and security if many of those states without nuclear weapons, whose nuclear power facilities the International Atomic Energy Agency monitors at great cost, actually changed course and sought to build nuclear weapons. Unfortunately, those states with the strongest motivation to acquire nuclear weapons are precisely the states most likely to trouble regional stability. Bailey's work has underlined the basic impotence of the nuclear nonproliferation regime even with respect to one of its fully safeguarded signatories, namely, Iraq. That recent experience should not have come as any surprise. Similarly, in the 1930s Nazi Germany's desire to find a cover for its aggressive diplomatic program and for naval rearmament motivated the Anglo-German Naval Agreement of 1935.[29] The idea that arms-control agreements might serve for purposes of deception has remained underappreciated among the cohorts of professional arms controllers well into the 1990s.

Negotiated arms-control regimes work only as long as contracting parties judge the constraints to be in their net interest. But a determined cheat can systematically exploit international regimes for arms control, or for other aspects of security, immensely to its own advantage. The misbehavior of Germany, Italy, and Japan in the interwar years, and of the Soviet Union and Iraq more recently, attests to the unreliability of arms-control arrangements as a pillar of international security.[30] Arms control failed in the Cold War because it could not succeed. States and alliances that believe they may have to fight will not constrain their military preparations in meaningful ways, even though putative foes also confront constraints.[31] Arms control, even disarmament, registered apparent successes in the early 1920s and again in the late 1980s and early 1990s precisely because it was largely irrelevant to international security.

The current nuclear proliferation regime has some notable structural advantages over the process of Soviet-American arms control during the Cold War. Specifically, the contracting, declared states with nuclear weapons share a common interest in maintaining their nuclear oligopoly. It is easy to agree to deny access to others to what one enjoys oneself. Second, the purpose and the measure of success are plainer for the nonproliferation regime — retard or stop the growth in the number of nuclear-weapons states — than was the case for strategic arms limitation. Because strategic arms limitation was ultimately about reducing the risk of the outbreak of war, it was always next to impossible to argue conclusively that any particular set of treaty terms would, or would not, warrant acclaim as success. If one lacks a robust understanding of the causes of war, and if arms control fundamentally is about war prevention/peace promotion, how can one distinguish better arms-control policies and agreements from those that might be worse? The mainstream of arms-control theory has quite simply missed the import of that question.

Entry into the rank of nuclear-armed states is now easier than was third-party access to the level and scale of strategic weapons capabilities that would have perturbed Soviet-American relations during the Cold War. Nuclear states can genuinely cooperate in the attempt to restrict their number to a degree impossible in Cold War strategic arms control, but these "have" states possess less ability to control membership in the nuclear club to any meaningful degree.

The theory and practice of arms control have never convincingly coped with the arms-control paradox, which holds that agreement is possible only when not needed, and that the reasons why agreement is needed are the very reasons that prevent agreement. The apparent successes of arms control, including those of the nuclear nonproliferation regime, in handling easy cases are no indicator of any ability to tackle the hard cases. Indeed, who cares whether or not deeply peaceable polities solemnly agree not to acquire military capabilities they have no intention of acquiring? An Imperial Japan, a Nazi Germany, an Iraq, or an Iran—these are the only litmus tests of arms control that really matter.

Fallacy 5: A taboo on the use of nuclear weapons, much strengthened by the nuclear nonproliferation regime, has helped delegitimize nuclear weapons in a useful fashion.

Foolish arguments, through repetition, come to enjoy an authority they do not merit. In the litany of fallacies that hinder a clear perspective on nuclear weapons, the idea of a nuclear taboo deserves special notice. The hypothesis is that an informal convention has gained momentum over the past three decades that all but prohibits the threat, or use, of nuclear weapons in support of policy. Arguing prescriptively, a leading American expert on nuclear proliferation has expressed this fallacy as follows: "A commitment to reducing the role of nuclear weapons and fostering a global nuclear taboo against their use would also contribute across the board to containing the scope of nuclear proliferation and its consequences."[32] A British authority has ventured a complementary judgment: "Playing down the significance of nuclear weapons in their [nuclear-weapons states'] security policies will in itself serve to reinforce the nonproliferation norm, by denying to potential proliferators evidence of the utility of proliferation, either as a usable source of military or political power or as a means to counter nuclear threats from the existing nuclear weapons states."[33]

As with such fallacies, the belief in a nuclear taboo is not wholly without merit. There is no doubt that the word *nuclear* has acquired negative connotations. Reinforced by the evidence of accidents at Three Mile Island and especially at Chernobyl—to cite only the most celebrated of near, and actual, disasters—popular attitudes in much of the liberal, democratic world have become less tolerant of all things nuclear.[34] Nevertheless, no public protest has yet to register a significant victory over and against nuclear-oriented defense policy.

As "nuclear" has ceased to be novel, so the decades have accumulated during which nuclear weapons have neither been used nor even brandished explicitly in attempts at coercive diplomacy. Taking off from Bernard Brodie's famous 1973 argument that nuclear weapons have "utility (only) in nonuse,"[35] an argument that he *initially* rehearsed nearly three decades earlier,[36] the idea has gained ground that there is a taboo against the use of such weapons. Admittedly, one cannot deny the fact of a half century of nuclear nonuse any more than one can deny "the [current] strength of the international political consensus" opposed to nuclear proliferation.[37] The question that really matters, however, is whether there is really a taboo with policy makers where and when the use of such weapons might prove useful.

In fact, there is a circularity to the argument about the supposed nuclear taboo. As with deterrent effect, a taboo exists only in the mind; inherently it is vulnerable to skeptical assay. Taboos are weakened or destroyed if they are challenged roughly and persistently. The nuclear taboo, no matter how desirable, has a reality confined either to those disinterested in the possession of nuclear weapons (formal or more or less covert) or to those determined to preserve the relative exclusiveness of their nuclear privileges.[38]

First, any attempt to exclude nuclear weapons by a taboo cannot help but represent a two-edged sword. Weapons uniquely worthy of a taboo on their threat or use are weapons of unique potential. Whatever psychological power such weapons lacked previously, any taboo will surely provide. A broad international consensus in favor of nuclear nonproliferation or nuclear nonemployment by those states possessing such weapons does not necessarily indicate that such weapons are irrelevant to national and international security. Singularization intends to render nuclear weapons singularly lacking in strategic utility, but in practice such an approach is at least as likely to reinforce the strategic judgment that such weapons are singularly useful.

Second, historical experience and common sense suggest that the hypothesis of a nuclear taboo is about as robust as were the taboos against war itself in the 1920s and 1930s and against the use of poison gas in World War II. It is no exaggeration to claim that many Europeans, especially in Britain and France, believed that there was a taboo against war—certainly a repeat of another great war in Europe—in the 1920s and 1930s. Indeed, the Kellogg-Briand Treaty outlawed war on 27 August 1928. The problem was that many Germans and certainly the post–January 1933 leader of Germany failed to share in such a belief.[39] Taboos are never as strong as the breadth of consensus behind them; rather they are only as strong as the absence of powerful challenges to their authority. The fact that most governments, and certainly most individuals, even in Germany, did not want war in 1939, is beside the point. Hitler wanted war in 1939—he had wanted war in 1938, but British appeasement had thwarted his aim—and really that was all that mattered.[40]

By way of minor illustration, there was also a perceived taboo against the use of chemical weapons (i.e., poison gas) in the 1930s and 1940s (as today). Such a taboo sprang from the experience, or perception of experience, in the Great War and was enshrined in the Geneva Protocol of 17 June 1925. The reasons why the combatants refused to use gas during World War II, however, do not speak persuasively to the robustness of any taboo against its use. Unlike the situation in 1918, when the use of gas shells was entirely tactical (i.e., used only on the battlefield), in World War II the participants recognized gas as a strategic weapon—particularly given the possibility of a delivery by bombers against cities. Nonetheless, the British fully intended to employ gas in 1940 against any beachhead secured by German invaders, while later in the war, Hitler was deterred from using newly developed nerve gases only by the belief that the Allies might respond against German cities.[41] Consequently, belief in a nuclear taboo is unrealistic in the truly hard cases where its effect is really needed and only restrains nuclear-oriented behavior that would not have been forthcoming anyway.

Third, states will not subscribe to behavior consistent with a nuclear taboo if such behavior is contrary to their survival or vital interests. A nuclear taboo certainly can raise the costs of the acquisition of nuclear weapons. For example, covert uranium-enrichment or plutonium-separation facilities are expensive and indeed would impose extraordinary opportunity costs on a relatively poor country. Similarly, international political suspicion that a country is driving toward a nuclear arsenal, illegally within, or legally outside, the Non-Proliferation Treaty's safeguards, could lead to the imposition of substantial international penalties.[42] It is possible, even probable, however, that candidate nuclear "rogue" status could produce considerable benefits if the guardians of the nonproliferation regime sought to bribe the errant power back onto the paths of righteousness.

A regional power that refuses to be bullied either by a nuclear-armed regional enemy (e.g., a Pakistan facing India, or one day possibly an Islamic-fundamentalist Egypt confronting Israel) or by a nuclear-conventional superpower (e.g., Iraq or Iran facing the United States, or the Ukraine facing

Russia) is not going to be a polity moved by taboos fashionable among the defense intellectuals in the developed world. However attractive, the hypothesis of a lasting nuclear taboo is fundamentally naive. Scholarship in anthropology shows that social taboos—against incest, for example, or against the poisonings of wells in warfare among desert-dwelling nomads—tend to be strongly functional. For a nuclear taboo to stop nuclear proliferation, threats, and use, it must express the interests of many, perhaps all, would-be proliferants. Plainly, that benign condition is far from likely for the foreseeable future.

Fourth, long before the international army of arms controllers invented the idea of a nuclear taboo, governments had registered the extraordinary nature of nuclear weapons. In the West, at least, the proposition that nuclear weapons are weapons of last resort had received wide-scale acceptance by the late 1950s. The nuclear taboo in effect represents a projection of Western, and especially American, self-interest as the leading conventional military powers on the rest of the world. Other powers might share an abhorrence of nuclear weapons, but there are, and will be, those polities that will overcome their distaste in the interest of advancing their national goals. A broad international consensus against nuclear weapons will no more retard the pace of nuclear proliferation than the like consensus against war prevented World War II.

The Second Nuclear Age

The professional literature of arms control is rich in the unfolding technical details of the second nuclear age. The argument in this chapter has purposefully refused to engage that literature in detail. The reason is that the literature and the topics it addresses—the 1995 review conference on the Non-Proliferation Treaty, for example, or improvements in the rigor with which the International Atomic Energy Agency safeguards inspections might be conducted—comprise second-order matters. The first-order topics are the character of world politics, the limitations of power (even of the world's only superpower), and the permanence of military-technological "progress." What 1990s policy makers do not need is a set of bold new policies to address *the* problem, or *the* challenge, of "horizontal" nuclear proliferation in order to cope with the post–Cold War nuclear age; there is no single such problem or challenge.

The United States and other leading members of the Non-Proliferation Treaty can occasionally bribe would-be nuclear states not to pursue further the path to nuclear weapons. And the United States and its functional allies can noticeably increase the costs of nuclear-weapons status. The bribes in question can include varieties of assurances and material assistance, while the costs can include financial, social, other military, or economic penalties. Furthermore, as a general rule, the United States should do what it can at modest cost to retard the pace of nuclear proliferation. In other words, this analysis is entirely supportive of mainstream arms-control arguments that further nuclear proliferation is more or less undesirable and that the United States should impede proliferation to the degree practicable. To register those points, however, is not to ignore several qualifications: nuclear acquisitions are not uniformly unfortunate for regional security; in rare instances, nuclear status will be of net benefit for regional security (in the case of Israel, for example); and even where one can greatly deplore proliferation, opposition to that proliferation is unlikely to be an overriding security interest of the United States, or of others for that matter. To illustrate the final item, the United States is indeed interested in discouraging North Korea from acquiring nuclear weapons. However, the record of the past several years demonstrates clearly that the United States is even more interested in avoiding war on the Korean peninsula.

This second nuclear age is of uncertain duration, but it has distinctive features as well as features familiar from the first nuclear age. In summary form, the following items merit ascription as defining characteristics of the new period:

- *No central political structure.* There is no dominant, organizing geopolitical relationship in the world politics of the 1990s. The consequence of this situation is that the one remaining superpower does not effectively know what it should be doing, against whom, or when. A great popular democracy finds it difficult to function in a steady, purposeful way in the international arena when it cannot discover a simple algorithm (Does action A or B contain Soviet power and influence?) to provide policy guidance.

- *An unfamiliar age.* Not only do American policy makers lack the convenience of a Soviet threat to order their world, they also do not understand the world that is emerging as a transitional second nuclear age. What are the issues that really matter? Which issues are interrelated and which are not? Which of the Cold War habits of mind, military capabilities, strategic ideas, political assumptions, and so forth, retain authority in the new period? The defense and, naturally, arms-control communities have agreed with the Clinton administration that a "Counterproliferation Initiative" is a sound proposal.[43] But is that agreement a matter more of organizational interest and convenience than of conviction or genuine strategic thought? After the sad fashion of the "war on drugs," the counterproliferation initiative seems to promise a great deal more than it can possibly deliver.

- *New nuclear forms.* In the innocent and simple 1960s when the United States and Soviet Union so painfully negotiated the Non-Proliferation Treaty, they could assay the relevant world in terms of two binary distinctions: (a) there could be nuclear states or nonnuclear states, and (b) there could be parties to the Non-Proliferation Treaty and those who declined to participate.[44] The second nuclear age of the 1990s suggests a more complex structure. In addition to the basic distinctions just cited, there are also (a) fragmented nuclear states (e.g., the former USSR); (b) suspected nuclear states not party to the Non-Proliferation Treaty regime (e.g., India and Israel); (c) would-be undeclared and renegade nuclear states party to the Non-Proliferation Treaty (e.g., nuclear by ambition, though not achievement to date, Iraq and North Korea).

- *Weak instruments of international order.* Collective security, arms control, U.S. peace keeping and UN and other peace-making, superpower, and great-power intervention, and alliance discipline will remain fragile for the foreseeable future. Collective security and arms control are more than fragile, they are literally impracticable. Arms control worthy of the name is feasible only when not needed, while collective security cannot tackle the truly hard cases because states continue to ask how events affect their particular interests rather than how best they might serve some notionally global interests. Countries with divergent levels of interest in an issue cannot pull together in the spirit of "all for one and one for all." UN peace keeping remains an artifact of Cold War conditions, whereas the requirements of peace making typically far exceed the legal, political, economic, and military resources that organizations such as the world community can command. In practice, super- and great-power intervention to keep or restore order is a small and unreliable stick in a disordered world. In the absence of a central focus for their foreign policies, the larger, and especially the largest, powers are incapable of maintaining a steady strategic course. The intervention against Iraq in 1990–91 appears not so much as the defining event for new world order as a unique episode unlikely to be repeated.

- *Denial strategies are ineffective.* It would not be entirely just to claim that the decade of the 1990s has been "proliferation friendly." It is expensive to acquire nuclear weapons, particularly the necessary fissile material, and it is doubly expensive if a proliferant believes that it needs to develop or otherwise acquire efficient weapon designs, technically safe weapons, high-quality delivery vehicles, and even a secure second-strike capability. If, in addition, the proliferant has concerns about environmental pollution and the concealment of key aspects of its nuclear program from the International Atomic Energy Agency's inspectors, not to mention the various means of nuclear monitoring, then the cost of military nuclear status becomes prohibitive for many. Nonetheless, a number of factors will characterize this second nuclear age: the diffusion of nuclear knowledge (scientific and engineering); the relative availability of trained experts from many countries (especially from the former Soviet Union and its allies); the global spread of state-of-the-art (certainly good enough) computational technology and information processing skills; a huge, and rapidly growing, surplus of weapons-grade fissile material;[45] and the breakdown of law and order (including export controls) in Eastern Europe. Non-Proliferation Treaty powers should note that, although they have learned much from Iraq about how a renegade member can proceed covertly toward nuclear weapons, would-be proliferants have also learned from Iraq's successes as well as its failures. In sum, although it is expensive to acquire nuclear weapons, and the costs are multidimensional, it has never been easier to do so. A wealthy state, or a state with wealthy backers, quite literally cannot be denied nuclear weapons in this second nuclear age.

- *To opportunity, add motive.* To the opportunities of acquiring nuclear weapons, via purchase, theft, national development or, more likely, some mix of all, one must add the strength of political motive. Some writers on nuclear proliferation have appropriately stressed the significance of motive. The more sophisticated among those writers recognize that proliferation, along with all defense issues at their heart, remain political subjects. Where even perceptive writers err, however, is in an implied belief that something useful can be done to alter the cost-benefit analysis of nuclear weapons by candidate proliferants. That is not to suggest that attitudes, certainly policies, do not change; of course they do. But, one must recognize that outside influences from the Non-Proliferation Treaty regime, or from particular states or groups of states, are not likely to shift a possible proliferant's policy course. The nuclear taboo, let alone the rising potency of conventional weapons, actually reinforces the strategic utility of nuclear-weapons status, rather than reducing it. No regional power is likely to be encouraged by the lessons of Desert Storm to embark on a nonnuclear battle with a U.S.-led coalition. And there is no evading the fact that nuclear weapons can and do act as the ultimate guarantor of a country's survival and vital interests, physical as well as political. As fewer countries judge themselves guaranteed adequately, let alone reliably, against international threats, so the motive to take the path of nuclear self-help will fuel policy decisions to that end. Most countries, most of the time, will lack the strength of political motive needed to move down the nuclear-weapons road, but, it should be recalled, most countries wanted peace in the late 1930s.

This discussion of the second nuclear age yields a short list of broad policy points. First, it is generally sensible to attempt to slow the pace of nuclear proliferation, but the United States should not be surprised when proliferation occurs. A period of enforced delay could provide time for radical change in the domestic or external dynamics that fuel a policy course of nuclear acquisition. With a most careful regard for national peril, the United States and other members of the Non-Proliferation Treaty regime should look quietly at a broad range of active counterproliferation measures. Second, the United States should not be shocked when the first nuclear weapons to be used in anger since 1945 explode in a regional conflict. Nuclear employment is a fact both waiting and all but certain to happen; only the local details are unpredictable.

Third, it is essential that we do not exaggerate the importance of nuclear proliferation. It is, after all, in a literal sense unstoppable, even though its pace can be slowed and individual cases might be contained. Nuclear proliferation is not the worst development in world politics. Indeed, there will be cases in the future where a nuclear-based defense would protect a state from aggression by ambitious and malevolent neighbors. It is all too easy to adhere to the decision rule of risking error on the side of the angels by talking up nuclear peril. Unfortunately for those believing in neat analysis and policy focus, security benefits, as well as costs, accrue to those possessing nuclear weapons.[46]

Conclusion

The truth about nuclear proliferation, shocking though it will seem, is that it cannot be halted or reversed and that assuredly it will result in the actual use of nuclear weapons sometime in the next century. No amount of moral posturing, hand-wringing, or provision of well-meaning technical or strategic advice by Americans is going to alter matters fundamentally. So much for the bad news. The better, if not good, news is that the United States and its counterproliferation allies are in a position to dissuade some would-be proliferants, to retard the pace of nuclear proliferation by others, and even to defeat the military nuclear power of the occasional "rogue" proliferant.

Western countries should understand, if any polities do, why the strategic demand for nuclear weapons will remain a permanent factor. If maintenance of some nuclear capability is nonnegotiable to American, British, and French (and Russian and Chinese) leaders, there should be little surprise about the attractiveness of nuclear weapons to deeply insecure regional states.

There is no magical solution, no golden key, for solving the problem of nuclear proliferation. Given the permanent importance of world and regional order, however, and the no less permanent menace posed by weapons of mass destruction, the United States urgently needs to develop several instruments of alleviation. It cannot eradicate "the scourge of nuclear proliferation," because it cannot shape the political motives of would-be proliferants or deny them the wealth with which to give (nuclear) physical expression to those motives. But, the United States, with other like-minded polities, certainly is capable of developing and deploying the means to defeat, or at least blunt, the physical threat posed by some proliferants. A superior intelligence network, tied to state-of-the-art active air and missile defenses (theater and area in scope), would provide much of the defensive answer. In addition, long-range, information-led conventional striking power, assisted by special operations forces, would provide a complementary sword vital to the above defensive shield.

Offensive and defensive military means that counter proliferation are essential and important, but they cannot solve the problem(s) reliably. Americans should recall their debate in 1990 about whether or not the liberation of Kuwait was "worth" the high level of casualties that many military "experts" claimed the Iraqis could and would inflict on a U.S.-led expeditionary force. How would an American debate proceed early in the next century if the issue were active military intervention against a state known to possess nuclear weapons? What "stakes" would be worth the risks of nuclear war? Regardless of what the United States should be willing to undertake to restore international order, any prospect of nuclear opposition in a regional crisis must dramatically lower the probability of U.S. military action.

Sun Tzu emphasized the need for a polity to know itself, while Clausewitz drew attention to the ubiquitous and cumulative military phenomenon he called "friction."[47] When one considers the adverse consequences of the events in Beirut (1983) and Mogadishu (1993) for the steadiness of American policy, it is obvious that any recommendations that require a president to send American troops into nuclear harm's way for less than all but self-evi-

dently vital interests are simply nonstarters. In the twenty-first century the
United States is probably going to have to learn to live with the occasional
nuclear war between other states while developing active and passive counterproliferation capabilities to permit intervention in the truly exceptional
case when U.S. survival or vital national interests are engaged. Welcome to
the second nuclear age!

Chapter 7

Strategy and Resources: Trends in the U.S. Defense Budget

Mackubin T. Owens

This chapter examines the relationship between emerging U.S. strategy and the increasingly severe budgetary constraints that will have an important, and perhaps decisive, impact on the course that American defense policy pursues over the next several decades *regardless of what the legislative and executive branches may wish.* Even with a prodefense Republican majority in both houses of Congress, a number of factors will most likely conspire to constrain future defense spending. The most important of these are the federal budget deficit, caps on discretionary spending, and the continued growth of entitlements.

Most critical is the budgetary environment, especially the trends associated with the federal budget. What is the impact of the growth of future entitlements? What are the implications of growing budget deficits? What are the effects of discretionary spending caps on defense spending? What might this mean for the Pentagon's share of future national output and federal spending?

Consequently, the relationships between strategic requirements and the defense budget demand examination. Its shortcomings notwithstanding, the Bottom Up Review provides a strategic context within which to examine the crucial question: how much is enough? In attempting to relate the defense budget to strategy and force structure, three sets of questions suggest themselves:

- The first set concerns the adequacy of the Bottom Up Review. Does the review represent an adequate strategy? Is it capable of achieving the national security goals of the United States? Is the review's emphasis on two nearly simultaneous major regional contingencies an appropriate strategic requirement? If the answers are no, there may well be a policy/strategy mismatch. What then is the resulting level of risk from such a mismatch?

- The second set concerns the match between the review's strategic objectives and the budgeted forces. Can the review's force structure realistically achieve the objectives established by this strategy, given the resources likely to be available for defense even under the most advantageous of circumstances? If the strategy is too ambitious for the budgeted force, the result will be a clear strategy/force-structure mismatch. What level of risk would such a mismatch create?

- The third set of questions concerns the review's programmed force. This issue is related to the previous one but is not identical. It rests more on the technical budgetary issues such as the validity of the costing assumptions underlying the allocation of resources at home. If the funding is inadequate, what will the impact be on the U.S. military in the short term as well as the long run? If the strategy requires a force structure that the budget cannot support, readiness may suffer in the short run, while in the long run, there may be fewer resources for modernizing the force. What does that mean in the future if a large "peer competitor" were to emerge to contest U.S. preeminence?

The issue of the Bottom Up Review's adequacy as a strategy and the possibility of a policy/strategy mismatch are issues that are beyond the scope of this article. But the strategy/force mismatch issue is central to the analysis in this chapter. Is the strategy too ambitious for the budgeted force? Are we asking the review's forces to achieve impossible goals, particularly in light of the budgetary constraints?

Finally, this chapter will explore the implications of a possible underfunding of the defense budget. Estimates of the magnitude of this potential underfunding vary from the Pentagon's own figures of $49 billion to the General Accounting Office's $150 billion. What then would be the consequences of such underfunding on readiness, modernization, and the future force structure?

How Much Is Enough?

The debate over the level of defense spending must take into account two conflicting demands: (1) the demands established by the *budgetary process*—the allocation of scarce resources for defense in light of competing claims, private as well as public; and (2) *strategic requirements*—the purposes established by national policy for which those resources will be employed. Both are important. Unfortunately, the debate usually ignores the latter. But defense budgets cannot realistically be analyzed independently of strategy.[1]

Strategy should serve three critical purposes: (1) to clarify the ends of policy by establishing priorities, (2) to relate these ends to the available resources, and (3) to conceptualize the available resources as means. Resources are not yet means until strategy has provided some understanding as to how they will be employed.

Strategy must answer the question: *What plan will best achieve the ends of national policy, given scarce resources for defense?* In theory, planners first identify national interests and the objectives necessary to realize those interests. They then assess the ability of potential adversaries to disrupt and thwart those interests and interfere with the achievement of national objectives. Finally the planners forge a strategy for countering threats to national interests, develop a force structure to implement the strategy, and then budget the money to acquire the necessary forces.

Reality has, unfortunately for social scientists, a nasty habit of intruding into the process and disrupting the theoretical conceptions of how the process works. Strategic decisions must always compete with the demands of domestic politics, in what Samuel Huntington has called "structural decisions."[2] To the credit of the Clinton administration, its defense planners, especially former Secretary of Defense Les Aspin, understood that it was necessary to establish a strategic framework for any defense budget. The result was the Bottom Up Review. The review, completed in October 1993, aimed at providing "direction for shifting American forces away from a strategy designed to meet a global Soviet threat [to a strategy] oriented toward the new dangers of the post-Cold War era."[3] A central element in the review is the requirement that the United States be able to "field forces capable, in concert with its allies, of fighting and winning two major regional contingencies that occur nearly simultaneously."[4] To do so the review calls for the forces that Table 7–1 compares to the 1990 force structure and President George Bush's "Base Force." However, this Bottom Up Review force structure must rely on budgetary decisions to achieve reality. Consequently, the Clinton budget is the deciding factor, not the strategic goals of the Pentagon.

Table 7–1. Force Structure Alternatives

	FY 1990		Bush Base Force FY 1997		Bottom-Up Review FY 1999	
	Active	Reserve	Active	Reserve	Active	Reserve
Army						
Personnel	751,000	736,000	536,000	567,000	495,000	575,000
Divisions	18	10	12	6	10	5
Brigades/regiments	5	22	5	4	4	15
Navy						
Personnel	583,000	149,000	502,000	118,000	394,000	98,000
Aircraft carriers	15	0	12	0	11	1
Other ships	514	31	411	16	314	16
Air Force						
Personnel	539,000	198,000	436,000	201,000	390,000	190,000
Fighter wings	22	12	15	11	13	7
Marine Corps						
Personnel	197,000	45,000	159,000	35,000	174,000	42,000
Divisions	3	1	3	1	3	1
Total personnel	2,070,000	1,128,000	1,633,300	921,000	1,453,000	905,000

Source: Adapted from John M. Collins, *Military Preparedness: Principles Compared with U.S. Practices*, CRS Report 94 – 48 S, Jan. 21, 1994, p. 10.

The Budgetary Context

In February 1994, Clinton presented his first detailed defense budget to Congress. That budget for FY 1995 requested $263.7 billion in net budget authority and projected $269.7 billion in outlays.[5] The president's budget request represented a decline in budget authority of 1.1 percent in real (inflation-adjusted) terms compared to FY 1994 and a reduction of 34.3 percent since the peak year (FY 1985) of the Reagan buildup.

The outlays projected by the FY 1995 defense budget represented a 26 percent decline in real terms since their recent peak year of 1989.[6] As Table 7–2[7] and Figure 7–1 show, reductions in defense spending will continue at least through FY 1999, when budget authority will have declined in real terms by 42 percent since FY 1985. At that time, according to administration predictions, defense spending will claim 2.9 percent of U.S. gross domestic product, the lowest proportion since before World War II. (See Figure 7–2.)[8]

Table 7–2. National Defense Funding
(*Current year and constant FY1995 dollars in billions*)

	Actual FY 1993	Estimated FY 1994	Requested FY 1995	Projected FY 1996	Projected FY 1997	Projected FY 1998	Projected FY 1999	Total FY 94–99
Budget Authority								
Current year $	281.1	260.9	263.7	255.3	252.0	258.7	265.1	1,555.8
Constant FY 1995 $	293.9	266.7	263.7	248.8	238.0	238.4	237.6	1,494.0
Real growth/decline		−9.3%	−1.1%	−5.6%	−4.0%	−0.2%	−0.4%	−10.9%
Outlays								
Current year $	293.9	277.0	269.7	260.5	256.4	256.6	257.5	1,577.7
Constant FY 1995 $	296.4	283.1	269.7	253.9	243.0	236.5	230.9	1,517.2
Real growth/decline		−4.5%	−4.8%	−5.8%	−4.3%	−2.7%	−2.4%	−18.5%

Note: Figures exclude costs associated with Operation Desert Shield/Desert Storm (affecting only outlay figures). OMB, Washington, D.C.

Figure 7–1. DoD Military Budget Authority Trend (42% Real Decline from 1985 to 1999; 1999 Level Same as Lowest Cold War Level)

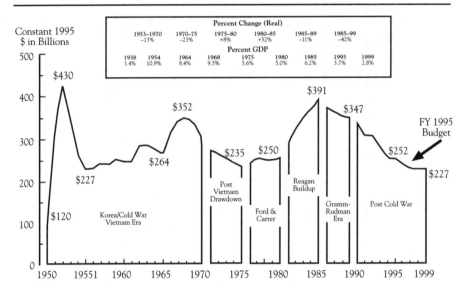

Figure 7–2. National Defense Outlays as a Percentage of GDP: FY 1947–99

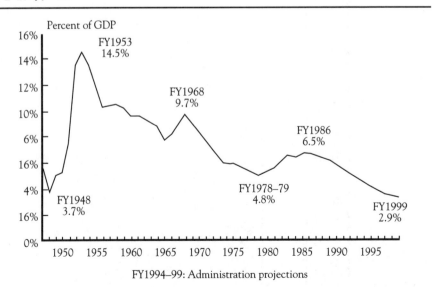

FY1994–99: Administration projections

The FY 1995 defense budget request included $252.2 billion for the Pentagon's military functions, $10.6 billion for the atomic energy defense activities of the Department of Energy, and $900 million for defense-related activities of other agencies. In September 1994, Congress essentially approved the president's request; it cut no major programs and made only minor changes in the budget.[9] During the debate over the FY 1995 defense budget, Clinton vowed that he would not cut defense spending below the level represented by his budget request. But two sets of critics have attacked the administration's funding level for defense. On the one hand, some have argued that defense spending has come down too far and too fast. They maintain the world is still a dangerous place and that if the United States is to remain safe, it must retain more robust military capabilities than those funded by the current budget.

On the other hand, others point out that in real terms, the FY 1995 defense budget equals that of FY 1980, when the Soviet Union constituted a formidable threat. While that budget was undoubtedly too low given the Soviet capabilities (President Jimmy Carter asked for significant increases for FY 1981), the equivalent budget is now more than enough for a world, which, while far from peaceable, represents no great threat to American interests. On 1 December 1994, in apparent deference to those who believe that defense spending is too low, Clinton announced he would seek an increase of $25 billion in defense spending over five years, beginning with the FY 1996 budget request.[10] Table 7–3 indicates the Clinton defense proposal for FY 1996.[11]

Table 7–3. Clinton Defense Proposal
(Billions of dollars in new budget authority; fiscal years)

	Fiscal Year						
	1995	1996	1997	1998	1999	2000	2001
Previous Clinton plan	$252*	$244	$241	$248	$254	$261	$268
Proposed increase	—	2	2	3	3	6	9
New budget request	—	$246	$243	$251	$257	$267	$277

Source: Department of Defense.
*The fiscal 1995 total does not include a planned supplemental spending request of more than $2 billion to cover unanticipated overseas military activities.

The president indicated that in addition to his $25 billion long-term additions, he would request a $2 billion emergency supplemental appropriation to offset the cost of unprogrammed military operations in FY 1995. Republican members of Congress welcomed the president's announcement but made it clear that they would seek even greater increases: the House Republicans' "Contract with America" would boost defense spending by $60 billion over the next six years.[12]

Yet an examination of the FY 1995 defense budget in the context of the federal budget as a whole raises serious concerns about future defense spending. As the Congressional Budget Office has observed, ". . . the overall outlook for the federal budget and the deficit may dictate future defense budgets as much as requirements for defense spending derived from [Pentagon] planning scenarios."[13] Several factors will constrain future defense spending, even with a Republican majority in Congress. The federal budget deficit, caps on discretionary spending, and the continued growth of entitlements are the most important.

The Budget Deficit

In March 1994, the Congressional Budget Office projected a decline in the deficit from $255 billion in 1993 to $180 billion in 1996. In 1997, it calculates the deficit will rise again in absolute terms and eventually reach $213 billion in 1999 but will remain at approximately 2.5 percent of gross domestic product. After 1999, according to an internal memo written by the director of the Office of Management and Budget and leaked to the press in October 1994, if current policies continue, the deficit will increase to $397 billion by 2004 (3.6 percent of gross domestic product) and reach an incredible $1.5 trillion per year by 2020. Such projections *cannot help* but place downward pressure on future defense spending.[14]

Entitlements

A major reason for pessimism about future deficits is the continuing growth of entitlement programs. Congress does not have to authorize or appropriate funds for these programs on an annual basis. Individuals who meet the criteria established by the law receive the various benefits, and the numbers increase year by year. There are four major categories of entitlements. Approximately half of entitlement spending goes to *cash insurance programs*, including Social Security (the largest of these programs), railroad retirement, unemployment compensation, veterans' compensation and pensions, and agricultural price supports. Slightly less than one third of entitlement spend-

ing goes to *government health care programs*, Medicare for the elderly and disabled and Medicaid for the poor. One tenth goes to government pensions,
and another tenth funds means-tested assistance programs for the poor: Supplemental Security Income for the elderly and disabled; Aid to Families with
Dependent Children; food stamps; and refundable earned income tax credits.[15]

Over the last thirty years, mandatory spending on entitlements has con-
sumed a growing share of national output as well as federal budgets. Spending
on entitlements as a percentage of gross domestic product has doubled from
6 percent in 1962 to 12 percent in 1994, and as a portion of the federal budget from 30 percent to 54 percent. If present trends and policies continue, entitlements could, by the turn of the century, constitute 14 percent of gross
domestic product and two thirds of federal budget expenditures.[16]

The Congressional Budget Office projects that the most rapid future
growth in entitlement spending will occur in Medicare, Medicaid, and earned
income tax credits.[17] Figures 7–3 and 7–4 illustrate the growth of mandatory
spending for entitlement in comparison with total discretionary spending, less
than half of which goes to defense. As Figure 7–4 suggests, mandatory spend-

**Figure 7–3. Components of Federal Spending as a Percentage of GDP:
1962–2004**

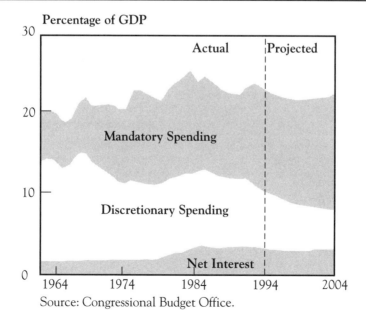

Source: Congressional Budget Office.

Figure 7–4. Domestic Discretionary, Defense, and Mandatory Outlays: Cumulative Real Changes FY 1990–1999

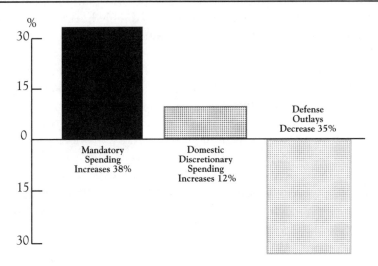

ing will increase by 38 percent from FY 1990 to FY 1999, while defense outlays decrease by nearly 35 percent, unless major changes occur in discretionary programs.[18]

Caps on Discretionary Spending

The budget divides total discretionary spending into three categories—defense, international, and domestic—which encompass programs funded by annual appropriations bills. The Budget Enforcement Act of 1990 established caps on discretionary spending; Congress extended these caps through 1998 by the Omnibus Budget Reconciliation Act of 1993. The caps apply to both budget authority and outlays.

From 1991 to 1993, Congress applied separate caps to defense spending. This so-called "wall" between defense and nondefense discretionary spending prevented raids on the defense budget by those who wished to increase nondefense programs. From 1994 through 1998—the last year of the Omnibus Budget Reconciliation Act—defense spending must compete with other discretionary programs under an overall cap on nominal budget authority that rises from $518 billion in 1995 to $553 billion in 1998. This even more restrictive cap in outlays rises during the same period from $545 billion to $550 billion.

But these nominal caps rest on inflation projections that are lower than economists now expect. The programs under the caps, however, must make reductions in real terms. The administration has concluded that the total real reduction in discretionary spending over the 1995–98 period necessary to keep pace with inflation is $120 billion. According to the administration plan, defense will absorb 80 percent of this reduction, a total of $97 billion.[19]

These three budgetary factors make it unlikely that, in the absence of any unforeseen national emergency, defense spending will increase in the near future. Indeed, budgetary pressures may conspire to reduce further future defense budgets, contrary to Clinton's pledge and notwithstanding a Republican Congress.

The Strategic Context

Commentators continue to debate whether the Bottom Up Review's force structure is capable of meeting its central strategic requirement, to be able to fight and win two nearly simultaneous major regional contingencies. The main reason to question the capability of the review's force to do so is the fact that fighting and winning two such conflicts was the objective of the Bush administration's larger Base Force.[20] To meet the same requirement, the Clinton Pentagon proposed spending $104 billion less over five years and fielding a force with 180,000 fewer personnel.

The Joint Staff originally concluded that the best the review's force could do in the event of two simultaneous major regional contingencies was to conduct the main effort in one theater while carrying out economy-of-force measures in the second. Once the United States had won the first conflict, forces would shift to a second theater. This "win-hold-win" strategy received widespread criticism once it became public, and Aspin eventually abandoned it. He then declared that U.S. strategy would return to the two-major-regional-contingencies standard, notwithstanding a considerably smaller force structure.

Even the Clinton administration has given mixed signals regarding the capability of the review's force to achieve this strategic objective. On the one hand, the chief coordinator for the Bottom Up Review, Assistant Secretary of Defense for Strategy and Requirements Edward L. Warner III, has stated, "Our strategy is an ambitious one, and . . . within the available dollars, it is an extremely tight fit. . . . [Nonetheless] we still feel the general sizing [and] character of the force we selected is the right one."[21] But Secretary of Defense William J. Perry has called the standard into question on several occasions. In March 1994 while testifying before the Senate, he noted, "It's an entirely implausible scenario that we'd fight two wars at once," and in July 1994 he stated that the review's force structure could not meet the two-major-regional-conflicts requirement "with the force structure laid out right now."[22]

Several general officers have also contradicted the claim that the review's force structure can execute the two-major-regional-conflicts strategy. Testifying before the Senate Armed Services Committee on 3 March 1994, General Joseph P. Hoar, USMC, then commander in chief of the U.S. Central Command (the unified command responsible for operations in Southwest Asia) challenged the sufficiency of strategic lift to support two major contingencies: "Strategic airlift in this country today is broken," he said. "I'm not sure it is workable today for one major regional contingency."[23] And the commander of the U.S. Air Force's Air Combat Command, General John M. Loh, has argued that the budget does not support the number of bombers the nation would need to execute the review's strategy.[24]

On the other hand, the Congressional Budget Office contends that the programmed Bottom Up Review's force structure is sufficient to prevail in two major regional contingencies. Employing more optimistic assumptions than those of the services and the joint staff, it argues that U.S. forces would achieve favorable force ratios in both southwest Asia and Korea in a relatively short time.[25]

The administration's *National Security Strategy of Engagement and Enlargement* reflects this ambivalence about the review's assumptions. While early drafts, reflecting the language of the *Bottom Up Review* itself, state unequivocally that the United States would maintain the unilateral capability to fight and win two nearly simultaneous major regional contingencies, the final version is less certain:

> To deter aggression, prevent coercion of allied or friendly governments and, ultimately, defeat aggression should it occur, we must prepare our forces to confront this scale of threat, preferably in concert with our allies and friends, but unilaterally if necessary . . . with programmed enhancements, the force the administration is fielding will be sufficient to *help* defeat aggression in two nearly simultaneous major regional conflicts.[26]

An increasing emphasis on "operations other than war" (OOTW), a category of military operations that includes peace keeping, humanitarian operations, and refugee support, further complicates the sufficiency of the Bottom Up Review force to meet the two-conflicts standard. In recent months, the U.S. military has conducted operations in Somalia, Haiti, Bosnia, and Rwanda. Such operations are in keeping with the administration's policy of "enlargement." The *National Security Strategy* lists as a task for the U.S. military "Contributing to Multilateral Peace Operations." U.S. forces "must pre-

pare to participate in peace keeping, peace enforcement and other operations" in support of "multilateral efforts to broker settlements of internal conflicts and bolster new democratic governments."[27]

Critics of the administration's defense policy argue that operations other
than war only worsen the risks created by the potential strategy/force mismatch. They contend that such operations contribute to increased operations'
tempo and decreased readiness, both of which undermine the war-fighting effectiveness of U.S. forces.

> On top of the basic warfighting requirement established by the Bottom Up
> Review, enlargement has the clear potential to pile open-ended "peace-
> keeping" missions on the U.S. military. But forces engaged in peace keep-
> ing cannot maintain the level of readiness necessary to carry out their
> warfighting missions. The greater the commitment to peace keeping, the
> less capable will U.S. force be to fight a war if called upon to do so.[28]

"Operations other than war" have had the effect of expanding commitments at the same time that the force draws down. The review's forces, which,
while preparing to fight two nearly simultaneous conflicts must also carry out
an increasing number of such operations, are significantly smaller than the
Bush-era Base Force, which was primarily a war-fighting force.

The evolution of the national military strategy reflects operations other
than war. The 1992 version, the *National Military Strategy,* emphasized the regional war-fighting capability of U.S. forces. The 1994 revision makes war
fighting only one of the three "strategic tasks" for the review's forces. (See
Figure 7–5.)

Affordability: Is the Bottom Up Review Force Underfunded?

The Bottom Up Review's force/strategy mismatch is exacerbated by the
likelihood that it is underfunded. Will the five-year defense budget proposed
by President Clinton and passed by Congress prove sufficient to fund the review's force structure? If it is not, what will have to give? Critics maintain
that the review's forces, their possible lack of capability to fight and win two
nearly simultaneous regional conflicts aside, are seriously underfunded. Estimates of the shortfall range from a low of $40 billion over the five-year de-
fense plan (the Pentagon's Comptroller) to a high of $150 billion (General
Accounting Office).

The critics attribute underfunding to two main culprits: overoptimistic
assumptions about future inflation and congressionally mandated pay raises

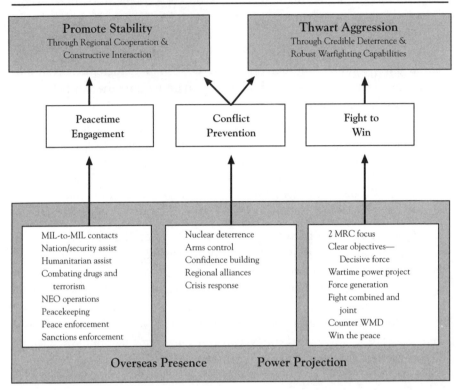

Figure 7–5. Strategy to Objectives

Source: NMS 94.

for military personnel and Pentagon civilians not programmed by the administration. The Clinton administration has acknowledged that it underestimated inflation by $20 billion over the budget period. Additionally, Congress approved a 2.6 percent pay raise rather than the administration's 1.6 percent, which will increase defense costs by at least $15 billion over the five years covered by the FY 1995 budget.

There are three other possible sources of underfunding:

- Overly optimistic estimates of savings from revamping federal procurement. The administration assumes that it will save $12 billion over five years as a result of these acquisition reforms. The Pentagon spends 75 percent of the federal procurement budget and, as a result, would have to cover the bulk of any shortfall were these reforms not to produce assumed savings.

- Higher than anticipated costs of carrying out base closures slated for 1995.

- The expected burden of a $31 billion cut over five years in total discretionary spending mandated by the Exon-Grassley Senate deficit-reduction amendment to the 1995 Budget Resolution. Though defense was spared in FY 1995, it may not fare so well in the future, since the Pentagon spends approximately half of the discretionary funds from which the cuts would be made.[29]

The Pentagon Comptroller has admitted to a shortfall of $40 billion ($49 billion through FY 2000), primarily the result of underestimating inflation and escalating defense payrolls.[30] The General Accounting Office and the Heritage Foundation are considerably more pessimistic. The latter has projected a $100 billion shortfall,[31] while the former contends that underfunding totals $150 billion. The General Accounting Office argues that in addition to the $21.6 billion in cuts yet to be made, the Pentagon's estimated savings from acquisition reforms and base closing were $32 billion too high. It attributes the other $112 billion in underfunding to the increased cost of weapons, further rises in military pay, and the unanticipated costs of environmental cleanup.[32]

Most observers contend that the General Accounting Office has been too gloomy. But some believe that the problem of underfunding is systemic. Dov Zakheim and Jeffrey Ranney have argued that underestimated but continuously rising "operations and support" (O&S) costs and acquisition costs will limit the ability of the Pentagon to implement its acquisition program for the future.[33]

> The experience of the Cold War period has taught us that defense planners often ignored the very real constraints that previous defense decisions placed upon future levels of resource availability and, as a consequence, on new directions in defense programming. Instead of projecting realistic real growth in the O&S and acquisition accounts, they planned for no real growth in the former and too little growth in the latter.[34]

Zakheim and Ranney claim that operations and support costs have grown at a real annual compounded rate of 1.9 percent, while acquisitions costs have risen by an average of 4.5 percent.

Although Zakheim and Ranney completed their analysis before Clinton submitted his first defense budget, they examined a force structure close in size to the Bottom Up Review's force, an option provided by Aspin when he was still chairman of the House Armed Services Committee. They concluded that this force would require a defense budget equal to 4.5 percent of gross domestic product (instead of the 2.9 percent projected by the administration) and that over the FY 1994–1999 period, the force would cost 29 percent more than Bush's considerably larger Base Force. Their analysis is consistent with that of the Heritage Foundation.[35]

If Zakheim and Ranney are correct, the Bottom Up Review's forces are not affordable unless the country reverses course and increases spending on defense by a considerable amount. Indeed, the largest force that the 3 percent of gross domestic product projected by the administration for defense would support would have 363,000 fewer personnel than the review's force and consist of ten army divisions (seven active, three reserve); two active marine expeditionary forces; thirteen air force tactical fighter wing equivalents (eight active, five reserve); and 224 navy surface ships and submarines, including six carrier battle groups.[36]

Congressional Budget Office memoranda released in November 1994 tend to support the arguments advanced by Zakheim and Ranney. Examining the long-term costs of the Bottom Up Review force, they concluded that even with optimistic assumptions, projected resources are inadequate to support the administration's plan for the three military departments through 2019.[37]

Consequence of Underfunding

Underfunding the defense budget will have serious consequences for the Pentagon, both in the short and long term. These consequences primarily result in increased competition among the four pillars upon which military capability—the ability to achieve specified wartime objectives—rests. These pillars are as follows:

- Readiness: the capacity of forces to deploy quickly and perform initially in wartime as designed.

- Force structure: the number, size, and composition of military units.

- Modernization: the technical sophistication of the forces, weapon systems, and equipment.

- Sustainability: the logistical "staying power" of the forces, usually measured in number of days.[38]

During a period of constrained resources, the Pentagon must weigh the benefits of increasing the relative funding of one pillar against the potentially adverse effects of decreasing the relative funding of others. It does not appear to have done so.

Readiness

The administration has made clear that readiness is the first priority in its defense budget. In testimony before the Senate supporting the FY 1995 defense budget, Secretary of Defense William J. Perry argued:

> We are taking [the savings from a smaller force structure] and investing them in operations and maintenance accounts as the most direct way to preserve readiness. While the force structure will decrease 7 percent between FY 1994 and FY 1995, we have increased operations and maintenance funding by 5.6 percent. We have also fully funded service [operations' tempo] requests. . . . The services were told that readiness is the first priority and that all other guidance could be traded off if they needed to program funds for improved readiness.[39]

Congress has ratified the administration's budgeting preferences in an attempt to ensure that U.S. forces maintain a high level of current readiness.

The emphasis on readiness is a result of the experiences of the 1970s. In 1980, the army chief of staff, General Edward C. Meyer, used the term "hollow army" in testimony before a subcommittee of the House Armed Services Committee to describe the mismatch between available combat personnel and the number of army divisions.[40] "Hollow force" soon came to mean shortages not only of personnel, but of training, weapons, and equipment. As measured by the U.S. military at the time, less than 40 percent of all active component divisions, squadrons, and ships received the rating of being fully or substantially combat ready. Conditions were even worse in the reserves.

The cause of these readiness problems was the result of the decision, as the Vietnam War came to an end, to retain the historic Cold War force structure, even as real defense expenditures fell by 31 percent from 1969 to 1975. Rising oil prices and increased personnel costs associated with the shift from the draft to an all-volunteer force exacerbated the negative effect of the decline in defense spending. As a result, the services delayed modernization until the end of the decade. To compensate for this delay, procurement of modern weapons then received priority over readiness.[41]

Whether modernization should have received emphasis at the expense of readiness during this period is still open to debate. But these examples illustrate that defense planners must make trade-offs among the pillars of military capability, especially during those periods when resources are severely constrained. The United States faces such a period now. For the moment several studies have indicated that current readiness levels are acceptable. A Pentagon task force on readiness released a report in June 1994 concluding that "the readiness of today's conventional and unconventional forces . . . is acceptable in most measurable areas."[42] A March 1994 Congressional Budget Office report contends that "overall, the readiness of deployable units is high now relative to historical levels."[43]

But both reports raise red flags concerning the future. The readiness task force stated that there are "'pockets of unreadiness' [forming as] a result of changes taking place in the armed forces and the turbulence created by these changes." The task force expressed concerns about the maintenance backlog due to "operations other than war"; the increasing use of operation and maintenance funds to "pay fact-of-life bills [such as] utility bills, port operations, etc."; the availability of support unit equipment to implement two major regional contingencies and carry out "operations other than war"; and reduced readiness due to decreased training tempo.[44]

Meanwhile, the Congressional Budget Office warned that trends in several areas might indicate problems with future readiness. For instance, the high fixed costs associated with the Pentagon's infrastructure of bases and depots "could significantly increase the level of operations and maintenance of spending per capita that is needed to maintain readiness."[45] Indicators point to similar problems in depot maintenance, the supply system, and maintenance of real property. More troubling yet is the fact that while overall mission-capable rates and resource ratings (C-ratings)[46] are currently high, "some . . . have fallen below peak levels seen in the late 1980s, and in a few cases the declines appear to be significant."[47]

Some analysts contend that readiness problems are more serious than either the Pentagon's readiness task force report or the Congressional Budget Office would indicate. In particular, the Heritage Foundation as well as members of Congress have called into question the adequacy of current defense spending levels to fund readiness.[48] For some time, anecdotal information concerning "pockets of unreadiness" has supported the pessimists. Flight hours for carrier squadrons awaiting deployment have significantly dropped. The navy is also substantially behind on its maintenance of aircraft and aircraft engines.[49]

While the average temporary deployment of AWACS crews and F-15 pilots has almost doubled since the early 1990s (a factor cited as a cause of the friendly fire shootdown of two army helicopters in northern Iraq by air force F-15s in 1994), overall air force readiness is down by 4 to 5 percent, "mostly for lack of money for jet-engine maintenance," according to the commander of the Air Combat Command.[50]

Despite this disquieting sign, the administration has maintained that readiness is high. In October 1994 Deputy Secretary of Defense Deutch held a special news conference to rebut claims that military preparedness has declined; he argued that U.S. forces were "more ready and capable than ever before." But on 15 November 1994 Defense Secretary Perry acknowledged that three of the army's twelve divisions had received readiness ratings of C-3, "marginally combat-ready." These divisions had been forced to cancel training to save money.[51]

A major cause of readiness problems is the speedup in operations' tempo resulting from an increase in "operations other than war." In August, Perry admitted before Congress that "humanitarian and peace-keeping operations were bleeding the Pentagon's budget." In a letter of 15 November 1994, he further confessed that "the problem [is] basically too many missions and not enough money."[52] Unplanned operations in Haiti, Somalia, Bosnia, Southwest Asia, Rwanda, and Korea, as well as refugee support operations in Cuba, cost the Pentagon $1.7 billion more than budgeted in FY 1994. Although Congress approved $1.2 billion of the Pentagon's supplemental request, the funds did not become available until after the end of the fiscal year ending 30 September 1994. In the meantime, the services had to cover the costs of these operations out of their own budgets. The result was a direct and adverse impact on short-term readiness exemplified by the base of the army divisions. "To keep front-line units prepared, the army was forced to raid the budgets of lower-tier forces."[53]

The $25 billion that Clinton has added to the defense budget beginning in FY 1996 is designed primarily to improve readiness. Improved readiness is also the goal of his $2 billion emergency supplemental defense appropriation for FY 1996. The supplemental appropriation aims to cover the continuing cost of unplanned operations in the hopes of avoiding a similar funding crunch for the services at the end of the current fiscal year.

Modernization and Defense Investment

Problems with near-term readiness are serious, but the connection of those problems along with the maintenance of administration priority on current readiness, personnel, and morale will increasingly tempt defense planners to shift funds from the modernization account to readiness accounts. This creates the danger that on some future battlefield, U.S. forces will find themselves at a serious disadvantage. This zero-sum game between near-term readiness and modernization seems inevitable given the administration's commitment to the Bottom Up Review's force and the likelihood that it is underfunded.

As Figure 7–6 indicates, Pentagon investment (procurement and research and development) has declined continuously in real terms since FY

1985.[54] Indeed, investment now constitutes a lower percentage of defense spending than at any time since 1980. Procurement has borne the brunt of the cuts in defense spending so far; it has contributed 60 percent of the $87 billion real reduction in the annual Pentagon budget from 1990 through 1995. While one would expect procurement to decline as force structure was reduced, spending on procurement has fallen considerably more than the spending on forces.[55]

The administration's intent was to reduce procurement in the short run, but only after a "holiday" to increase spending on improved weapons. Because the Pentagon bought large quantities of weapons during the 1980s, administration planners believed that stocks would suffice into the next decade. Thus, in the short term reduced spending on weapons would not incur an unacceptable risk.[56] However, at some time in the next five to ten years, modernization must resume. But this may be difficult to achieve because of the factors suggested by Zakheim and Ranney.

Figure 7–6. DoD Investment and Operations Budget Authority: FY 1985–1995

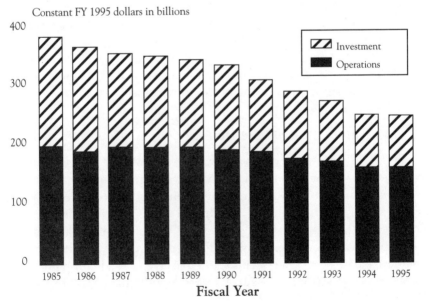

FY 1994–95: Administration Projections

Source: CBO, CRS-11.

Figure 7–7.

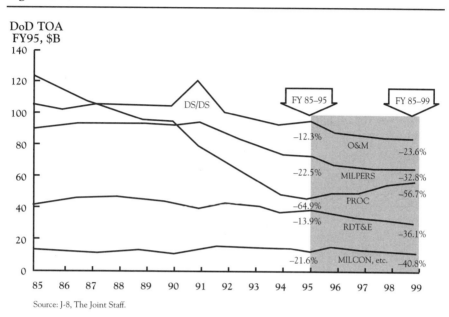

Source: J-8, The Joint Staff.

The administration expected to fund renewed modernization in the near future by saving on operation and maintenance costs as force structure declined. In submitting the FY 1995 defense budget to the Senate, Perry told committee members that procurement funds would increase 20 percent between 1996 and 1999.[57] Figure 7–7 suggests the projected upturn in procurement and the continued decline in operating and maintenance funding after FY 1995. But as predicted by Zakheim and Ranney, operation and maintenance did not decline as projected. "There is a constant gnawing at the modernization budget by the operations and maintenance budget," Zakheim has observed, exacerbated by manpower-intensive, low-technology operations such as Somalia and Haiti.[58] This commitment to "operations other than war" suggests that the administration cannot reverse the decline in procurement.

If modernization does not resume soon, the result could be an unprecedented fourteen-year decline in investment. This will created a "bow wave" of procurement bills in the future, which, combined with expected increases in procurement costs, will make it difficult to buy the required weapons at the rate necessary to equip any significant force. Figure 7–8 compares current procurement of selected weapons with their "steady state" procurement rates implied by the Bottom Up Review.[59]

The emphasis on current readiness at the expense of modernization has culminated in a Pentagon review of major weapon systems. In August 1994, Deutch, seeking to save $80 billion, ordered the services to prepare plans to delay or cancel nine programs, to include:

- Canceling the army's Comanche helicopter scout;

- Delaying by up to four years purchase of the air force's F-22;

- Stretching out purchase of the navy's Arleigh Burke-class Aegis destroyer (DDG-51);

- Canceling the marine corps' V-22 Osprey.[60]

Senator Sam Nunn, then chairman of the Senate Armed Services Committee, contended that implementing Deutch's plan would seriously undermine the ability of the Bottom Up Review's force to meet its objectives.[61] Then-Chairman of the Senate Appropriations Subcommittee on Defense Daniel Inouye lamented that "the services. . . are eating their seed corn."[62]

Figure 7–8. Historical Procurement Data: Numbers of Weapon Systems

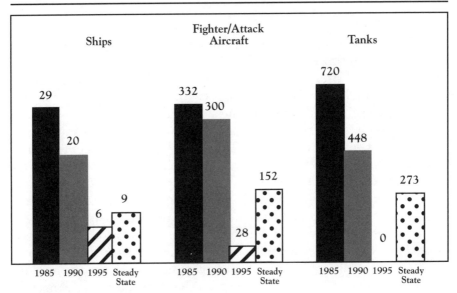

SOURCE: Congresional Budget Office.

NOTE: The steady state estimate is the number of weapons DoD needs to buy each year, on average, to support pleased 1999 forms.

Although these systems were, for the most part, spared from cuts in the FY 1995 defense budget, they are back on the block again in FY 1996. Deutch has estimated that the FY 1996 defense budget will have to cut $12 billion by canceling or stretching out programs from this list of candidates.[63] Trends in research and development, the other main component of defense investment, reinforce concerns about the ability of the United States to field modern, capable forces in the future. While research and development were protected through FY 1993, Congress made major cuts in FY 1994 with a 10 percent overall decline from the previous year. The FY 1995 defense budget reverses this decline in the short run but accepts roughly a 25 percent reduction in research and development funding by FY 1999. If this reduction holds, annual research and development will fall to a level below the Cold War average of $31 billion (FY 1995 dollars) and substantially below the average of the last decade ($42 billion in FY 1995 dollars). Figure 7–9 indicates the relationship between procurement and research and development.

Continued tensions between readiness and modernization seem inevitable if the Bottom Up Review's force structure, driven by the requirement to fight and win two major regional contingencies, is maintained. Combined

**Figure 7–9. Modernization Funding
(in Constant 1995 Billions of Dollars)**

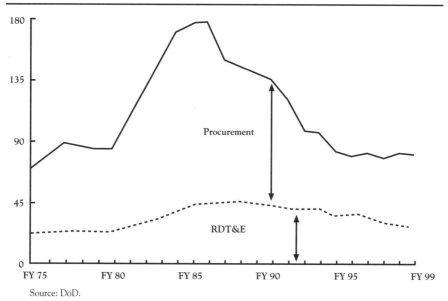

Source: DoD.

with the current operations' tempo of "operations other than war," the strain on the military will be intolerable.

Matching Strategy and Resources: The Defense Budget Dilemma

The options confronting defense planners in the wake of the mismatch between the administration's ambitious foreign policy and the cash that it is willing to devote to the military—or is politically able to devote—are limited:

- Spend marginally more money on defense.

- Reduce operational demands on military forces.

- Reallocate the existing defense budget.

- Shift to a less ambitious strategy and reduce force structure.

The Heritage Foundation is the strongest advocate of the first alternative. One of its analysts advocates spending $298 billion a year on defense, pending a thorough, bipartisan review of the nation's defense requirements.[64] But even with the realignment of Congress after the 1994 election and the ascendancy of a Republican majority in both houses, fiscal reality makes it unlikely that the downward trend in defense budgets will dramatically alter.

Although there are considerable limits on its ability to increase spending on defense, a Republican-dominated Congress may be able to reduce the demands on U.S. military forces by limiting their participation in "operations other than war" and by reducing those parts of the defense budget that do not enhance combat effectiveness. Comments of senators during a Senate Armed Services Committee hearing in September 1994 foreshadowed likely Congressional opposition to open-ended defense commitments.[65] Deploring the Pentagon's plan to cut or delay weapon modernization, senators suggested that U.S. commitments around the world might have to be cut back. In the words of Republican Senator William Cohen of Maine, "We cannot maintain the same kind of commitments that currently are on the board, not at a time when you are cutting many of the industrial base items that we need to furnish the troops with."[66]

Politicians have also expressed similar sentiments about the funding of items in the defense budget that are not directly related to traditional military capabilities.[67] The General Accounting Office has reported that $4.5 billion of the FY 1995 operations and maintenance budget activities such as commissaries, transient housing, and welfare and recreation facilities do nothing to improve readiness.[68] Another General Accounting Office report identified $10.4 billion for nondefense items in the Pentagon budget from 1990 to 1993.[69] According to the Heritage Foundation, this means that the Pentagon's nondefense spending increased by 238 percent during the period as the Pentagon's budget authority declined by 19.8 percent.[70]

The Pentagon's own figures tell a similar story (see Table 7–4). The total nondefense spending (including health care costs for dependents and retirees) has increased from $11.6 billion in 1990 (3.9 percent of the defense budget) to $23 billion in 1995 (9.1 percent of the defense budget). Some $5.7 billion, or 2.5 percent of the FY 1995 defense budget, will go to environmental cleanup. Over the next five years, $20 billion are targeted for "defense conversion," which one observer describes as "a simple job subsidy that keeps no planes in the air, ships at sea, or tanks rolling."[71]

Not surprisingly, Congress mandated many of these expenditures in the aftermath of the Cold War. But such expenditures reflect the priorities of a very different body than the 104th Congress seated in January 1995. These funds may possibly shift back from nondefense-spending operation and maintenance and modernization accounts in order to shore up both near-term and future readiness.

Table 7–4. Internal DoD Budgetary Pressures: Programs Not Directly Related to Combat Capability
(Budget Authority, in Billions of Dollars)

Program	1990	1992	1993	1994	1995 Request
Defense conversion —					
Worker and community programs	—	2.3	3.5	2.4	2.4
Post Cold-War reductions —					
i.e., base closures, chemical demilitarization	0.7	1.0	2.1	2.6	3.1
Environmental programs	1.4	4.4	4.0	5.4	5.7
Health program for dependents and retirees	7.6	8.8	9.0	9.1	9.2
Drug interdiction and counterdrug activities*	0.6	1.0	0.8	0.7	0.7
International assistance	—	0.3	0.5	0.5	0.9
Dependent education	1.2	1.2	1.3	1.2	1.1
Total	**11.6**	**19.0**	**21.2**	**21.8**	**23.0**
Percent of total DoD budget	**3.9%**	**6.7%**	**7.9%**	**8.7%**	**9.1%**

Source: DOD Comptroller.
*Does not include OPTEMPO funding.

While such shifts might ease the tension between readiness and modernization, many believe that the only way to ensure that the United States can field a ready, modernized force in the future is either to modify significantly the Bottom Up Review force or to change the strategy and cut force structure in the near term. William Kaufmann of the Brookings Institution has advanced the first alternative. He contends that a different balance among air, land, and sea forces would provide the same combat power as the review's force: "smaller U.S. forces on the ground, but larger air force fighters [*sic*] than are programmed by the Bottom Up Review, combined with fewer carrier battle groups, would achieve virtually the same results as the Base or Bottom Up Review Forces—and at a significantly lower cost."[72]

The best-known advocate of the second alternative is Andrew Krepinevich of the Defense Budget Project. He argues that the United States is in a "threat trough. . . . History would tell you that the greatest dangers for us don't lie in the near term, but in the mid and long term."[73] Krepinevich believes that, in the absence of more money for defense, the current force structure is too large because it is designed to execute an unlikely mission—to fight and win two nearly simultaneous major regional contingencies.

> Refusing to acknowledge the existence of a plans/funding mismatch in defense and attempting to execute the Bottom Up Review recommended defense program with the currently programmed budgets for defense involves the greatest risk to U.S. security. The United States will find itself wasting scarce resources in a vain attempt to maintain military capability at the expense of its future military potential. The result could be a United States that finds itself in the "out years" with both insufficient military capability, and demands for undertaking another military buildup.[74]

Krepinevich would cut current force structure, reducing active duty personnel by another 250,000. This would relieve the strain on personnel accounts and readiness and also free up funds for modernization.

What Is to Be Done?

The trends visible in the FY 1995 defense budget will, absent a national emergency, continue for the foreseeable future. Defense spending will continue on a downward track. If increased defense spending is not forthcoming, the only way to bring resources and strategy into line is to change the strategy and reallocate the existing budget. Reductions in strategic requirements would permit a further decline in force structure.

A conventional force of eight active army divisions, two and one-half marine expeditionary forces (MEFs), eleven air force tactical fighter wing equivalents, and a navy of 320 ships, including ten carriers, would provide a force more than capable of handling a single major conflict while conducting economy-of-force measures in a second if necessary. This force would cost about $250 billion annually in FY 1995 dollars while providing sufficient resources for modernization. Such a strategic requirement, in reality, does not differ greatly from the existing one. For all its talk of responding to two "nearly simultaneous" major regional contingencies, the Bottom Up Review's timeline is not so much simultaneous as sequential, and the real burden of conducting operations in the second theater actually falls on reserve forces.

To free up further funds for modernization, the Pentagon would have to match a reduction in requirements with a decline in force structure. The national leadership would have to reduce operations other than war. Reducing such operations should not, however, become a first step in strategic disengagement. American military forces must continue to underwrite the liberal, transoceanic trading regime created by the Cold War. Overseas presence is an important element of a liberal world order.[75]

As various analyses cited above suggest, the Pentagon can also adjust its budget internally. The cost of the defense infrastructure is too high for existing forces, much less for a reduced one. In particular, Congress must find a way to close unneeded bases. In addition, any part of the defense budget that does not directly enhance the ability of U.S. forces to carry out their military missions must be closely examined.

Given the likely fiscal environment, the great danger facing the American military establishment is that the high tempo of current operations, resulting from the combination of expanded commitments and smaller forces, will deplete resources for modernization. If the United States is to avoid a replay of the 1970s or, more important, a debacle on some future battlefield, defense planners must reduce those commitments and take whatever other steps are necessary to bring resources and strategy into line.

Peacekeeping and Power Projection? Conventional Forces for the Twenty-first Century

John R. Galvin and Jeffrey S. Lantis

T he United States is at a critical juncture in the use and commitment of its conventional forces around the world. With troops in ninety-one countries, the Pentagon is fighting the main battle here at home: how to avoid "going hollow" within its force structure while at the same time maintaining the qualities that won the Gulf War. Shrinking defense budgets, a changing and sometimes vague national strategy, and unanticipated military operations compound the problems.

While conventional forces represent a key component of U.S. defense policy and strategy, the scope and pace of the downsizing of conventional forces suggest that the United States will soon be unable to support *both* unilateral power projection and international peace keeping in coming decades. American commanders, however, can still configure their forces in a unique fashion to support multilateral military operations and thus allow international leaders to play to American military strengths in a new era.

Conventional Forces in the 1990s

Between 1990 and 1992, during operations Desert Shield and Desert Storm, the Bush administration began the process of defense cuts and reductions in conventional forces. As the Soviet threat faded, Secretary of Defense Richard Cheney and Chairman of the Joint Chiefs of Staff General Colin

Powell orchestrated a controlled drawdown of military forces by implementing the Base Force plan in 1992 as part of a new strategy of regional defense. According to this plan, active-duty army divisions would decrease from fourteen to twelve, navy ships from 443 to 387, carrier battle groups from fourteen to twelve, and air force fighter wings from sixteen to thirteen. The new Base Force was to total 1.6 million active-duty personnel: 1,405,000 based in the continental United States, 184,000 in Europe, 105,000 in the Asia-Pacific region, 17,000 in the Middle East, and 10,000 in Africa.

However, in terms of U.S. commitments, nothing changed. The drawdown and reorganization failed to prevent the administration from making significant conventional force deployments to support multilateral peacekeeping operations. This was, in part, a response to high-profile crises in northern Iraq and Somalia, but it also reflected a mood of optimism about American potential in the post–Cold War era. The 1992 *National Military Strategy of the United States* listed the "strengthening of international organizations like the United Nations" as one of the "enduring national security interests and objectives" of the United States. It estimated multilateral operations in the UN context as a means to augment the projection of U.S. power, and clearly, the "New World Order" meant more than the passive peacekeeping of the Cold War.[1]

It was no surprise, then, that the Clinton administration adopted many elements of the Bush defense strategy in its first year in office. In his campaign, Clinton did not take issue with the general thrust of Bush's foreign policy, nor had he spoken out against maintaining visible forces abroad as well as at home. While he did call for a reduction of an additional 200,000 troops from the base force, Clinton, after he became president, maintained that "the need to deploy U.S. military forces abroad in peacetime is an important factor in determining our overall force structure."[2]

The new administration took this commitment a step further. It emphasized the continued importance of "engagement" in international affairs and the "enlargement of the world's free community of market democracies."[3] The idea of *engagement*, though complex, was fairly clear, but *enlargement* was another matter. The president apparently was willing to assume greater responsibilities for the democratic community of nations by using American forces to "counter the aggression of states hostile to democracy and market economies" where necessary.[4] Such a goal would require decades of sustained political, economic, and social trial and error to reach. And throughout this demanding period, the United States would have to keep its forces constantly ready for major expeditionary operations.

The Reality of Operations' Tempo in the Clinton Administration

A major obstacle to the pursuit of such goals as enlargement and engagement was the reality that American forces were already overextended at the beginning of the Clinton administration. At the same time, U.S. foreign policy boosted the operations' tempo (the scope and pace of operations) for American forces: since the fall of the Berlin Wall, operations' tempo has increased by over 300 percent.[5] Troops deployed for peacekeeping and peacemaking operations, as well as for training in traditional and nontraditional missions. At home, deployments of U.S. forces took place in response to domestic disasters in 1994. National guard, reserve, and active-duty troops helped to fight forest fires across broad areas of the Pacific Northwest during the summer. In Washington State, for example, thousands of marines, along with army and air force reservists, worked hand in hand with civilians to bring wind-driven fires under control. Such cooperation occurred in Idaho, California, Montana, Oregon, Wyoming, and Arizona, where active-duty and reserve troops provided logistical and air support for fire fighting.

Altogether, U.S. forces maintained thirty-five other operational deployments around the world in 1994. Sixty navy and coast guard vessels operated in the Caribbean to interdict Haitian and Cuban "boat people," while approximately 1,100 soldiers deployed to Guantanamo Naval Base to process refugees. The air force flew 2,300 sorties in the region in support of Operation Maintain Democracy. In Africa, approximately 30,000 soldiers deployed to Somalia and neighboring countries from December 1992 to March 1994, as air force personnel flew over 11,100 support sorties. The humanitarian crisis in Rwanda prompted another U.S. response that involved more than 2,000 soldiers.

In the Middle East, American forces enforced two no-fly zones over northern and southern Iraq. Since 1991, the military operation in northern Iraq (part of Operations Provide Comfort I and II) has involved some 1,350 ground troops and 63,000 sorties. At the same time, the no-fly zone over southern Iraq (as part of Operation Southern Watch) has included a staggering number of sorties—137,000 since 1991. The continuous presence of naval expeditionary forces in the gulf has supported these operations.

American military forces have participated in crisis response and humanitarian relief operations in the Balkans since 1991. Twenty-four members of the U.S. European Command staff serve in Kiseljak, Bosnia as part of the United Nations Protection Force (UNPROFOR) headquarters staff, while another fifty members have been in Zagreb with the Joint Task Force Forward Staff. Since 1992, a battalion of soldiers from the U.S. forces serving in Germany has provided border security in Macedonia. About 3,000 air force personnel participated in Operation Deny Flight and Operation Provide Promise in and over Bosnia—where by December 1994 they had flown 9,700 fighter sorties and 2,301 airdrop missions. The navy also maintained four ships from Sixth Fleet—including amphibious assault ships—in the Adriatic to monitor the UN arms embargo.

Some commitments with a long history have become second nature to the U.S. military and the public. Approximately 100,000 American troops remain in Europe in 1994 as part of the NATO integrated command structure formalized in 1949. This deployment has totaled approximately 10 million troops, or perhaps better stated, 30 million troop-years. The United States has also maintained a continuous, long-term naval commitment to the region, the Sixth Fleet, in the Mediterranean since NATO came into existence. In the Middle East, American battalions have rotated through the multinational peace-keeping and observer forces in the Sinai for over twelve years. Another 8,500 air force personnel have served in the Gulf since the end of the war, where they have flown some 170,000 sorties in the last three years.[6]

In Asia, the United States has maintained a long-term commitment to South Korean security with a presence of approximately 35,000 American soldiers on the peninsula. The escalation of north-south tensions in early 1994 prompted deployment of an additional 700 air defense artillery troops as an indicator of U.S. resolve to protect its Korean ally. And in Latin America, members of the 24th Aviation Brigade have deployed to the Bahamas for counterdrug operations since 1984. An average of fifty members of 7th Special Forces Group have been in Colombia since 1985, along with air force personnel who have flown over 400 AWACS reconnaissance sorties as a contribution to the antidrug effort.

Over 160,000 American troops deployed overseas and acted to carry out specific tasks and responsibilities. The scope of all these military operations is impressive but represents an obstacle to changing defense policy and strategy. This pattern of operations presents a near-term challenge for the attainment of the goals of "engagement" and "enlargement."

The Web of Worldwide Logistics

The complex logistical support structure on which each operations deployment depends multiplies the effect of such extensive deployment. Communications, transportation, maintenance, and supply lines stretch out from the United States in a giant web of worldwide logistics. Whether soldiers deploy to the Bahamas or Australia, they rely on a vast air, sea, and ground network, which in turn involves a substantial level of committed military forces and an infrastructure of airfields, naval bases and ports, storage depots, and pipelines, all linked by an integrated communications network to regional commanders and the national chain of command.

Even after eliminating more than 500 Cold War installations in Europe and the Far East, the Pentagon in 1994 still maintained 495 major bases in the United States and 1,650 base facilities overseas.[7] Worldwide depots such as Kwajalein and Guam in the Pacific and Diego Garcia in the Indian Ocean provide the foundations for operational deployments. In sum, this web of worldwide logistics, sustained into the indefinite future, is but one aspect of the commitment required if the United States expects to implement its declared strategy of "engagement" and "enlargement."

Training Deployments

Operations are, of course, the fundamental reason for the existence of military forces, but operational deployments do not always improve training and enhance readiness. In fact, unit overall readiness when deployed on particular missions gradually decreases because of concentration on the specific tasks at hand and a lack of time to maintain combat proficiencies.

Among those forces not engaged on operations, there is a third level of military activity that constitutes an ongoing, major commitment of conventional forces: training deployments. In the first half of 1994, there were at least forty-two training deployments around the world. In the Caribbean, troops preparing for a possible invasion of Haiti in summer 1994 trained in Antigua, the Bahamas, Barbados, the Dominican Republic, Grenada, and St. Kitts. Two aircraft carrier battle groups remained in the area for training operations through to the end of the year. In the Middle East, approximately 1,300 members of the 24th Infantry Division participated in field training exercises in Kuwait prior to the arrival of a full brigade in the fall.

Training deployments continued in Europe and Asia despite the drawdown of U.S. forces in the region. In Asia, 5,350 soldiers from selected units deployed to Korea for a command post exercise in 1994. The USS *Constellation* and its supporting battle group also participated in training operations in the region. Finally, army training and construction projects were under way in Micronesia, Fiji, Australia, Mongolia, Tonga, Thailand, Kwajalein, and the Seychelles in summer 1994.

The Effects of Operations' Tempo on Decision Making

Operations' tempo is the key to American military training. Operational and training deployments, along with the supporting web of worldwide logistics and administrative infrastructure, constitute a quotidian effort that top U.S. decision makers must consider when they make military responses to events around the world. Scarce defense resources in the post–Cold War era make it more likely that the worldwide webs of logistics and infrastructure will serve as constraints on the use of force in at least two ways.

First, new commitments mean difficult choices, including the removal of forces from other areas. New commitments present a dilemma for regional commanders who must often shift specialized units and unique assets without jeopardizing current commitments. In addition, the United States participated in five of seventeen ongoing UN peace operations in 1994, and the administration has faced difficult political choices about participation in these operations when faced with threats elsewhere. These include the recalcitrance and bellicosity of North Korea's resisting nonproliferation of nuclear weapons, the continuing demonstrations of Saddam Hussein's designs on Kuwait and his restless aggressiveness, and the unpredictable future of Russia's relationship with its neighboring states.[8]

Second, any use of conventional forces has long-term implications for weapons stocks, procurement, and training schedules. The Gulf War significantly depleted the stock of precision-guided munitions, and procurement of new systems was a high priority for the Pentagon in the early 1990s. Troop deployments also interrupt training schedules. Together, increasing operations' tempo and support for the goals of enlargement and engagement placed great pressure on acquisition, training schedules, and budgets.

The pace of current military operations is frenetic, and the results remain surprisingly good. But the cost of such activities in the post–Cold War era has made many Americans unhappy, and the search is on for ways to cut back. One approach is to construct defense budgets that do not anticipate contingencies and to insist that unprogrammed expenditures come "out of hide."

"Out of Hide" Defense Expenditures

Another important set of constraints on American security policy exists in the defense budget process itself. The Clinton administration has committed itself to remain actively engaged in world affairs, but military leaders have had to absorb unanticipated costs such as peacekeeping operations in their annual budgets. This has created short-term budget problems in many categories, slows maintenance and training schedules across the board, and has serious ramifications for readiness. Nevertheless, the administration has tasked the military to do more with less, and unanticipated expenditures have become a regular part of the budget game in the post–Cold War era.

The year 1994 confronted policy makers with a considerable number of crises and conflicts. New and more serious confrontations materialized inside and between states. American interests appeared threatened by a lineup of countries with checkered histories with the United States, including Iraq, Iran, Syria, Libya, North Korea, and even China and Russia. U.S. leaders either explicitly or implicitly identified these nations as potential adversaries in the post–Cold War period, and many of these countries maintained large military arsenals, including long-range delivery systems and nuclear, chemical, and biological weapons capabilities.

Regional conflicts around the world also attracted American attention. For example, despite administration efforts to avoid involvement in Rwanda—a visceral response to the deadly clashes in Somalia that drove the United States to an ignominious retreat—international pressure and media attention forced an American response. U.S. troops deployed to Rwanda and neighboring central African states in summer 1994 to support a multilateral response to the refugee crisis. Troops participated in a joint task force as part of Operation Support Hope and deployed to Ethiopia, Zaire, Uganda, Zimbabwe, Rwanda, and Kenya.

These unanticipated military operations in 1994 were all expensive. Congressional critics grumbled about the cost of the operation in Rwanda (an estimated $120 million). But the cost of "engagement" did not stop there. The response to refugee crises in the Caribbean cost the military $260 million, while the unanticipated heightening of tensions with Iraq and North Korea cost another $550 million. The Pentagon estimated that the total expenditures in 1994 for unanticipated military operations were approximately $1.7 billion. Clearly, checklists of criteria for the use of force did not last long when circumstances—including especially media attention—demanded an American response.

Although the impact of the media on political decision making has received much attention, it is still underrated: in case after case, governments around the world have reevaluated policies, decisions, and even major military actions as a direct result of the media (more often than not television, rather than the print media) and its ability to place simultaneously any event before a world audience. National administrations have constantly misjudged the capability of graphic media to impact their decisions in places from Tienanmen Square to Mogadishu to Grozny. Increasingly, the collective visceral reaction of a world of television eyewitnesses has become an extraordinary and growing power over the political response to internal and external crises: the policy maker can feel the citizens, his constituents, looking over his shoulder as he studies his options.

Uncertainty About the International Security Environment

The administration has appeared uncertain about its response to this new world disorder. Official pronouncements have represented a broad range of thinking about the emerging international security environment. The administration's major documents on defense policy are, in fact, somewhat incompatible—the *Report on the Bottom Up Review*, the FY 1995 *Annual Report to the President and the Congress*, and the 1994 *National Security Strategy of Engagement and Enlargement* promised active international engagement but demonstrated ambivalence about continuing disorder in the world. The *Bottom Up Review* and the *Annual Report* articulated military preparations for two regional conflicts sometime in the distant future. But the president's *National Security Strategy* focused on the post–Cold War era as a unique opportunity to downsize the military. Taken together, the documents described a search for high-quality military forces at bargain-basement prices.

A major aspect of the Bottom Up Review was its assessment of current and future threats to U.S. national security. That assessment served as the key to prescriptions about defense strategy, force structure, and personnel policy for the new administration.[9] The review recognized a considerable number of potential threats to American security, including the proliferation of weapons of mass destruction, nuclear arsenals in the Commonwealth of Independent States, "major aggression in regions important to the United States," instability in new democratic and free-market states, and economic threats to American security.[10] The review then defined an integrated response to regional conflicts, each of which would require four or five army divisions, four or five marine brigades, ten air force fighter wings (plus up to one hundred bombers), and four or five carrier battle groups.[11] Although it was no doubt speaking directly to the restructuring and belt-tightening prescribed by Clinton during the 1992 presidential campaign, the review paid little attention to other budget categories, including nontraditional operations.

This trend continued in Secretary of Defense Les Aspin's FY 1995 *Annual Report* to Congress, which sought to balance current and future defense needs in an austere budget environment. Aspin acknowledged that hard choices had to be made among priorities for research and development, procurement, personnel, and other aspects of the force structure. But he focused almost solely on readiness at the cost of other categories.[12] Even though defense outlays would eventually fall to 2.8 percent of the gross national product (the lowest level since before Pearl Harbor) and troop cuts would reduce active-duty military strength to 1,525,700 in FY 1995 (down from 2,174,000 in 1987), Aspin maintained that the new structure and budget would not compromise readiness.[13] He reiterated the administration's commitment to active engagement in the international system and described a force structure that could respond to regional conflicts, unilaterally if necessary.[14]

The *National Security Strategy of Engagement and Enlargement*, released in July 1994 by the White House,[15] also underlined a number of key contradictions and ambivalence in administration thinking that had already emerged. On the one hand, the strategy maintained that the end of the Cold War had not reduced the need for American efforts in furthering international security wherever possible.[16] As in earlier documents, the president argued that U.S. forces should be robust and flexible: "so long as we retain the military wherewithal to underwrite our commitments military strength would be used to play a leading role in defending common interests and help ensure that the United States will remain an influential voice in international affairs."[17]

On the other hand, in spite of a broad range of commitments, the strategy cited "unparalleled opportunities" to downsize American military strength and the need to "husband scarce resources."[18] The strategy offered criteria for guiding tough decisions on how and when to employ American forces abroad. These included determining whether the benefits of commitment would outweigh the costs, whether the burden of international commitment could be shared, whether nonmilitary means would offer a reasonable chance of success, and whether there were adequate assurances of achieving the operation and its objectives.[19] Thus, while the administration had set out a commendable goal for itself in the post–Cold War era—enlargement and engagement—these goals were seemingly a narrow portion of the calculus for force commitment.

A survey of these documents setting forth U.S. national security policy suggests that the administration has not yet settled on a coherent vision of the emerging post–Cold War security environment. Some have labeled the documents incompatible. The *Review*, for example, described the post–Cold War world as "an era of new dangers," while the *National Security Strategy* focuses on new, "unparalleled opportunities to make our nation safer and more prosperous."[20] References throughout the administration's pronouncements to the criteria for the use of force in the new era also seemed contradictory. For example, after bold suggestions about engagement in the *National Security Strategy*, the president hedged that U.S. "international involvement will be more circumscribed when other regional or multilateral actors are better positioned to act than we are."[21]

A wish to avoid any costly unilateral force deployments or those in which America pays the major part of the bill matches American ambivalence concerning the commitment of U.S. military forces to UN command. This adds a political aspect to the administration's strategic outlook and gives other nations around the world the strong impression that the United States is not as predictable, not as willing to lead, not as committed to its declared strategy as it might have been in the past.

Out of Hide: Planning Problems and Budget Shortfalls

The nation and its representatives expect the military to be ready for any deployments during a given year, but unanticipated operations create serious ripple effects throughout planning, readiness, and budgeting areas. Both the *Report on the Bottom Up Review* and Aspin's last *Annual Report* agreed that engagement of U.S. forces in peacekeeping or humanitarian operations might inhibit the ability to respond to other threats. The first step in responding to any major regional conflict, according to these documents, would have to be the cancellation of involvement in peacekeeping or humanitarian assistance duties to focus and conserve military resources.[22] However, a comprehensive army study on the feasibility of redeploying forces from peacekeeping operations to regional conflicts will not be ready until mid-1995.

Presidential Decision Directive 25, released in May 1994, reinforced the administration's emphasis on peacekeeping. This document agreed that participation in UN peacekeeping operations would be a "force multiplier" in efforts to promote peace and stability around the world. The administration did set out "more rigorous standards of review for U.S. support for, or participation in, peace operations . . . with the most stringent applying to U.S. participation in missions that may involve combat." These criteria would likely restrict the degree of American involvement in future operations.[23]

Because unanticipated military operations like peacekeeping missions complicate an already difficult budget environment, another portion of the administration's plan attempted to define a separate line in the defense budget for peace-keeping operations. The FY 1995 defense budget included a request for a special $300 million fund for such operations. However, administration officials failed to give the fund high priority in their lobbying efforts, and Congress subsequently described the request as vague and cut the line item in August 1994.[24] Given the fact that the United States was responsible for 30 percent of the peacekeeping bill, the administration would find moving away from these political and military constraints difficult to accomplish even when faced with threats elsewhere.[25]

There are practical concerns about the utility of the two-major-regional-conflicts concept for defense planning in the post–Cold War era. The *Army Times* reported in mid-1994 that almost no one in the Pentagon thought the new construct would work because budget cuts would undermine readiness.[26] This echoed an earlier statement from Aspin in his testimony to the House

Armed Services Committee that the five-year defense spending totals in the administration plan were "essentially built upon a macroeconomic basis not on a threat analysis basis . . . they were just kind of pulled out of the air."[27] The FY 1994 *Annual Report* also included confusing statements about readiness. Aspin described readiness as the Pentagon's "top priority"; he further emphasized its importance for foreign and security policy success and for troop morale. However, he also pointed out problems with readiness created by budget cuts and drawdowns:

> Indeed, drawdowns have structural characteristics that inherently eat at readiness [including] turbulence in personnel as units disband and individuals are rapidly reassigned; insecurities in an uncertain future for military professionals that make it difficult to recruit and retain the best people; turmoil in the management of materiel as portions of the industrial base shrink or close down . . . and sluggishness in the divestiture of bases and other infrastructure that often requires short-term spending to reap long-term savings.[28]

Overall, the administration has thus far failed to address the fact that the Bottom Up Review's forces will remain underfunded for the next several years by a considerable amount. Congress approved the full FY 1995 defense budget request for $263 billion in October, but the Pentagon and Congress differed over projected deficits in the budget. The General Accounting Office released a report in early 1994 claiming that the review force will experience at least a $150 billion shortfall in the coming five years and concluding that the defense budget plan "contained more programs than the president's current funding projections will support."[29] Pentagon officials responded with a projection of a $40 billion shortfall in the coming years and charged that the General Accounting Office vastly overestimated potential cost increases for equipment, overseas operations, and personnel.[30]

Even the lesser Pentagon estimate presages near- and long-term problems for defense policy planning, and the administration has had to prioritize budget commitments in that context. Officials have clearly chosen to emphasize readiness at the cost of needed modernization and procurement programs.

❦

U.S. Conventional Forces: Uniquely Configured to Support Multilateral Operations in the Post–Cold War Era?

Existing military commitments, budget shortfalls, downsizing, and policy ambivalence impose constraints on defense policy. This is a growing concern in a world that has seen ninety conflicts since the Berlin Wall came down. Because these trends will continue, administration officials must emphasize the inherent strengths of the American military in the post–Cold War era by focusing support on multilateral operations.

Capabilities

U.S. conventional forces are uniquely configured to support multilateral operations around the world. The United States currently enjoys an enormous superiority in technology, resources, and firepower over any potential opponent in the post–Cold War era. U.S. support for multinational operations can come in the form of logistics, training, intelligence, communications, and even firepower.

Today, the foundation of American superiority in conventional forces lies in two factors: technology and command and control. First, the U.S. military has created technologically superior forces for use in high-intensity conflicts as a result of its long contest with the Soviet Union. This advantage is a function of aggressive research, development, and procurement efforts, and it has allowed American leaders superiority in all aspects of force deployment. Advances in laser and radar technology have improved targeting accuracy, and U.S. forces benefit from advanced communications and intelligence systems. The global positioning system, for example, allowed troops to carry out difficult maneuvers in the featureless desert during Operation Desert Storm. Precision-guided weaponry brought pinpoint accuracy to the same war, while advanced munitions like the "Brilliant" antitank munitions and the triservice standoff attack missile will provide a needed edge in future conflicts.[31]

Second, the current configuration of U.S. military forces lends itself to the support of multilateral operations because of superior command, control, communications, and intelligence. These assets allow American leadership to orchestrate a highly potent combination of aircraft, missiles, fast-deployment ships, ground firepower and mobility, long-range communication, reconnaissance and surveillance capabilities, and worldwide logistics for any operation. In short, they provide a versatility that remains unique in the modern era.

Capability is also a function of numbers and sustainability. Most experts insist that the force structure would be stretched to the breaking point in responding to two regional conflicts simultaneously.[32] In 1993 the Congressional Research Service estimated that any future regional conflict at the levels experienced in the Gulf War would require considerably more personnel and equipment than the Bottom Up Review provides.[33] Other military and civilian experts have suggested that the two-major-regional-conflicts scenario is really a derivative of the Cold War; others call it a worn-out construct from recent U.S. experiences, a Gulf War hangover.

Some also worry that American airlift and sealift may represent the Achilles' heel in the new force structure. Engagement in multiple operations requires the rapid transfer of tens of thousands of troops and equipment from one theater to another.[34] Such a move would run into serious difficulties given the reduction in merchant marine support and the production delays with the C-17. The commander of Central Command recently noted: "It was all we could do to fly troops and equipment to the peace operation in Somalia, while at the same time delivering war material to Egypt for a training exercise."[35] One response was that the air force commissioned a study on the requirements for shifting assets between conflicts, but it will not be out until fall 1995.

To their credit, the administration has responded to these immediate concerns. Secretary of Defense William Perry has admitted that the Bottom Up Review force could not fight two wars at once "for at least several years" because it lacked necessary modernization programs and weapons upgrades.[36] Pentagon officials have identified needed enhancements in airlift, sealift, and precision-guided munitions programs that will be available by the year 2000. In December 1994, the White House announced a $25 billion increase in the topline budget request to address short-term readiness and personnel problems over a six-year period.

Support for Multilateral Operations

The administration has produced a number of documents that demonstrate a long-term commitment to support multilateral operations in the emerging strategic environment. In the *Report on the Bottom Up Review* and the FY 1995 *Annual Report*, Aspin reiterated the administration's commitment to active engagement in the international system and defined an elaborate plan to sustain a high level of involvement.[37] In the July 1994 *National Security Strategy*, the president reiterated basic American intentions on this question and went one step further. He maintained that the ending of the

Cold War had not reduced the need for American efforts to enhance international security wherever possible. The president argued that the United States was the world's "premier economic and military power, and its premier practitioner of democratic values." Finally, he added that active American leadership would continue to be necessary to keep threats down.[38]

The strongest statement of administration support for multilateral operations came in Presidential Decision Directive 25. In it the administration recognized that "U.N. and other multilateral peace operations will at times offer the best way to prevent, contain, or resolve conflicts that could otherwise be more costly and deadly." The directive argued that the United States benefits from involvement in multilateral operations by reducing its share of the military burden and gains legitimacy by "invoking the voice of the community of nations."[39]

Although sponsoring withdrawal from Somalia and displaying little interest in involvement in a large-scale military response in Bosnia, the administration has been willing to use American forces to support other multilateral operations. U.S. forces provide close air support, airdrop humanitarian relief supplies, and monitor the no-fly zone over Bosnia, as well as over northern and southern Iraq. American forces led a peaceful invasion of Haiti in summer 1994 and continue to provide support for the multilateral police force there. U.S. airlift was also employed in Rwanda and Zaire to provide humanitarian relief.

Efficiency

Nevertheless, there continues to be ambivalence, and in fact debate, over the shaping of a force with a major mission of collaboration with foreign military organizations in international coalitions. One route has been a greater emphasis on conventional force structures designed to contribute to NATO's strategic concept, emphasizing cooperation and dialogue, crisis management, conflict prevention, and response to multidirectional threats. The president has argued in several major documents that multilateral cooperation could be a force multiplier. Together with the other options, this is seen as the way to a reduced U.S. defense posture in the early part of the twenty-first century.

The administration's efforts to build a multinational coalition for the invasion of Haiti in fall 1994 was an example of operations that probably will become more common. This operation involved approximately 15,000 active-duty American troops, but it also required the call-up of 10,000 reserves to operate with a coalition of countries committed to participation in the postinvasion peacekeeping force. Even with a strong and early commitment of reserve forces, such operations produce longer term concerns about troop rotation, training, and maintenance.[40]

By 1996, only approximately 100,000 American troops will remain in Europe, a major reduction from the heights of the Cold War. Still, U.S. troops committed to NATO are forward deployed and well equipped. They provide a solid operational and logistical foundation for crisis response. The influence of their presence over the years has resulted in extraordinary compatibility (in NATO terms, "interoperability")[41] among the forces of member nations. The new NATO concept formulated at the November 1991 Rome summit emphasized crisis management as the foundation for further international coordination. Moreover, the United States has taken an active role in development of the NATO Rapid Reaction Corps, which presently consists of a number of divisions immediately available for operations under NATO corps command. These forces can respond to regional and out-of-area contingencies using the available NATO infrastructure of bases, pipelines, long-range communications, and storage facilities.

Furthermore, the North Atlantic Cooperation Council provides a forum for consideration of security issues across Western, Central, and Eastern Europe. The Partnership for Peace program brings the European nations together on politico-military questions, while the Conference on Security and Cooperation in Europe plays a strong role as a forum for confidence-building measures and nonproliferation issues, among other tasks.[42] The Western European Union is also available for service if NATO does not wish to step in to address a European problem.

The United States can offer support for multilateral operations but only if it places a major focus on maintaining its edge in technology; otherwise, current U.S. technological advantages will disappear in the face of the efforts by other major powers. It will be difficult, however, to keep up a commitment to procurement, research, and development programs in the Pentagon when funds are so short and operational demands are great. Increased reliance on other, more efficient means for maintaining readiness—such as simulation systems for joint training exercises and even major changes in the research, development, and procurement process—needs further study.

Today, the U.S. military is turning to "recapitalization" (refurbishing) programs to extend the life of equipment, but one must not confuse such efforts with modernization or product improvement. There is also more interest in the Pentagon in the application of engineering development programs whereby the military would invest in private research and development in the short term but plan to produce prototypes that would then go on the shelf in programs where industry might delay indefinitely full production and acquisition. Such changes would not necessarily be welcomed by industry, and would be expensive because of low volume of production, but they could serve to maintain the American edge in conventional forces and facilitate multilateral operations.

Defining Roles and Missions

Restructuring the military and reassigning roles and missions should be a high priority given the changes in strategy, tactics, and force structure in the post–Cold War era. In fact, a major review of service roles and missions formally began in 1994. But to a great extent the administration remained ambivalent about restructuring, and uncertainty within the Pentagon about future defense budgets reinforced the traditional reluctance to shed roles and missions. Military leaders are looking for a fuller understanding of the implications of jointness for war-fighting doctrine as well as for organization, training, and materiel requirements.[43]

One major area currently under review is the question of coalition interoperability. U.S. military leaders are examining the extent to which their forces should train for, plan, and pay for multilateral operations in the emerging operational environment. Projected changes in unified command plans, along with an emphasis on multilateral operations and a modified distribution and posture of American military forces, have increased the complexity of the debate.[44] Nevertheless, this issue remains at the heart of questions about future American defense policy and strategy, the efficiency of overseas deployment, and specialization in (and budgeting for) peace operations.

The Pentagon confronts a number of specific concerns about roles and missions in the post–Cold War era. These include the integration of air forces and reassignment of responsibilities for close air support and interdiction. With the success of attack helicopters and with the arrival of missile power on the battlefield, the army has defined a larger role for itself in ground support and challenged the air force role in this capacity. Sealift has also emerged as an object of considerable debate between the army and navy. Theater air defense has also generated severe infighting, since that responsibility devolves on the army, the air force, and even the navy (just as air defense has played a larger role more recently in the navy's littoral strategy). The services have also struggled over control of space assets and activities, battle damage assessment, combat search and rescue operations, depot maintenance management, and central logistics support, among others.

Many such issues are a function of the new international order, while others emerged in the wake of the 1986 Goldwater-Nichols Defense Reorganization Act. For example, the shift of authority to regional commanders in chief dictated by Goldwater-Nichols has meant that decisions about shifting of assets between conflicts as well as the availability of specialized units would be a function of regional control rather than the services themselves.

The administration itself has only just begun to address the roles and missions question. The president sanctioned the formation of the independent commission and tasked it to deliver a final report on these matters to the Congress by May 24, 1995. Since its establishment, the president has strengthened the commission by expanding membership from seven to eleven, while Secretary of Defense William Perry further stipulated that at least one new member have high-level experience with national guard and reserve forces.

The commission subsequently released a list of twenty-five major issues related to roles and missions that it would examine; it highlighted military and congressional interests in certain specific changes and their budgetary implications. Nevertheless, members chose not to address issues relating to the national guard and reserve forces, sealift, and counterproliferation because of opposition from the services themselves. The redefinition of roles and missions involves a complex set of negotiations about appropriate responsibilities, with each service branch articulating its "core competency" and specializations. This debate has already spurred unusually hardbitten debate as the services vie for their slice of a shrinking budget.[45]

To date, the administration had made relatively little progress. At such a critical time, roles and missions need fundamental restructuring to support coalition interoperability for traditional and nontraditional operations. The civilian leadership must provide the impetus and guidance for this reorganization in order to overcome traditional resistance from the services. Presidential leadership could set the tone for necessary changes in the structure that supports defense policy and strategy.

Conclusion

U.S. military resources are greatly overstretched—160,000 soldiers deployed in ninety-one countries—and the Pentagon faces an enormous struggle for solvency and strength in the post–Cold War era. Political and security goals are contradictory in this environment, while shrinking defense budgets, unanticipated military operations, and training and maintenance backlogs all compound the uncertainty.

The administration's pronouncements on defense policy seem incompatible and demonstrate ambivalence about the security environment and defense policy. This has contributed to uncertainty in Congress and the Pentagon about force commitments, as demonstrated in recent debates over support for multilateral operations and cooperation with the United Nations. The scope and pace of the downsizing occurring in the forces, coupled with frenetic operations' tempo, make support for unilateral or even multilateral power projection and international peacekeeping in the twenty-first century highly problematic.

The Pentagon needs to make at least four major changes in policy and strategy to allow the United States to project power successfully in the twenty-first century. First, the administration must move to make the limited and overstretched forces of the Bottom Up Review more robust, flexible, and versatile than current policies would allow. Second, there is need for greater emphasis on conventional force structures designed to contribute to NATO's new strategic concepts of cooperation and dialogue, crisis management, conflict prevention, and international response to multidirectional threats. Third, the Pentagon must carefully review and revise service roles and missions to focus support on multilateral operations. Fourth, U.S. leaders must move beyond the rhetoric and recognize the political and economic limits on defense policy and strategy. They must build innovative modernization and procurement programs and explore new, more efficient ways to support a modern military organization.

Conventional force planning can go one of two ways. The administration can favor short-term solutions—which will result in dangerously overstretched forces pursuing a myriad of political goals. Such an approach will largely compromise any long-range approach to American security. On the other hand, the administration can build consensus by reorganizing and limiting its overseas commitments, enhance multilateral crisis response options, and ensure that the Bottom Up Review's force is adequate to its tasks. The second option requires political bipartisanship to face the challenge of change and real leadership from civilians as well as military. This will not be easy with the new political alignment in Washington.

Chapter 9

Great Powers
No More

Lawrence Freedman

I n 1960 Dean Acheson, the former U.S. secretary of state, caused something of a stir in London with his observation that Britain had "lost an Empire" but had "not yet found a role."[1] Many in Britain received Acheson's remark as a graceless put-down at a time when London was wondering whether its views carried the same weight as before in Washington. At another level many recognized the remark to be little more than a candid statement of the blindingly obvious—Britain was no longer the power it once had been, now that it had relinquished its empire. Yet at another level still, it set a challenge, and this came to be the most enduring legacy of Acheson's remarks in Britain.

The challenge was to find a "role," a unique contribution that only Britain could provide with its global perspective and contacts, long traditions, and diplomatic skills. British statesmen offered all sorts of formulations. Their proposals normally involved "bridge building": between Washington and Moscow (reflecting memories of London as a junior member of the Big Three); or between the United States and Western Europe, as the linchpin of NATO; or between North and South, via the Commonwealth. All had their moment and, on occasion, real substance, but somehow they never added up to a lasting "role." Here is where Acheson did his real disservice. By kidding his hosts he suggested that there really was a distinctive international position that might compensate for Britain's loss of empire and satisfy a lingering sense of national greatness. In some way the British wanted to feel responsibility for the international order. Without such responsibility, Britain was just another middle-rank power. Being ordinary is what countries like Britain fear most.

This essay is about the United States, not Britain. One should be wary about assuming that national histories follow the same trajectory. Thought of Britain inevitably kindles images of decline in American minds, as the fate of aging parents casts shadows over the most vigorous middle age. Perhaps this is because a Briton, Paul Kennedy, sparked the great debate in the 1980s on America's decline, precisely by drawing parallels with the experience of past great powers.[2] Yet despite all the cultural, liberal, free-trade, maritime, and alliance connections, the two situations are not comparable. Without its international associations, the United States is still of a size and wealth that must always put it in the rank of the first rate; stripped of its colonies, Britain shrank to the second rank, at best.[3]

If there is a similarity between British debates in the early 1960s and those in the United States in the late 1980s, it lies in the assumption that what was at stake was a comparative position within an international frame-work that in its essentials all took largely as given. The idea of a "role" im-plies some concept of an international system whose stability is a function of the fashion within which key units behave. In the contemporary American debate there is the familiar presumption that the problem lies in identifying and articulating a role that domestic and international audiences alike can appreciate. At the start of the 1990s, with the United States in an unassail-able position as the only remaining superpower, such a task momentarily ap-peared easier than ever.

This chapter explores a contrary assumption: that the search for a role has become anachronistic. An international system shaped by a multitude of factors and containing large numbers of diverse units imposes inherent limits on the influence that even the strongest units can exert. The changes in the international system over the past few decades—to some extent obscured by the "great-power politics as usual" character of the Cold War—mean that the traditional great-power roles for states no longer exist.

The International System

How might one define a great power's international role? The idea that one could usefully describe the primary elements in the international system as consisting of great powers goes back at least five centuries.[4] The descrip-tion of some powers as "great" gained currency at the start of the nineteenth century, though a rank order had emerged well before then. From the earliest, the notion carried a dual implication. The status of great power said something about a particular state's ability to defend itself as well as its contribution to the system as a whole. Initially, it sufficed for the system that great powers considered only the demands of their own security. Eventually, theorists accepted the idea that it was necessary to employ a wider conception of international security.

A wider concept—based on the presumption that states must use the status of great power most properly in the service of the international community—legitimized the possession of such power and possibly comforted those who wielded it. Such a concept remained, nonetheless, an uneasy companion to the belief that states do not seek to accumulate or to dispose of great power unless convinced that their own special interests are well served. The status of great power means relief from the rules considered appropriate for lesser powers on the grounds that more vital interests are at stake. Despite this reassuring thought, which occurs naturally in the capitals of great powers—that what is good for a particular great power is good for the system as a whole—others are more likely to be painfully aware of the instances where such is not the case.

Until comparatively recently theorists took for granted that the natural vocation of great powers was to expand and, when frustrated on land, to do so overseas through the acquisition of distant colonies. Over time the ability to reach beyond borders became critical. Here, maritime powers found their great advantage with the ability to control the sea lines of communication.

A system containing a number of expansionist great powers generated two types of insecurity. The first was a fear among small powers that they could not sustain independence, but risked conquest by neighboring predators. The second was a belief among the great powers that their interests were bound to collide. Each harbored fears of how others might displace it in the international hierarchy and strip it of earlier acquisitions. The system could cope so long as there were outlets for the expansionist urges of the great powers. However, the limits on available territory meant that at some point the powers would collide. As the great powers gobbled up territory around the globe, confrontations were inevitable—at the imperial peripheries if not the metropolitan centers.

As "power" was always military, the ability to impose will through force distinguished the ranks of the major powers from the minor in the hierarchy of powers. War provided the mechanism through which great powers rose and declined, though, of course, the explanation for the shifts in fortune had much to do with underlying economic and social factors. The basic challenge of the international order was how best to accommodate the entry of rising great powers and the exit of those declining by means other than war, and how to accommodate great powers that refused to play by any set of rules.

The Treaty of Westphalia in 1648, which by general account established the rules, reflected a view that anything was better than constant conflict in the name of religion. Respect for sovereignty was one way to establish a modus vivendi, a form of peaceful coexistence, between Protestants and Catholics, and to prevent imposition of any new imperium comparable to the Holy Roman Empire. This was a highly conservative doctrine. Having sorted out one theological/ideological dispute, it denied legitimacy to further challenges to the political establishment of states.

In a system of noninterference the only test of a regime's claiming sovereignty over a territory was that it was sovereign in practice: that it could maintain internal order and survive, and possibly prosper, in war. At its simplest, the settlement did not allow for challenges based on higher claims of justice or righteousness: the only challenge that mattered had to rest on power. The solution to the apparent problem that if effective power were the basis of legitimacy, then superior power would in all cases be more legitimate lay in an understanding that unregulated anarchy would be disastrous and that some form of self-regulation was necessary.

The doctrine of the balance of power sought to turn the respect for raw strength into a basis for restraint. The balance of power could provide a source of stability to the international system because of the number and diversity of the states in the system. If any state were to become too powerful, the others could combine in an alliance and, if necessary, fight. The balance of power certainly did not prevent war. The Europeans, in fact, fought many in its name. Nonetheless, the balance of power represented an ideology of international order in which the players already preferred a plural system to a hegemonic one.[5]

Under the influence of Newtonian physics and then market economics, Europeans came to see the balance of power as the natural order of things, and thus it provided the language by which states justified their foreign policies, whatever the reasons. Even in the most self-serving cases, one can lose the legitimizing function with excessive cynicism. Here were at least principles that recognized the claims of others; noninterference in internal affairs and the importance of preventing a monopoly of power could serve as standards against which one statesman might judge the behavior of other nations. There was thus a ready fit between the pursuit of interests by great powers and the international order, so long as the participants were all of a conservative disposition.

The problems began as particular states generated new, irreligious ideologies that set transcendent, often democratic, grounds for social organization, such as republicanism, liberalism, and socialism. The internal stability of a regime based on an ideological view of the world depends on other states' adopting the same view and thus necessitates the internal destabilization of those states yet to "reform." Disinterest in the internal affairs of other states is only possible for states when their respective ideologies remain on a similar course.

The course of the French Revolution and the subsequent Napoleonic wars underline this point. Once the European powers had successfully mastered this challenge, their instinct was to manage the international system once again through a common set of rules that essentially conservative states would have little difficulty in following in pursuing their international interests: hence the shared hostility toward revolutionary ideologies that not only provided for the accumulation of power and territory but also contested the very legitimacy of others. During the course of the nineteenth century the rise of liberalism subverted authoritarian regimes and generated demands for self-determination. These demands still confounded all attempts to establish a system of international order based on fixed borders. Nationalism inevitably led to demands for new aggregations of states, as with Italy and Germany, as well as the fragmentation of others, as in the Ottoman and Austro-Hungarian empires.

From their own perspective, individual states, therefore, judged a particular international order not only by the threats it generated, or by the opportunities it provided for trade, but also by the support it provided to particular political philosophies. Thus, those who considered their national interests best supported by the system had a broader interest in its sustenance. Only great powers could protect this interest, but this fact demanded that they think about more than their immediate security. The designation of great power, therefore, came to imply responsibility for the system as a whole, and thus duties as well as rights. The two remained linked; a central position in the system's management ensured that states could protect their particular interests. In this way, the retention of the status of a great power became an interest in itself.

In gatherings such as the Congress of Vienna in 1815, the League of Nations in 1919, and the United Nations in 1945, the key task was to establish the rights and duties of those designated as great powers and to establish the mechanisms through which these powers would operate. Each followed the defeat of a threatening ideology—revolutionary republicanism, antidemocratic authoritarianism, and racist nationalism. In each case, the powers hoped that a new consensus could rest on a common set of shared principles. The ensuing consensus failed when new ideological fault lines opened up.

If there had been a universal political philosophy, then the problem of order would have been easier to resolve. Attempts to establish the rule of international law, or even to move toward world government, assumed that such concepts could rest on the core principles of liberalism—the right to liberty of individuals and to self-determination for nations. As long as there was mutual respect for such rights, then there would be no problems. The challenge for the international order, as with the domestic, was to ensure that the community as a whole protected such rights against those who sought to deny them. This required a theory of political obligation, always a difficult area for liberalism, in that it qualified the basic freedom to ignore the problems of others.

The notion that great powers had an obligation to help small powers developed in the eighteenth century and almost immediately led to doubts as to whether the constant wars to protect the liberties of the latter were truly consistent with national interests. Certainly, during the nineteenth century, small powers learned not to rely on the great powers but to look to self-defense, which depended on size, in terms of both territory and population. So small states combined to form Germany and Italy. By and large, the great powers took order to be a higher priority than the rights of the smaller states. During the twentieth century, victimization of small states prompted a number of great powers to respond against the offender—but only when they recognized patterns of behavior that ultimately threatened everyone. This factor has provided a spur to those who have sought to develop forms of international organization that are more reliable guarantors of international security than a sense of duty on the part of the great powers.

The point of the realist's critique of liberal internationalism has been that maintenance of order and protection of the weak against the strong have never sensibly been a matter of learning how to honor the rule of law, but rather have been matters of power and interest.[6] The realists, however, have been vulnerable to the charge of cynicism in assuming that power and interest were all that mattered. Contrary to the view that domestic politics in the great powers were an irrelevance and that individual states related to each other on the basis of a straightforward calculus of power—varied by alliances and occasional wars—ideology has always been central to concepts of the international order. The system has been sensitive not only to acts of aggression but also to subversion, and the boundary between the two was never as clear-cut as realist theoreticians would have it.

Any attempt to assess the potential role of a great power must, therefore, assess three tensions. The most obvious lies between a general responsibility for the international order and specific security problems of great powers themselves. One can suppose that requirements of international order are taken most seriously when they coincide with the strategic imperatives of great powers. The second tension relates to the competing requirements within the concern for international order between the prevention of violence on a large scale—and in particular escalation to conflict among the great powers—and a concern for the rights of small states. The third tension is linked to the previous one. If threats to international order do not simply take the form of criminal, aggressor states who discard the rules, but rather challenge the ideological basis upon which power *within* individual states rests, then the responsibilities of a great power unavoidably tend toward a form of hegemony. Here the tension arises from the specific ideology of liberalism. Liberal ideology has survived the authoritarian and totalitarian challenges of the past two centuries but, precisely because concepts of democracy and liberty are at its core, liberalism, if taken seriously, is inherently disorderly.

America's Rise to Superpower Status

We might turn to consider how the United States has managed these tensions during its rise as a great power, through to the end of the Cold War. The United States was unusual in having the western half of the North American continent available for expansion through the nineteenth century. America did seize territory from Mexico, but its most substantial struggle was to hold the union together rather than to expand its boundaries. As the century closed, the frontier reached its limits; the United States then engaged in a degree of local imperialism. It had sought (via the Monroe Doctrine) to define the Americas as an exclusive sphere of influence—in return for its abstention from meddling in European spheres of influence. Gradually, in spite of itself, the United States found that such a position was not tenable and inevitably it became drawn into a leading role in the world system.

Though America had forged its identity, in part, as an escape from, and in contrast to, Europe's decadence and cynicism, the challenges of the first half of the twentieth century demonstrated that the United States could not safely stand apart from the international state system. The residual strength of mercantilism led to the assumption that a trading nation must secure its markets rather than rely only on a competitive edge. It was also hard for a polity proclaiming its democratic nature to express disinterest in the fate of those proclaiming the same values elsewhere. Moreover, as the reach of the potentially hostile powers grew, the United States could no longer assume that its favored geographic location would afford it protection.

World War II confounded both the isolationist view that the United States could avoid external entanglements and internationalist hopes for a system of collective security. The new American diplomatic line, as it emerged after the war, accepted an interest in global order *and* recognized that this goal required the protection of American power. Former great powers, victors and vanquished alike, were more than happy to accept American leadership after 1945 in the face of the Soviet threat. Initially, the West saw this

threat as dangerous in its ideological form. Communism had a natural attraction in those societies where the right bore much of the responsibility for
the depression of the 1930s. Moreover, communism received the boost of the
apparent success of state intervention in wartime economies, its role in Europe's resistance movements to Nazism, and the awe with which so many
viewed the Soviet Union's own struggle against Nazism.[7]

The United States, however, lacked a communist party with anything approaching mass support. Such support as it had remained confined to intellectual circles. The bulk of the party's actual members were probably FBI
agents informing on each other. But the readiness of the ideological right to
blame international reverses (such as the "loss" of China to communism in
1949) on a Moscow-orchestrated subversion only magnified its strength. Mc-
Carthyism, and Senator McCarthy himself, lasted well into the Eisenhower
administration.[8] In this fashion, U.S. strategic policy during crucial moments
contained an ideological input, even if based on willful exaggerations of local
communist influences.

Fortunately, the Truman administration recognized that explanations
based on subversion were less helpful than a recognition of the unsettled economic and political conditions that could only serve as the wellsprings for the
extension of Soviet influence. Once Europe had achieved a degree of stability—to a large extent through the application of American economic
power—then the threat became less one of internal subversion and more one
of external aggression, which required the continuing presence of American
military power.

For four decades the United States worked to contain threats from the
East until communism disintegrated from within. With half of the continent
organized by Moscow into a formidable military alliance, only the United
States could ensure an effective balance. The implications became evident
during the "great debate" in the 1950s in Congress on the basing of American
troops in Europe.[9] There were at the time hopes that U.S. support would be
only a temporary matter—until the Western Europeans had sorted themselves out and could contain Soviet power on their own or until the fundamental issues of the Cold War resolved themselves. In any event, it took two
generations before the Europeans could begin to think seriously about assuming a greater responsibility for their own security—and even then this
came only with reluctance.

During the intervening years, the culture of dependence created by such
an asymmetrical alliance was not without critics on both sides of the Atlantic.
In Europe some, particularly the French, bristled at what seemed a humiliat-
ing dependence on the United States. In Washington there was a persistent
suspicion that Europe was taking the United States for a ride and that the

Cold War required Americans to accept the dangers of an excessive nuclear bias in strategy as well as the unfairness resulting from the inadequate contributions of some alliance members to the collective defense. Yet despite grumbles, the Washington consensus accepted the logic of the strategic imperative. European security was a truly vital interest and required a decisive American role. Americans could only understand this reality in terms of the language of balance, spheres of influence, hegemony, alliance, and comparative military strength. Posed in these terms the confrontation settled naturally into the preservation of the status quo. In 1961, during the course of the Berlin crisis, it became apparent that the United States would defend what was already part of the West but would not take the risks required to liberate what lay under Soviet control.[10]

In the presence of nuclear weapons, and with due respect to Soviet power, the West had to accept the limits on the ideological confrontation. This fact remained problematic for those who saw the defeat of communism as a moral imperative; yet it soon became apparent that such logic carried with it the danger of a war that would eliminate capitalism as well as communism. Although antagonistic, the two superpowers accepted a shared interest in preventing their antagonism from getting out of hand. Nonetheless, no real peace could be called into being in such a battle of ideas. The Cold War competition continued in terms of working out two alternative forms of economic and social organization, even while proposals for liberating crusades—on both sides—lost their edge.

The 1960s began with a presumption that the two systems would eventually converge, with the logic of Western democracy marrying with Eastern economic planning. Even as it became apparent in the 1970s that the socialist planned economy was a dismal failure, many in Europe still widely supposed that somehow the injection of Western technology and financing could support economic and political reform in the East. In any event, the coexistence of two such sharply differentiated systems remained inherently unstable, especially once one system demonstrated an unassailable superiority in satisfying the economic, as well as the political, needs of its people. This reality gnawed away at the bipolar balance in Europe until, eventually, the ideological foundation of Soviet power collapsed.[11]

The Cold War's preoccupation with European security meant that the West did not fully explore the implications of developments beyond Europe. Here the balance between ideology and strategy was different. In Europe, the competing ideologies had superpower sponsors. Elsewhere, the most dynamic ideological force was neither capitalism nor communism but anticolonialism. The United States could claim its own anticolonial credentials. As with Russia, its own colonization had been on a continental rather than a maritime basis. For a while, the old colonial powers of Britain and France attempted to demonstrate that communism had inspired and sustained anticolonialism. Gradually, they had to accept the authenticity of anticolonial movements and dispose of their empires.

The United States perceived this process not as an opportunity to acquire more colonies of its own but rather as one to encourage the spread of Western ideology. The Soviets took a similar view with state socialism. As a result, the connections with the wider ideological struggle and the consequent temptation to obtain external support through ideological claims often complicated the struggle for power within the newly independent states. In regions lacking the discipline of the European-style balance, Washington could imagine how internal instabilities in some countries might lead them to fall under Moscow's influence. On this basis, the United States backed regimes that were demonstrably anticommunist, often with no more than a faint hope that U.S. help might eventually be reciprocated by allegiance to liberal political values.

U.S. foreign policy emphasized less and less the promotion of American values and more and more resistance to Soviet-backed advances and was thus vulnerable to manipulation by those claiming that any measures with an apparently socialist inspiration represented a strategic challenge. Over time the superpowers realized that an attempt to shape the politics of the Third World was a costly and wearisome game. By the end of the 1980s both contestants viewed regional conflicts with greater discrimination and evident reluctance to commit resources, and certainly troops, unless vital interests were at stake.

America's Response to the End of the Cold War

This brings us to the situation that has developed since the Cold War's end. The United States' successful conclusion of that conflict, combined with its success in the Gulf War, resulted in the appearance of the United States as holding a position alone, not even primus inter pares among great powers but as the sole superpower.[12] The United States appeared to have everything going for it: the implosion and then apparent taming of its main adversary; established alliances with most of the other great powers; the demonstrated superiority not only of its armed forces but also of its political principles, social values, and economic philosophy. President George Bush proclaimed a "new world order."

However, this new world order was an aspiration and not a reality. It was either banal, in noting a sharp discontinuity in world politics, or else a rhetorical device that ignored the existence of basic tensions in responding to the demands of the new strategic environment.[13] This chapter has identified three possible tensions in strategic policy making: between a general responsibility for international order and the specific security problems of the great power itself; between the prevention of large-scale violence and a concern for the rights of smaller states; and between the promotion of liberalism and the inherent, disorderly implications of taking this ideology seriously.

The United States conducted the crisis, which began with the Iraqi invasion of Kuwait on 2 August 1990, in a manner consistent with its determination to enforce the traditional principles of international order, with particular respect for states' rights. For Bush the novel element in the pursuit of world order was simply the readiness of the Soviet Union to cooperate in this task. Despite his talk of justice, he had little interest in the United States' assuming responsibility for the universal protection of human and minority rights. Bush had no desire to govern foreign, and notoriously difficult, countries, hence his unwillingness to order American forces to advance to Baghdad to remove the Iraqi regime after its forces had collapsed in battle.

U.S. indifference to the domestic conduct of the Iraqi government proved impossible to maintain after Saddam moved with characteristic ferocity against the Kurdish and Shia insurrections in March 1991. Bush, along with other international leaders, appears then to have become carried away with the idea that in the new world order, individual and minority rights would exist equally alongside state rights as an international interest, each deserving determined action by the United Nations. The Kurdish precedent helped establish the conception. The new doctrine appeared to assert that when governments pursued vicious and repressive policies—as in Iraq and Haiti—or where there had been a complete breakdown of law and order—as in Somalia—then human and minority rights could take precedence over state rights. This, as mentioned earlier, is the principled but disorderly logic of liberalism.

There was a view that would take such logic much further, toward denying the existence of strategic imperatives—not so much modifying, as sweeping aside, the belief in a great-power state system. According to this view, states were becoming increasingly irrelevant, obliged to bow before the demands of global markets and communications. Critics posit that transnational actors and problems that could only be addressed on a global scale were now mocking traditional notions of sovereignty. Out of such models emerged hopes for a calmer future based on the triumph of liberal democracy and free markets. This view argued for a mission to ensure this triumph by targeting countries, large and small, still struggling to unburden themselves of the shackles of authoritarian government, dogmatic ideologies, and closed economies.

There were elements of such a view within the Clinton administration, which prepared to define the promotion of democracy as a core foreign policy objective. Here it could claim to be riding the crest of a historical tide. Coupled with a concept of a unipolar world, the task of American foreign policy appeared indubitably hegemonic. Yet, if the United States were to follow such logic, it must also be ready to interfere in the politics of all regions of the world, to take on exactly that role as "world policeman" that American politicians readily disavow even as they accept some limited, international responsibilities. Questions of power and interest, as well as the stubborn refusal of dark and aberrant practices to yield to progress, could still contradict the great mission. The Clinton administration has had to contemplate a state system notable as much for its fragmentation and consequent diffusion of power as for its global, integrative forces.

In such circumstances, the more parochial concerns of a self-interested state with limited resources to spare for external affairs came to qualify profoundly the hegemonic logic of a universalist philosophy. A widespread sense in the United States that the nation had already paid too great a price for its role as leader of the Western world reinforced tendencies toward caution. The political elites had become convinced of a declining national tolerance for the sacrifices entailed in substantial military interventions, although the evidence suggests that the key factor was whether American forces suffered casualties to no obvious purpose. The 1983–84 debacle in Beirut probably crystallized American attitudes here as much as the Vietnam experience. The Gulf War was the exception to the rule: its positive image reflected the small price (both in financial and human terms) and the speed of the battlefield success—even though Saddam Hussein's dogged grip on power in Iraq eventually deprived the victory of much luster. For these reasons, any American president forming an administration at the start of 1993 would have been reluctant to dabble in the problems of distant regions, or to assert foreign over domestic priorities.

Experts saw the wellspring of Clinton's success in 1992 as the result of popular irritation with the American government's neglect of domestic problems—particularly health care, education, and urban violence—along with an excessively lenient attitude toward the unfair trade practices of allies who had proved all too ready to bite the hand that had protected them against communism. American political leaders could rationalize sensitivity to these domestic discontents in terms of a universalist liberal philosophy, that is, a belief in free trade, but their practice tended toward the unilateral pursuit of the particular complaints of hard-hit industries and regions. Domestic economic weaknesses also influenced the provision of the international reserve currency, in the form of the dollar. The shift in the position of the United

States from a creditor into a debtor nation, set firmly in motion by the Reagan administration, complicated even more the interaction between national interests and international responsibilities.

Moreover, in contrast to Bush, Clinton represented a generation with good reason to be uncomfortable with the exercise of American power—its perspectives shaped not by the fight against Nazism nor the early simplicities of the Cold War, but by the moral dilemmas of Vietnam and the broader confusion of a world that no longer seemed divided into a battleground between good and evil. Clinton came to appreciate that patriotism and sacrifice were not to be mocked and that leaders who disclaimed interest in military force as an instrument of policy were likely to incite even more awkward challenges. But those of his generation remain genuinely troubled by the use of force. They know too well the reasons why it is likely to be unpopular, and they have rehearsed, in past speeches and policy platforms, the many ways in which military interventions go wrong. They do not trust the military—a feeling the military reciprocates. They expect the exercise of American power to serve a high moral purpose and thus prefer to exercise it in the name of ideological values, such as democracy and free trade, and as part of a multilateral effort in which they can forge and act upon the broadest possible international consensus, with contributions according to capacities. Yet, they dare not push international interests too far at the cost of perceived national interests.

For all these reasons, Clinton was never going to lead a "pay any price, bear any burden" administration; nor was he, however, ready to tear up America's international commitments. The new administration was going to have to find a balance among the competing pressures on American policy makers. Clinton's uncertain touch as he established his presidency meant that these pressures intensified rather than eased, especially in view of inordinate attention paid to the discordant voices of Congressional opinion.

Not surprisingly, the overriding impression of the first two years has been one of confusion and inconsistency in the conduct of foreign policy, policies moved by events rather than long-term philosophy. Even the pursuit of more selfish goals, the pursuit of domestic rather than international needs, was often hesitant and displayed a sense of the limits rather than the potential of superpower. In Somalia and Bosnia, and initially in Haiti, the overriding impression was of aversion to any risks. The Clinton administration took tough stances in rhetoric but failed to follow through in practice. In Bosnia, the British and French became exasperated over the American tendency to occupy the moral high ground with everything but troops and with the general lack of seriousness in the development of U.S. policy. The Clinton determination to promote democracy in China by using trade as a weapon crumbled as it became apparent that such an approach risked the United States' jeopardizing its position in a fast-growing, massive economy. Meanwhile, the devaluation of the dollar to hurt Japanese exporters made it harder to attract funds into the United States to meet the deficit. Even in areas where American diplomats made great progress—for example, the Middle East—the administration appeared to be following events rather than shaping them.

During the administration's second year, there was evidence that it had learned some hard lessons. Its Bosnian policy remained beyond redemption, and its every move seemed to worsen matters—threatening relations with key allies and undermining the United Nations while doing little for the Muslims. Elsewhere, Clinton had opportunities to stand tough and look determined. In October 1994, he authorized a substantial deployment of troops to Kuwait in the face of menacing Iraqi maneuvers close to the border, though this was in support of an established commitment rather than the creation of a new one. In Korea the administration apparently curtailed Pyongyang's military nuclear options in return for substantial help in developing its civilian nuclear options. The most substantial interference in regional politics, other than the continued economic destabilization of Cuba, came with the successful replacement of the military rulers in Haiti with President Aristide (although how successful the reconstruction of Haiti will prove remains to be seen). As in Korea, the ubiquitous Jimmy Carter played a last-minute role as quasi-official mediator. The administration was now willing to recognize the limits to economic pressure; it would have to back up coercive diplomacy with a credible threat of force as well as the availability of a credible negotiated outcome.

When Clinton entered office, there were reports that he hardly saw his secretary of state: by the end of the first two years he had personally involved himself in Middle Eastern shuttle diplomacy—gaining a Jordanian-Israeli Treaty and pushing Syria and Israel toward some sort of deal. At a time of tumultuous transition within Russia, Clinton worked at reassuring the Russians that he was not trying to exploit their weakness. At the same time he urged them not to use American policy as an excuse to intimidate others, especially the Baltic states. When the Republicans captured both the Senate and the House of Representatives in November 1992, commentators assumed that the president's inability to achieve much on the home front would lead this most domestic of presidents to increase his interest in international politics. On the other hand, the Republican agenda threatened to diminish his freedom of maneuver by cutting overseas aid budgets and U.S. support for the United Nations and by emphasizing a preference for unilateral action over the multilateral—even if that meant inaction in practice.

America's Role in the Future

The pattern of American foreign policy is not simply a function of the competence or transitory interests of the president, nor does it reduce to a struggle between isolationist instincts and international responsibilities. The United States can no more disengage from the world than it can organize distant regions according to its own designs. It remains the world's most substantial great power, but the limits on its power are profound. The world no longer works in such a fashion that great powers can decide the fate of lesser powers amongst themselves or sustain expansive and ambitious objectives beyond their immediate neighborhoods.

An attempt to define a "world role" is therefore liable to be a futile exercise. The United States must be discriminating in terms of targeting efforts and resources. Two areas of influence are of central importance to American interests. The first is Central America and the Caribbean. Here disruptive local events could impinge upon domestic American politics, most notably in the form of refugees. The second area covers the core alliance commitments in Western Europe, East Asia, the Middle East, and the Gulf. Other areas will be of marginal interest to the United States. Thus, despite its past involvement in the politics of Liberia, the United States was passive in the face of the recent collapse of that country.

In its areas of interest the United States has not followed a single set of policies but has juggled competing concerns in the promotion of democracy and human rights, the defense of national interests, and the pursuit of "order." In its own neighborhood, the United States has shown the capacity and the will to act in a decisive fashion to support such objectives. Matters become more difficult in the context of relations with established allies. By and large, with the exception of the Gulf and parts of East Asia, support for these alliances does not contradict support for liberal democracy. There were intimations during the Gulf crisis of a distaste on the part of some Americans for supporting nondemocratic states, and to the extent that this theme remains, it may limit support to Gulf states in the face of indigenous threats. The fate of the Shah of Iran is eloquent in this respect, but so is the fate of post-Shah Iran. Domestic challenges to Gulf regimes provide the obvious areas where the tension between a concern for order, especially when backed by clear national interests, and a belief in democracy may well manifest itself.

Trade issues provide a more serious source of disruption to critical alliance relations. This risk has grown with the shifting balance of interest within Washington between traditional strategic rivalries and contemporary economic competition. Those of a "realist" persuasion warn of great power struggles to come as a replacement for the Cold War and tend to see new challengers emerging from among the current set of U.S. allies (Japan or Germany). Such challengers would derive their power, at least in the first instance, from economic strength.

The United States has certainly turned on the pressure in trade negotiations with both its European and Asian allies. However, Washington's interests in trade, and the domestic salience of the issue, derive from weakness rather than strength. The complexity of contemporary international trade limits the capacity for advanced states to wage trade wars with confidence and, eventually, commercial profit (unless one supposes that states might be able to wage such wars for market share). As with democracy, the trade issue may not be one that will by itself tear the alliances apart, but it could limit commitments at crucial moments.

By and large, America's allies are not a disorderly bunch. They represent the wealthier and more stable parts of the world. While all may have domestic travails and some have been through substantial internal upheavals, it is only nondemocratic nations that have serious question marks about their long-term prospects. Nor, at the moment, are most of America's industrialized allies seriously challenged by the kind of strategic threat that inspired the formation of the original alliances. As these are all states with whom the United States will want to maintain cordial relations, and as the current demands of alliance do not seem so great, the inclination will be to hold existing alliances as steady as possible. It is not so much a sense of shared threat, but the positive impulses of shared values and inertia that will hold the center.

If the requirements of order involve sustaining a congenial alliance in conditions without great threat, then the demands of foreign policy do not appear too arduous. As it is, the crises that gain media attention and require emergency sessions of the Security Council tend to be in marginal areas of the world. Such crises impinge on the alliances but do not represent a core threat. The concerns of German policy makers with regard to Eastern Europe or of the French with regard to North Africa may have more to do with the knock-on effects of economic chaos and the social consequences of mass migration than old-fashioned aggression by hostile states. Such problems need not directly threaten the allies and certainly will not affect the United States. As a result, one can suppose that American policy will become semidetached, leaving it up to those most closely involved to set the terms of a Western "line." America will still provide some support, probably confirming rather than clarifying matters.

The most important and difficult relations are liable to be with those two great powers outside of the old U.S. alliance systems—namely, Russia and China. No longer are either on collision courses with the West. The

"Dengist" revolution in Chinese foreign policies and economics long preceded the collapse of the Soviet Union. Yet Russia and China remain problematic, the former because of its accumulating weaknesses, the latter because of its growing strength, and both because of their nuclear arsenals. American interest remains largely one of ensuring that there are no external repercussions as both follow paths away from state socialism. Managing this kind of great-power politics is qualitatively different from the power politics of the past. There will also be the awkward tensions between the interests of small countries in the vicinity of great powers, made no less difficult by their great-power neighbors' being in internal disarray, and between the vision of universal democracy and the immediate requirements of order and stability. However, such power politics are more complex and ambiguous than those that led in the past to fears of world war on the one hand and condominium on the other.

Conclusion

All this explains why the search for a great-power role has become anachronistic. It is a notion rendered anomalous through the passing of an international system dominated by a few such powers upon whose relations the fate of all depended. Some insist that the international system still generates imperatives for great-power competition, so that whatever its current protestations and even alliances, the United States is almost doomed to find itself in an economically generated conflict with Japan.[14]

Yet the resemblance between the contemporary international system and that of earlier periods is slight. One does not have to overstate the importance of economic interdependence, or acknowledge the complexity of contemporary trade and financial relationships, or argue for the irrelevance of the modern state to recognize that the state has shed a number of its earlier functions. The most important changes, at any rate, are not in the economic but in the political and military spheres. The first is the dramatic decline in the territorial interests of great powers. The second is in the existence of many new states with the ability to thwart or frustrate any attempt by outside powers to organize their affairs. The arrogance with which great powers dealt with the meek until quite recently will no longer hold. As the contemporary system contains so many diverse units, inherent limits will exist on the influence that even the strongest can exert. With the single, and large, exception of nuclear weapons, engagement in the generality of international conflicts will increasingly be a matter of genuine choice rather than as a response to the demands of the system or of clear strategic imperatives.

This is particularly true for the United States, which can, for the most part, pick and choose *its* crises because most will have scant impact on the life of Americans. U.S. choices may reflect the concerns of allies, or the interest of segments of the American population, or even the whims of the president. Nothing here adds up to a role. By and large, states will sort out their relations with each other with slight interference from North America. When large issues arise they may still look to Washington for leadership, but with little confidence that they will get it.

There is no question that the United States remains the most substantial international power and can take a lead and enforce its will in most international crises if it desires to do so. The problem is that the potential costs of initiatives have risen substantially, or at least no longer seem proportionate to the national interests involved. The risk in such circumstances is that the United States will attempt to identify what one might describe as proportionate participation, that is, it will engage in the problems of the wider world to a level believed to be commensurate with its interests. However, the effort required to make a difference to a given problem may well, in these terms, be quite disproportionate—in terms of the resources required to provide a degree of economic stability or the forces needed to calm a conflict and enforce a peace. In which case, proportionate participation will only work if others participate as well in order to create a sufficiently large pool of resources. In turn, this will mean that the United States will need to develop a culture of multilateralism, which, for the moment, appears inimical to opinion in Washington.

For the United States, as for Britain earlier, the period in which it can exert power independently and separately from multilateral institutions is drawing to a close. The demands of the new situation may well appear to be messy and frustrating or not even worth the effort. The possibility that the United States may make such a choice is understood, and increasingly accepted, by America's allies. The alternatives are that the United States remains activist and engaged, but such a course would require either a readiness to commit substantial resources to problems of marginal interest or else a readiness to accept a more modest role as part of a broadly based effort. The option that is not available is a demand for the freedom of unilateralism combined with a parsimonious approach to commitments. That will simply result in halfhearted meddling, irritating allies for minimal achievement.

Defense Publications

T his list includes many books published during 1993 and 1994 on U.S. national security issues. Books are grouped in the following categories: arms control; defense budget and political issues; defense strategy; history; NATO and European security; nuclear weapons and strategy; multilateralism, peace keeping, and peace making; proliferation; regional security; terrorism; intelligence; yearbooks and databases; and other issues.

Arms Control

McGeorge Bundy, William J. Crowe, and Sidney D. Drell, *Reducing Nuclear Danger: The Road Away from the Brink* (New York, 1993), Council on Foreign Relations Press. 107 pp. A prescription for international action to reduce nuclear arsenals and stop proliferation.

Malcolm Dando, *Biological Warfare in the 21st Century* (London, 1994), Brassey's Ltd. 226 pp. An assessment of biological warfare and proliferation that concerns itself with the history of such weapons as well as the potential for their control.

Peter van Ham, *Managing Non-Proliferation Regimes in the 1990s: Power, Politics, and Policies* (New York, 1994), Council on Foreign Relations Press. 112 pp. The author provides an overview of the agreements, organizations, and issues of proliferation-control regimes concerning weapons of mass destruction.

Defense Budget and Political Issues

David A. Deese, *The New Politics of American Foreign Policy* (New York, 1994), St. Martin's Press. 336 pp. This collection of original essays surveys the roles and limitations of foreign policy actors—including public opinion, the media, Congress, and the executive branch—on developing and implementing policy.

The Presidential Commission on the Assignment of Women in the Armed Forces, *Women in Combat: Report to the President* (McLean, VA, 1994), Brassey's Inc. A broad coverage of key women's issues relating to military structures and developments. The Commission is composed of prominent Americans from both the public and private sectors.

Defense Strategy

Leon Aron and Kenneth M. Jensen, eds., *The Emergence of Russian Foreign Policy* (Washington, DC, 1994), United States Institute of Peace Press. 256 pp. This volume addresses defense and foreign policy issues facing Russia. Topics include relations with the Near Abroad and the Commonwealth of Independent States, the role of Russian peacekeeping in former Soviet states, and others.

Aspen Strategy Group Report, *Securing Peace in the New Era: Politics in the Former Soviet Union and the Challenge to American Security* (Queenstown, MD, 1994), Brookings Books. 150 pp. A report of proceedings at an Aspen Strategy Group conference that brought together leading experts on the newly independent states of the former Soviet Union to consider the high-stakes issue of managing U.S. relations with those states.

Barry L. Blechman, William J. Durch, David R. Graham, John H. Henshaw, Pamela L. Reed, Victor A. Utgoff, and Steven A. Wolfe, *The American Military in the 21st Century* (New York, 1994), St. Martin's Press. 530 pp. This work assesses likely roles and missions for the U.S. military in the next century in the service of national defense and foreign policy needs.

Paul Davis, ed., *New Challenges for Defense Planning: Rethinking How Much Is Enough* (Santa Monica, CA, 1994), Rand. 800 pp. A collection of essays by senior Rand analysts on a variety of topics on the structuring of new ways to examine post–Cold War defense planning.

Christopher Gacek, *The Logic of Force: Limited Wars in American Foreign Policy* (Irvington, NY, 1994), Columbia University Press. 370 pp. A study that explores the tension between decisive force levels and limits to the use of force through several case studies including Vietnam, the Gulf War, and Somalia.

Raymond L. Garthoff, *The Great Transition: American-Soviet Relations and the End of the Cold War* (Washington, DC, 1994), Brookings Books. 700 pp. A historical analysis of the perspectives and actions of the United States and the Soviet Union from 1981 through the collapse of the communist bloc that draws on many recently released or declassified sources.

David M. Glantz, *The Military Strategy of the Soviet Union* (Portland, OR, 1993), Frank Cass Publishers. 368 pp. A historical study of the development of Soviet military strategy focusing on political-military actions and incorporating key documentation hitherto unavailable in the West.

William W. Kaufmann, *Assessing the Base Force: How Much Is Too Much?* (Washington, DC, 1993), Brookings Books. 97 pp. An examination of the 1990 Defense Department Base Force as a relic of the Cold War that can be questioned and reduced.

History

Seyom Brown, *The Faces of Power: United States Foreign Policy from Truman to Clinton* (Irvington, NY, 1994), Columbia University Press. 712 pp. This second edition examines the premises adopted by American policy makers in shaping national interests and goals during the Cold War and beyond.

The Central Intelligence Agency, *The Secret Cuban Missile Crisis Documents* (McLean, VA, 1994), Brassey's Inc. 414 pp. A volume of recently declassified documents relating to the crisis and surrounding events. Introduction by Graham T. Allison Jr.

Richard Clutterbuck, *International Crisis and Conflict* (New York, 1994), St. Martin's Press. 388 pp. Through twenty-four different case studies, the author examines factors influencing crisis management and war in history and forecasts future patterns of conflict.

Eliot Cohen, ed., *Gulf War Air Power Survey* (Washington, DC, 1994), Government Printing Office. 5 vols. This ambitious work examines in detail the planning, operations, effects and effectiveness, logistics, training, tactics, and weapons of the air war in the Gulf. Professor Cohen headed a multidisciplinary team of airmen and scholars in this exhaustive study.

Henry Kissinger, *Diplomacy* (New York, 1994), Simon and Schuster. 912 pp. A study of modern diplomacy focused on the existence of the conflict between American idealism and realpolitik.

Diane B. Lane, ed., *The Diplomacy of the Crucial Decade: American Foreign Relations During the 1960s* (Irvington, NY, 1994), Columbia University Press. 376 pp. A collection that highlights the fight against communism, especially in the developing world, as the motivational force for American foreign policy of the 1960s.

Allan Millett, *In Many a Strife: General C. Thomas and the United States Marine Corps, 1917–1956* (Annapolis, MD, 1993), Naval Institute Press. 456 pp. A biography of an influential marine officer whose mustang career began at Belleau Wood and ended in the Cold War. His experiences help chronicle the transition of the marines from colonial infantry to Cold War force in readiness.

Allan R. Millett and Peter Maslowski, *For the Common Defense: A Military History of the United States of America* (New York, 1994), The Free Press. 701 pp. This expanded and revised edition places American military history within the broader reach of social history. It includes material on the Gulf War as well as the role of history in shaping future policy.

Williamson Murray, MacGregor Knox, and Alvin Bernstein, eds., *The Making of Strategy: Rulers, States, and War* (New York, 1994), Cambridge University Press. 680 pp. This collection of essays examines the process of making strategy from the Peloponnesian War until the present. From a common interpretive perspective, the studies analyze how states and rulers — tyrants, kings, and presidents — have made strategy.

William O'Neill, *A Democracy at War: America's Fight at Home and Abroad in World War II* (New York, 1993). The Free Press. 400 pp. A story of the struggle between democratic politics and the American war effort in the 1940s.

Inderjeet Parmar, *Special Interests, the State and the Anglo-American Alliance, 1939–1945* (Portland, OR, 1994), Frank Cass Publishers. 256 pp. An examination of the origins of the alliance during the Second World War, encompassing studies of the interaction of elites and institutions and of the relationship between democracy and the war effort.

Gerhard Weinberg, *A World at Arms: A Global History of World War II* (Cambridge, 1993), Cambridge University Press. 1,225 pp. This thorough, integrated history looks at the war with moral outrage at the individuals who unleashed this horrific spasm of violence on the world. *A World at Arms* will become the premier study of the Second World War.

James A. Winnefield, Preston Niblack, and Dana J. Johnson, *A League of Airmen: U.S. Air Power in the Gulf War* (Santa Monica, CA, 1994), Rand. 400 pp. An analysis of the influence of modern air war on the Persian Gulf War.

NATO and European Security

Martin Baldwin-Edwards and Martin Schain, eds., *The Politics of Immigration in Western Europe* (Portland, OR, 1994), Frank Cass Publishers. 200 pp. An analysis of the political and security implications of mass immigration in Europe, attending to specific problems in Western European countries.

Alexis Heraclides, *Security and Cooperation in Europe: The Human Dimension 1972–1992* (Portland, OR, 1993), Frank Cass Publishers. 217 pp. An in-depth examination of the Conference on Security and Cooperation in Europe, examining its achievements and the controversies relating to the human dimension.

Richard L. Kugler, *Commitment to Purpose: How Alliance Partnership Won the Cold War* (Santa Monica, CA, 1994), Rand. 635 pp. An analysis of the central role of the NATO alliance in Cold War events and policies.

Harold S. Orenstein, trans., *Soviet Documents on the Use of War Experience: Military Operations 1941 and 1942* (Portland, OR, 1993), Frank Cass Publishers. 280 pp. The final volume in a series examining what Soviet military theorists and commanders have learned from the study of their own military operations.

Trevor Taylor, ed., *Reshaping European Defense* (Washington, DC, 1994), Brookings Books. 128 pp. A brief but authoritative assessment of how Great Britain, France, Germany, Italy, and the Netherlands are reviewing their defense needs for the twenty-first century.

Nuclear Weapons and Strategy

Glenn C. Buchan, *U.S. Nuclear Strategy for the Post–Cold War Era* (Santa Monica, CA, 1994), Rand. 83 pp. A discussion by this veteran analyst of various "nuclear futures" that might involve and influence the United States.

Multilateralism, Peacekeeping, and Peace Making

Ashton B. Carter, William J. Perry, and John D. Steinbruner, *A New Concept of Cooperative Security* (Washington, DC, 1993), Brookings Books. 65 pp. The authors apply cooperative security as a mechanism for controlling weapons proliferation.

Robert W. Gregg, *About Face: The United States and the United Nations* (Boulder, CO, 1993), Lynne Rienner Publishers. 150 pp. A review and analysis of the turbulent relationship between the United States and the United Nations, which concludes with an examination of future possibilities for engagement.

Janet E. Heininger, *Peacekeeping in Transition: The United Nations in Cambodia* (Washington, DC, 1994), Brookings Books. 160 pp. A study of the United Nations' largest, most ambitious, and most costly peacekeeping operation, the United Nations Transitional Administration in Cambodia (UNTAC).

Rosemary Righter, *Utopia Lost: The United Nations and World Order* (Washington, DC, 1994), Brookings Books. 400 pp. An examination of the role of the United Nations in international peacekeeping and a critique of UN efforts to adjust to more active multilateral diplomacy and its new role in the international system.

Proliferation

Andrew J. Pierre, ed., *Cascade of Arms: Controlling Conventional Weapons Proliferation in the 1990s* (Washington, DC, 1994), Brookings Books. 385 pp. This book discusses the opportunities and obstacles for the neglected dimension of conventional arms restraints in the post–Cold War world.

Regional Security

John Coakley, ed., *The Territorial Management of Ethnic Conflict* (Portland, OR, 1993), Frank Cass Publishers. 230 pp. A survey of the way that states respond to and cope with ethnic conflict, using case studies from around the world.

Alexis Heraclides, *Self-Determination of Minorities in International Politics* (Portland, OR, 1993), Frank Cass Publishers. 291 pp. A study of separatist and secessionist movements, investigating the origins and dynamics of this multifaceted problem and its implications for international security.

John W. Holmes, ed., *Maelstrom: The United States, Southern Europe, and the Challenges of the Mediterranean* (Washington, DC, 1994), Brookings Books. 260 pp. A discussion of the prospects for cooperation in the Mediterranean between the United States and the nations of southern Europe to respond to new challenges in the world.

Susan L. Woodward, *Balkan Tragedy: Chaos and Dissolution After the Cold War* (Washington, DC, 1994), Brookings Books. 385 pp. An analysis of the causes of the Yugoslav wars and the role that international intervention has played in exacerbating the conflict.

Terrorism

Maxwell Taylor, *Terrorist Lives* (London, 1994), Brassey's Ltd. This book, based largely on previously unpublished interviews, examines the experience of personal involvement in terrorism. Professor Taylor looks at this behavior through an interdisciplinary lens of political science, psychology, and criminal justice.

Intelligence

Christopher Andrew and Oleg Gordievsky, *More Instructions from the Centre: Top Secret Files on KGB Global Operations 1975–1985* (Portland, OR, 1993), Frank Cass Publishers. 130 pp. An analysis of selected top-secret documents from KGB files secreted away by double agent Gordievsky. It offers a revealing insight into the attitudes, prejudices, and fears of the KGB during its declining years.

Yearbooks and Databases

The Central Intelligence Agency, *The World Factbook: 1994–95* (McLean, VA, 1994), Brassey's Inc. 420 pp. A comprehensive compendium of unclassified data on every country from Afghanistan to Zimbabwe.

Centre for Defence Studies, *Brassey's Defence Yearbook 1994* (London, 1994), Brassey's Ltd. 400 pp. This yearbook provides comment and analysis on current defense and security policies.

The International Institute for Strategic Studies, *The Military Balance 1994–1995* (London, 1994), Brassey's Ltd. An up-to-date annual survey of the world's armed forces that covers more than 160 countries.

Other Issues: The Environment and Economic Security

Martin Binkin, *Who Will Fight the Next War? The Changing Face of the American Military* (Washington, DC, 1994), Brookings Books. 220 pp. Addressing the military roles and influences of racial minorities, women, and the reserve components on military effectiveness, the author argues for the involvement of the public in shaping the post–Cold War armed services.

Paul H. Nitze, *Tension Between Opposites: Reflections on the Practice and Theory of Politics* (New York, 1994), Scribner's. 212 pp. The author, a distinguished public servant, sets down a brief set of theoretical observations about politics and applies them to some of the most famous policy makers and decisions of post–World War II international relations.

Caroline Thomas, ed., *Rio: Unravelling the Consequences* (Portland, OR, 1994), Frank Cass Publishers. 240 pp. An interdisciplinary collection of arguments about the potential impact of the Rio agreement on state coordination of policies to deal with environmental issues and on their implications for international security and stability in the new era.

The "Clash of Civilizations": The Debate (New York, 1994), Council on Foreign Relations Press. 64 pp. The complete text of Samuel P. Huntington's controversial 1993 *Foreign Affairs* article "The Clash of Civilizations?" and comments by seven distinguished critics. Critics include Jeane J. Kirkpatrick and Fouad Ajami.

Endnotes

Introduction

1. Thucydides, *History of the Peloponnesian War*, trans. Rex Warner (New York, 1986), p. 80.

2. On the argument that history had ended with the collapse of the Soviet Union or that we are about to enter a more peaceful and less contentious world see Francis Fukuyama, "The End of History?" *National Interest*, 16, Summer 1989; John Mueller, *Retreat from Doomsday: The Obsolescence of Major War* (New York, 1988); and Carl Builder, *The Icarus Syndrome: The Role of Air Power Theory in the Evolution and Fate of the U.S. Air Force* (New Brunswick, NJ, 1994). On the other side see Samuel Huntington's "The Clash of Civilizations," *Foreign Affairs*, 72:3, Summer 1993. For an instructive discussion on how history and human struggle have *not* turned out to reflect the hopes and aspirations of the optimists, see Michael Howard, *War and the Liberal Conscience: The George Macaulay Trevelyan Lectures in the University of Cambridge* (New Brunswick, NJ, 1978).

3. One must also note dark predictions that heavily emphasize overpopulation and the collapse of civil society, based on a harder look at much of the world than the optimists' views. See in particular Robert D. Kaplan, "The Coming Anarchy," *Atlantic Monthly*, February 1994; Thomas F. Homer-Dixon, Jeffrey H. Boutwell, and George W. Rathjens, "Environmental Change and Violent Conflict," *Scientific American*, February 1993; and Matt Connelly and Paul Kennedy, "The Rest Against the West," *Atlantic Monthly*, 25 August 1994.

4. We should not single out the American polity for its contempt of the past. After all, the Germans managed to repeat their grand strategic concepts and mistakes in two world wars with disastrous results not only for themselves but for Europe and the world. See Williamson Murray, *German Military Effectiveness* (Baltimore, MD, 1992), chap. 1.

5. Interestingly, in the late 1980s Andrew Marshall, Director of Net Assessment in the Pentagon, asked a group of historians to examine the governmental processes of net assessment in the late 1930s—a study that he believed would be particularly useful for examining the processes of strategic assessment in a world that was not dominated by two superpowers. The result was the study edited by Williamson Murray and Allan R. Millett, *Calculations, Net Assessment, and the Coming of World War II* (New York, 1992).

6. Thucydides, *Peloponnesian War*, p. 80.

7. Quoted in N. Thompson, *The Anti-Appeasers* (Oxford, 1971), pp. 156–57.

8. In an address to the Atlantic Pact Foreign Ministers on 3 April 1949, President Harry Truman commented: "The Atlantic Pact is a long step forward in the development of a common-offensive. . . . But none of us are under any illusions that the Atlantic Pact itself is more than a symbol of our common determination, a contract, as it were, under which our new partnership must now proceed to develop the concrete means of first containing, then defeating World Communism. When I say defeating, I do not mean nor countenance aggressive war. I mean rather the building up of a power balance sufficient to destroy the destabilizing fear of Soviet aggression and then, from this secure power base, taking active measures, on the one hand to remove in the non-Soviet world the social and economic pressures on which Communism thrives, and on the other hand to create active counterpressure to undermine the base of Soviet power itself." Memorandum of Conversation, The White House, 3 April 1949, Harry S. Truman Library.

9. Here one should remember that the opposition to the Marshall Plan and other manifestations of an American commitment to Europe came not just from the Henry Wallaces on the left but from the right wing and the likes of Robert Taft, not to mention the American mandarin in the Far East, General Douglas MacArthur.

10. Their victory as well as their lonely struggle against the tide of academic wishful thinking is well documented in an issue of *National Interest* (Spring 1993) devoted to their courage and integrity.

11. As the United States did during the Gulf War when it deployed its most modern and capable forces to protect the economic and strategic interests of the industrialized, democratic world from the megalomaniac overreach of Saddam Hussein.

12. Paul Kennedy, "British 'Net Assessment' and the Coming of the Second World War," in Murray and Millett, *Calculations*, p. 35.

13. Ibid.

14. The performance of the American military in Haiti and the considerable differences that current reporting has suggested between the contribution presently being made by special forces units—considerable—and those of the Tenth Mountain Division—about zero—underline the unsuitability of U.S. conventional forces to the ambiguities of many of the troubles in the Third World. See Anna Husarska, "Police State, A Military Tour of Haiti," *New Republic*, 23 January 1995.

15. For all intents and purposes, that occurred during the Korean War. The Truman administration viewed the outbreak of the war in Korea as the first step to wider communist moves, probably in Europe. Thus, not only did it deploy massive American forces to the Korean peninsula, but it sent newly formed divisions directly to Europe to deter, but if necessary to fight, the Soviets. This preparation to fight one war and prepare for another at the same time forced Truman to mobilize a substantial portion of America's economic strength, enforce a widespread draft, and even introduce wage and price controls.

16. Andrew Krepinevich, *The Army and Vietnam* (Baltimore, MD, 1986), pp. 104–112.

17. I am indebted to Mr. Robert Gaskin for this point.

18. Of course, during the Cold War we did not have the lift to get a substantial portion of the ground and air forces in the continental United States to Europe in time for the war. This is no reason to build the current forces on the mistaken approaches of the past.

19. We should avoid the trap that the army is apparently falling into at the present time of declaring all of its corps in the continental United States to be "intervention corps." By trying to have everybody prepare for every mission, the army will only create forces that are uniquely unprepared for specific missions.

20. The exercise "Quick Kick" that II MEF and XVIII Airborne Corps have been performing since 1962 suggests the kind of capabilities that we will need for major regional contingencies.

21. The army was not happy with the combat reserve forces that it called up during the Gulf War. This commentator at least suspects that a substantial portion of the problem was that the army had tailored its structure to depend on reserve units for political purposes—the no-more-Vietnam syndrome—but that most senior army generals, as their predecessors have since the days of Emory Upton, held reserve combat formations in unspoken contempt. The marines, however, felt that their reservists were marines just like any others. Consequently, they shipped those called up out to the desert, where they appear to have performed admirably.

22. See in particular Williamson Murray, *Operations*, Vol. II, Pt. I, and Barry D. Watts and Thomas A. Keaney, *Effects and Effectiveness*, Vol. II, Pt. II of *Gulf War Air Power Survey*, ed. Eliot Cohen (Washington, DC, 1994).

23. The author is aware of some apparent contradiction with his conclusion in the *Gulf War Air Power Survey* that the most effective air weapon against the morale of Iraqi forces in the Kuwaiti Theater of Operations was the B-52, which was also the most inaccurate. But the B-52 bombing strikes, because of their enormous size, had a terrible psychological impact on the Iraqis. As Lenin is reputed once to have said, "Quantity has a quality all its own."

24. It is clear the U.S. Army, for example, has not been under significant enemy air attack since early in 1943 in Tunisia. Yet because of the Soviet air threat on Europe's central front during the Cold War, it invested great amounts of time and resources in building up significant antiaircraft capabilities. But the central front has gone away, and so has the threat.

25. The marines have argued that they need their air power to provide the fire support that artillery provides the army. Considering that in any amphibious operations the marines—or the army for that matter—will not have artillery for a considerable period of time, then direct air support that can be used from relatively small ships and then deployed to bare operating areas has great justification. But the marines' own Harrier and helicopters seem much better tailored to this mission than the F/A-18.

Chapter 1
What History Can Tell Us About the "New Strategic Environment"

1. For this definition, see A. J. P. Taylor, *The Struggle for Mastery in Europe, 1848–1918* (Oxford, 1954), p. xxiv.

2. For this concept, which is strategic-analytical rather than psychoanalytical, see Yehezel Dror's classic, *Crazy States: A Counterconventional Strategic Problem* (Milwood, NY,

1980). Some of the realities behind it are at least as old as the Assyrian empire; see especially Karl A. Wittfogel, *Oriental Despotism: A Comparative Study of Total Power*, expanded ed. (New York, 1981).

3. On the consequences and dynamics, rather than the causes, of despotism, Wittfogel's *Oriental Despotism* remains instructive; of the contemporary dictatorships, the most extreme example, unparalleled even in the Middle East in the magnitude and variety of its atrocities, is naturally Ba'athist Iraq; see Kanan Makiya [Samir Al-Khalil, pseud.] *Republic of Fear*, rev. ed. (New York, 1990) and *Cruelty and Silence* (London, 1993).

4. See Simon Leys, "1977 Postscript: Maoism Mummified," in his *The Chairman's New Clothes: Mao and the Cultural Revolution* (London, 1977), p. 206.

5. See the Tocqueville of Japanese politics: Karel van Wolferen, *The Enigma of Japanese Power: People and Politics in a Stateless Nation* (New York, 1989).

6. See especially the reflections of Ian Buruma, *The Wages of Guilt* (London, 1994).

7. Van Wolferen, *Enigma*, passim, but especially chaps. 2 and 15.

8. The Thatcher government's assistance to the U.S. strike against Tripoli in 1986 is an exception that proves the rule of national egotism; Thatcher's domestic popularity suffered, while the French and other allied governments denied overflight rights and reaped domestic benefit.

9. For the embarrassed posturing of the European powers in 1973, see the pithy summary of Walter Laqueur, *Confrontation: The Middle East War and World Politics* (London, 1974), pp. 153–58 ("European Attitudes, or 9 X 0 = 0").

10. For the quoted phrase, see Taylor, *Struggle for Mastery*, p. xix.

11. For "capitalist encirclement," see Robert C. Tucker, "The Emergence of Stalin's Foreign Policy," *Slavic Review* 36 (1977), especially p. 571; for Stalin in 1940 (to Stafford Cripps) on the overthrow of the "old equilibrium," see Llewellyn Woodward, *British Foreign Policy in the Second World War* (London, 1970), 1:470 n. 1; for the final struggle with the United States, see R. C. Raack, "Stalin's Plans for World War II," *Journal of Contemporary History*, 26 (1991), pp. 219–20 and Kreve-Mickevicius report of June 1940 conversations with Molotov and Dekanosov, in U.S. House of Representatives, *Select Committee to Investigate Communist Aggression and the Forced Incorporation of the Baltic States into the U.S.S.R.*, *Third Interim Report*, 83d Cong., 2d sess. (Washington, 1954), pp. 458, 459, 462; and on Stalin's 1951 directive, see the testimony of Karel Kaplan, *Dans les archives du comité central: Trente ans de secrets du Bloc soviétique* (Paris, 1978), p. 165.

12. "Marxist theoreticians": Victor Louis, quoted in Henry Kissinger, *The White House Years* (New York, 1979), p. 185.

13. On the analogy of Italian politics under the First Republic (1946–94), where a *bipartitismo imperfetto* kept the Italian Communist Party from power.

14. See especially the summary of these trends in Paul Kennedy, *Preparing for the Twenty-First Century* (London, 1993), chap. 7.

15. See Alan S. Milward, *The European Rescue of the Nation-State* (London, 1992) and Milward et al., *The Frontier of National Sovereignty: History and Theory 1945–1992* (London, 1993).

16. For the phrase "international social work," see Eliot A. Cohen, "What to Do About National Defense," *Commentary*, November 1994, p. 31 ("social work masquerading as strategy").

17. The account in Liah Greenfeld, *Nationalism: Five Roads to Modernity* (Cambridge, MA, 1992), chap. 4, is exemplary, but for the anti-Semitic component see also Paul L. Rose, *German Question/Jewish Question: Revolutionary Antisemitism from Kant to Wagner* (Princeton, 1992).

18. See Greenfeld, *Nationalism*, for the preindustrial origins of nationalism, in contrast to Ernest Gellner, *Nations and Nationalism* (Ithaca, NY, 1983).

19. See Elie Kedourie, *Nationalism* (London, 1960), pp. 62–71.

20. Gellner, *Nations and Nationalism*, p. 1.

21. See especially Kedourie, *Nationalism*, chap. 3.

22. The widespread if often implicit concept of "liberal nationalism" is profoundly misleading as a guide to reality, since it lumps two very different phenomena: ethnic fanaticism based on a vision of the segmentation of the human species, and the "constitutional patriotism" found in the United States, in part in Britain, and since 1945 in a few other industrial democracies. (For the concept, see above all Yael Tamir, *Liberal Nationalism* [Princeton, 1993]).

23. See Rose, *German Question/Jewish Question*, especially pp. 40–43.

24. One notable (if unsurprising) exception to the rule was George Orwell in "Wells, Hitler and the World State" (1941): "Modern Germany is far more scientific than England, and far more barbarous."

25. For Nazism as a modern phenomenon rather than an "atavism" or "anachronism," see especially Jeffrey Herf, *Reactionary Modernism: Technology, Culture, and Politics in the Third Reich* (Cambridge, 1984) and Michael Prinz and Rainer Zitelmann, eds., *Nationalsozialismus und Modernisierung* (Darmstadt, 1991).

26. I borrow the term from Gellner, *Nations and Nationalism*.

27. I owe the Hapsburg comparison (which is perhaps a bit hard on the Dual Monarchy) to my late colleague and friend at the University of Rochester, Sanford Elwitt.

28. The most forceful statements of this thesis are Michael W. Doyle's, "Kant, Liberal Legacies, and Foreign Affairs," *Philosophy and Public Affairs* 12 (1983), pp. 209–17, and "Liberalism and World Politics," *American Political Science Review* 80:4 (1987). But some of Doyle's data and deductions are questionable. Was Robespierre's France a "constitutionally secure liberal state"? Did Britain become one only in 1832 (thus making the War of 1812 a war declared by a liberal state on a "nonliberal" one)? Did Italy really choose the Entente side in World War I from liberal fellow-feeling, rather than from a calculation of which side offered more and was most likely to win? ("Kant, Liberal Legacies, and Foreign Affairs," p. 209; "Liberalism and World Politics," p. 1156). For a useful survey of many of the major objections to the "democratic peace" thesis, see Raymond Cohen, "Pacific Unions: A Reappraisal of the Theory That 'Democracies Do Not Go to War with Each Other,'" *Review of International Studies*, 20:3 (1994), pp. 207–23.

29. On culture as the decisive source of post–Cold War conflict, see especially Samuel P. Huntington, "The Clash of Civilizations?" *Foreign Affairs*, 72:3 (1993), pp. 22–49, which overstates the novelty of cultural conflict—the Cold War was *also* a clash between the West and states that despite their Marxist ideological veneer were largely non-Western in culture.

30. ". . . yet has a negative object"; Carl von Clausewitz, *On War* (Princeton, 1976), p. 358.

31. Quotations from Charles Krauthammer, "The New Terrorism," *New Republic*, 13/20 August 1984, p. 12; and Tom Shales, "On the Air: The Drama Behind ABC's Coup," *Washington Post*, 20 June 1985, p. D1, respectively.

32. For the underlying cultural lacerations that have been further inflamed by Western media penetration, see Bernard Lewis, "The Roots of Muslim Rage," *Atlantic Monthly*, September 1990; on the function of anti-Western conspiracy theories (and not only in the Muslim world), see especially Daniel Pipes, *In the Path of God: Islam and Political Power* (New York, 1983), pp. 182–87.

33. While aggregate Soviet/Russian arms exports dipped after 1990 due to the collapse of the Soviet Union's external clients, the *quality* of arms and know-how exported—some of it clandestinely through criminal channels—increased markedly.

34. On this theme see above all Paul Kennedy, *The Rise and Fall of the Great Powers* (New York, 1987).

35. Cf. Francis Fukuyama, *The End of History and the Last Man* (New York, 1992).

36. See van Wolferen, *Enigma*, chap. 2; idem, "No Brakes, No Compass," *National Interest*, Fall 1991, pp. 26–35.

37. For a brief analysis, see Kennedy, *Twenty-First Century*, chap. 2; the graphs in C. McEvedy and R. Jones, *Atlas of World Population History* (London, 1978) also remain useful.

38. 1992 percentages calculated from World Bank, *World Development Report 1994* (Oxford, 1994), pp. 213, 228; projections, from idem, *World Development Report 1993* (Oxford, 1993), p. 289 (West: high-income Organization for Economic Cooperation and Development members, less Japan). With Japan the percentages are 14.6 (1992), 13.5 (2000), and 10.7 (2025).

39. Speech at Mannheim, November 5, 1930 (transcript, p. 5, Institut für Zeitgeschichte, Munich, IfZg Fa88, Fasz. 54).

Chapter 2
American Strategic Policy for an Uncertain Future

1. This article reflects the opinions of the author and does not represent the policies of the Defense Department or the United States Government. The author expresses his thanks to Robert Dujarric of the Hudson Institute and Lee Smith for their suggestions for the improvement of this article.

2. *National Security Strategy of the United States* (Washington, DC, 1993) pp. i, 7; *Public Papers of the Presidents of the United States. George Bush 1991, Book I—January 1 to June 30, 1991* (Washington, DC, 1992) [hereafter, *Bush Papers*], pp. 201, 575–77, 626.

3. *Economic Report of the President Transmitted to Congress February 1992* (Washington, DC, 1992), pp. 95–103, 115–24, 143–47; *Economic Report of the President Transmitted to the Congress January 1993* (Washington, DC, 1993) [hereafter, *Economic Report* followed by year], pp. 3, 19, 21, 35–39, 58, 225, 238.

4. *Bush Papers*, pp. 123–24, 221, 238.

5. "Bush Talks of 'Atrocities,'" *New York Times*, 16 October 1990, p. A19; "No Compromise on Kuwait, Bush Says," *New York Times*, 14 October 1990, p. A10.

6. *Bush Papers*, pp. 22, 25, 44, 51.

7. *A National Security Strategy of Engagement and Enlargement* (Washington, DC, 1994).

8. B. R. Mitchell, *International Historical Statistics: Europe 1750–1988*, 3d ed. (Washington, DC, 1992), pp. 890, 891, 894, 897.

9. Ibid., pp. 897, 905, 908; *Economic Report 1992*, pp. 225, 351.

10. Central Intelligence Agency (CIA), *World Factbook 1994* (Washington, DC, 1994), pp. 84, 203, 417; Patrick E. Tyler, "Daunting Challenges for China's Leaders," *New York Times*, 3 January 1995, p. C10.

11. CIA, *World Factbook 1994*, pp. 18, 57, 82, 178, 188, 219, 246, 355, 390, 445; James Brooke, "Higher Growth Seen for Latin America," *New York Times*, 3 January 1995, p. C10.

12. CIA, *World Factbook 1994*, pp. 27, 41, 109, 134, 136, 149, 156, 194, 199, 239, 281, 321, 368, 379, 415, 417. Expressed in purchasing power equivalents, the Central Intelligence Agency estimated the 1993 GNP of the United States as $6.38 trillion and that of the European Union as $5.97 trillion (including the fifteen European Union members as of January 1995).

13. Thucydides, *History of the Peloponnesian War*, trans. Rex Warner with an introduction and notes by M. I. Finley (New York, 1972), pp. 80, 404.

14. Most notably, Francis Fukuyama, *The End of History and the Last Man* (New York, 1992).

15. V. I. Lenin, "Socialism and War" in Robert C. Tucker, ed., *The Lenin Anthology* (New York, 1975), pp. 183–95; Sigmund Freud, *Civilization and Its Discontents* (New York, 1961), pp. 66–68.

16. K. Subrahmanyam, "Understanding Each Other," *Economic Times*, 12 October 1994.

17. The percentages of American GNP spent on defense in fiscal years 1948, 1949, and 1950 were 5.0, 5.1, and 4.6 percent, respectively. American defense expenditures in fiscal year 1992 came to 5.3 percent of GNP, or $315.5 billion. American GNP in 1995 should reach about $6.8 trillion, 4.6 percent of which would equal about $313 billion. The 3.6 percent of GNP that the Bush administration requested for defense in fiscal year 1995 would have amounted to some $245 billion. Fiscal year 1950 national security expenditures came to $13.1 billion in the dollars of the time, or about $75 billion in 1994 dollars. See John Lewis Gaddis, *Strategies of Containment: A Critical Appraisal of Postwar American National Security Policy* (New York, 1982), p. 359; CIA, *World Factbook 1994*, p. 418; Harry G. Summers, *On Strategy II: A Critical Analysis of the Gulf War* (New York, 1992), p. 250; Office of the Assistant Secretary of Defense (Comptroller), *National Defense Budget Estimates for Fiscal Year 1993* (Washington, DC, 1992), pp. 36, 126–27.

18. Clearly, unless the Indian Wars are considered as a single struggle, the Cold War was the longest conflict in American history. But "most expensive" could be applied to the Civil War in terms of loss of life, especially as a percentage of population, or to World War II in terms of the percentage of GNP spent annually. Nonetheless, because of its estimated cost of $11 trillion in 1995 dollars, the Cold War can be described accurately as the most expensive.

19. Department of Defense, *Soviet Military Power 1985* (Washington, DC, 1985), pp. 10, 116–17, 120, 122, 130.

20. CIA, *World Factbook 1994*, pp. 331, 417.

21. Ibid., pp. 329, 416.

22. International Institute for Strategic Studies (IISS), *The Military Balance 1994–1995* (London, 1994), passim. Among American allies are included the members of NATO, Egypt, Israel, Saudi Arabia, Oman, Qatar, United Arab Emirates, Bahrain, Kuwait, Philippines, Japan, South Korea, and Australia.

23. Ibid., p. 111; "Special Focus on Russia and Its 'Near Abroad,'" *Jane's Intelligence Review*, December 1994; Steven Erlanger, "Russia's Army Seen as Failing Chechnya Test," *New York Times*, 25 December 1994, p. A1.

24. CIA, *World Factbook 1994*, pp. 84–85; "War of the Worlds, Survey: The Global Economy," *Economist*, 1–7 October 1994, p. 4; David Shambaugh, "Wealth in Search of Power: The Chinese Military Budget and Revenue Base," and Paul Godwin "'PLA Incorporated,' Estimating China's Military Expenditures," both papers presented at the IISS/CAPS conference on "Chinese Economic Reform: The Impact on Security Policy," Hong Kong, 8 July 1994; IISS, *Military Balance 1994–1995*, p. 170.

25. Gerald Segal, *China Changes Shape: Regionalism and Foreign Policy* (London, 1994).

26. Paul Kennedy, *The Rise and Fall of the Great Powers* (New York, 1987), pp. 330, 369, 436.

27. Thomas W. Graham, "The Economics of Producing Nuclear Weapons in Nth Countries," in D. L. Brito, M. D. Intriligator, and A. E. Wick, eds., *Strategies for Managing Nuclear Proliferation* (Lexington, MA, 1983).

28. Gaddis, *Strategies of Containment*, pp. 79–80, 93; Carl von Clausewitz, *On War*, ed. and trans. Michael Howard and Peter Paret (Princeton, NJ, 1984), pp. 90–91.

29. Seymour M. Hersh, *The Samson Option: Israel's Nuclear Arsenal and American Foreign Policy* (New York, 1991), pp. 17, 66, 137–39, 174–77, 216, 220–34, 259–61, 285–87, 301.

30. Michael I. Handel, "The Evolution of Israeli Strategy: The Psychology of Insecurity and the Quest for Absolute Security" in Williamson Murray, MacGregor Knox, and Alvin Bernstein, eds., *The Making of Strategy: Rulers, States, and War* (New York, 1994), pp. 552–53; Colin S. Gray, "Strategy in the Nuclear Age: The United States, 1945–1991," in Murray, et al., *The Making of Strategy*, p. 587.

31. Martin C. Libicki, *The Mesh and the Net: Speculations on Armed Conflict in a Time of Free Silicon* (Washington, DC, 1994), pp. 1–50.

32. Andrew F. Krepinevich, "Cavalry to Computer: The Pattern of Military Revolutions," *National Interest*, Fall 1994, p. 40.

33. J. F. C. Fuller, *The Conduct of War, 1789–1961* (London, 1972), pp. 87–94; Archer Jones, *The Art of War in the Western World* (Urbana, IL, 1987), pp. 390–91, 395–96.

34. Summers, *On Strategy II*, pp. 1–149; Raymond L. Garthoff, *The Great Transition: American-Soviet Relations and the End of the Cold War* (Washington, DC, 1994), pp. 751–78.

35. It would be impossible to document fully this phenomenon in a reasonably limited space. A glance through any foreign *Who's Who* provides numerous examples of foreign political, business, and military leaders educated in the United States. Flipping through French and other foreign-language journals reveals the overwhelming number of references to American publications.

36. Daniel Pipes, "The Paranoid Style in Mideast Politics: From the Gulf War to Somalia, Fear of a Sinister Uncle Sam," *Washington Post*, 6 November 1994, p. C1.

37. See the questions, although not necessarily the answers, in Mickey Kaus, "The End of Equality," *New Republic*, 22 June 1992.

Chapter 3
How to Think About Defense

1. On American foreign policy in the early period, see Bradford Perkins, *The Creation of a Republican Empire, 1776–1865* (Cambridge, 1993), in Warren I. Cohen, ed., *The Cambridge History of American Foreign Relations*, 4 vols. One of the best introductions to American military policy in the early periods remains Walter Millis's *Arms and Men: A Study of American Military History* (New Brunswick, NJ, 1981). Allan R. Millett and Peter Maslowski's *For the Common Defense: A Military History of the United States of America* (New York, 1994) brings the story up to date.

2. Richard Cheney, "Remarks to the Navy League Meeting," *Federal News Service*, 16 April 1992, p. 6.

3. Mark Watson, *Chief of Staff: Prewar Plans and Preparations* (Washington, DC, 1950), p. 23.

4. U.S. Department of Commerce, Bureau of the Census, *Historical Statistics of the United States: Colonial Times to 1970* (Washington, DC, 1975), p. 1141.

5. See Thomas A. Keaney and Eliot A. Cohen, *Gulf War Air Power Survey Summary Report* (Washington, DC, 1993), pp. 248–51.

6. For a useful introduction to thinking about the revolution in military affairs see Andrew F. Krepinevich, "Cavalry to Computer: The Pattern of Military Revolutions," *National Interest*, 37, Fall 1994, pp. 30–42. A short Russian discussion is Vladimir I. Slipchenko's "A Russian Analysis of Warfare Leading to the Sixth Generation," *Field Artillery*, October 1993, pp. 38–41. Martin C. Libicki's "The Mesh and the Net: Speculations on Armed Conflict in a Time of Free Silicon," McNair Paper 28 (Washington, DC, 1994), is, at least, suggestive.

7. Eliot A. Cohen, ed., *The Gulf War Air Power Survey*, Vol. III, Pt. II, *Logistics* (Washington, DC, 1994) tells the story well. In December of 1990 alone, for example, Military Airlift Command generated over 2,500 heavy airlift sorties a month.

8. For evidence, one need only look at the spate of articles in *Foreign Affairs* triggered by Samuel P. Huntington's "The Clash of Civilizations?" *Foreign Affairs*, 72:3, Summer 1993, pp. 22–49.

9. This argument was made most famously by Francis Fukuyama, "The End of History?" *National Interest*, 16, Summer 1989, pp. 3–18. See also John Mueller, *Retreat from Doomsday: The Obsolescence of Major War* (New York, 1988).

10. Surely the success of the North Vietnamese in the period from 1965 to 1975 against the United States is a warning.

11. On the Clinton administration's plans see Les Aspin, *Report on the Bottom-Up Review* (Washington, DC, 1993). The best critique of the Bottom up Review is Andrew F. Krepinevich's *The Bottom-Up Review: An Assessment* (Washington, DC, 1994). See also Stephen Daggett, "Defense Spending: Does the Size of the Budget Fit the Size of the Force?" Congressional Research Service Report, 28 February 1994.

12. General Accounting Office (GAO), "Future Years Defense Program: Optimistic Estimates Lead to Billions in Overprogramming," GAO/NSIAD-94-210, 29 July 1994.

13. A useful selection of readings on American strategy in the nineteenth century, which dealt largely with the problem of defense narrowly understood, is Walter Millis, ed., *American Military Thought* (Indianapolis, 1966), Parts II and III.

14. Robert W. Coakley, *The Role of Federal Military Forces in Domestic Disorders 1789–1878* (Washington, DC, 1988), p. 314.

15. See John Diamond, "Air Force General Calls for End to Atomic Arms," *Boston Globe*, 16 July 1994, p. 3, for an interview with General Charles A. Horner, the retiring commander of the U.S. Space Command. Note that this declaration runs counter to government policy, further evidence of a phenomenon noted at the end of the article.

16. See Barry D. Watts and Thomas A. Keaney, *Effects and Effectiveness*, Vol. II, Pt. II of *The Gulf War Air Power Survey*, ed. Eliot Cohen (Washington, DC, 1994), pp. 312–30.

17. John Diamond, "Perry Is Told Peace Takes Toll: Bottle, Beatings Hurting Air Force," *Washington Times*, 5 October 1994, p. 17. Other indications of an overstretched military showed up in falling readiness rates—including, in September 1994, the grounding of 50 percent of the aircraft in twenty-eight navy and marine squadrons. See John D. Morocco, "Republicans Raise the Ante on Defense," *Aviation Week and Space Technology* 141:24, 12 December 1994, p. 21.

18. "Report of the Secretary of the Air Force," in Les Aspin, *Annual Report to the President and the Congress 1994* (Washington, DC, 1994), p. 276.

19. The 17 January 1993 attack used up forty-five missiles, of which thirty-seven hit; the 26 June attack used twenty-four, of which sixteen hit. Of the others, some exploded harmlessly, but others careened into residential areas and killed a number of civilians.

20. In any event, some in the navy argue that the large aircraft carrier may have outlived its usefulness as the capital ship of the modern navy. See Charles R. Girvin, "Twilight of the Supercarriers," *US Naval Institute Proceedings*, July 1993, pp. 41–45.

21. On the various service personalities, see Carl H. Builder, *The Masks of War* (Baltimore, 1989).

22. David LaGesse, "Pentagon, State Clash on Troops," *Dallas Morning News*, 17 June 1994, p. 1.

23. On the Yugoslav controversy, see Michael R. Gordon, "Powell Delivers a Resounding No on Using Limited Force in Bosnia," *New York Times*, 28 September 1992, p. 1; Colin L. Powell, "Why Generals Get Nervous," *New York Times*, 8 October 1992, p. A35.

24. Charles Dunlap Jr., Col., USAF, "The Origins of the American Military Coup of 2012," *Parameters*, Winter 1992–93, pp. 2–20. See also his article, "Welcome to the Junta: The Erosion of Civilian Control of the U.S. Military," *Wake Forest Law Review*, Summer 1994, pp. 341–92. See also Richard H. Kohn, "Out of Control: The Crisis in Civil-Military Relations," *National Interest*, Spring 1994, pp. 3–17; and "An Exchange on Civil-Military Relations," *National Interest*, Summer 1994.

25. For an example of a military reading along these lines, especially regarding civilian oversight, see Bill Gertz, "Ex-Commander in Somalia Hits Second Guessing," *Washington Times*, 22 October 1993, p. 1.

26. Winston S. Churchill, "Fifty Years Hence," in *Amid These Storms: Thoughts and Adventures* (New York, 1932), p. 279.

Chapter 4
Crack-up: The Unraveling of America's Military

1. John T. Correll, "The High-Risk Military Strategy," *Air Force Magazine*, September 1994, pp. 34–42.

2. William Matthews, "Is Leaner Meaner?" *American Legion Magazine*, August 1993, pp. 26–50.

3. Dov S. Zakheim, "How Much National Security Does America Need?" *The World and I*, June 1993, p. 98.

4. Ibid.

5. Richard L. West, Lt. Gen., USA, "Short Rations for the Army," *Army Magazine*, April 1994, p. 21.

6. William W. Kaufman, "Hollow Forces," *Brookings Review*, Fall 1994, pp. 24–29.

7. David C. Morrison, "Modernization Morass," *National Journal*, 26 March 1994, pp. 721–24.

8. John D. Morrocca, "Pentagon Eyes Savings to Boost Procurement," *Aviation Week and Space Technology*, 14 February 1994, pp. 22–23.

9. Kaufman, "Hollow Forces," p. 26.

10. Norman Augustine, Testimony Before the House Committee on Armed Services, 30 April 1992.

11. Morrison, "Modernization Morass," p. 721.

12. "Deutch: Pentagon Shortfall is $40 Billion, But Two War Strategy Still Viable," *Inside the Pentagon*, 22 September 1994, p. 3.

13. General Accounting Office (GAO), "Future Years Defense Program: Optimistic Estimates Lead to Billions in Overprogramming," GAO Report GAO/NSIAD-94-210, 29 July 1994.

14. Eric Rosenburg, "Look Out! Big Ticket Weapons Programs Are on the Ropes," *Defense Week* 15:34, 22 August 1994, pp. 1, 7.

15. Jeff Ranney, interview by author, Washington, DC, 8 September 1994.

16. Augustine, "Testimony."

17. Norman Augustine, *Augustine's Laws and Major System Development Programs* (New York, 1986), p. 52.

18. Jacques S. Gansler, "Reform of the Weapons Acquisition Process," paper presented at the meeting of Business Executives for National Security (BENS), 11 January 1991.

19. Michael P. Carns, Gen., USAF, Speech to Operations Director's (XO) Air Power Conference, 31 March 1993, Washington, DC.

20. Therese Hitchens, "Lean Manufacturing Reduces F-16 Costs," *Defense News*, 11–17 July 1994, p. 18.

21. David A. Fulghum, "Air Force May Delay JPATS, TSSAM," *Aviation Week and Space Technology*, 19 September 1994, p. 26.

22. Michael P. Carns, Gen., USAF, letter to the author, 31 October 1994.

23. Charlotte Twight, "Department of Defense Attempt to Close Military Bases: The Political Economy of Congressional Resistance," in *Arms, Politics, and the Economy* (New York, 1990), pp. 236–72.

24. Lyndon B. Johnson, "Military Authorization Act of 1965, Veto Message from the President of the United States, 21 August 1965," *Weekly Compilation of Presidential Documents* 1 (1965), p. 132.

25. Ibid.

26. Barry M. Blechman, "The Congress and Defense Resource Management," in *The Politics of National Security* (New York, 1990), p. 36.

27. Michael J. Dugan, Lt. Gen., USAF, "Memorandum to the Director, Joint Staff," 15 September 1988.

28. Colin L. Powell, Gen., USA, "Memorandum to the Secretary of Defense," 2 November 1989.

29. Richard Cheney, Secretary of Defense, "Memorandum to the Chairman, Joint Chiefs of Staff," 8 February 1990.

30. Robert W. Gaskin, "Restructuring the U.S. Military Establishment: BENS Spurs Critical Roles and Missions Debate," Business Executives for National Security (BENS) Policy Update, August 1992.

31. Senator Sam Nunn, "The Defense Department Must Thoroughly Overhaul the Services Roles and Missions," Floor Speech, U.S. Senate, 2 July 1992.

32. General Accounting Office (GAO), "Roles and Functions," GAO Report to the Honorable John W. Warner, U.S. Senate, GAO/NSIAD-93-200, July 1993, p. 2.

33. Robert W. Gaskin, "House Creates Commission for Roles and Missions Reform," BENS Policy Update, August 1993.

34. Andrew Krepinevich, "Roles and Missions: New Thinking in an Era of Changing Challenges and Scarce Resources," Testimony before the Senate Budget Committee, 9 March 1994.

35. Les Aspin, *Report on the Bottom-Up Review* (Washington, DC, 1993).

36. Ibid.

37. Joint Chiefs of Staff, "1992 Joint Military Net Assessment" (Washington, DC, August 1992).

38. Ibid.

39. "Defense Budget Decline Worsens, BUR Unattainable, Forecast Says," *Defense Daily*, 12 October 1994, p. 51.

40. Ibid.

41. Erik Rosenburg, *Defense Week*, 15:41, 17 October 1994, pp. 1, 12–16.

42. George C. Wilson, *Army Times*, 21 May 1994, p. 37.

43. Correll, "High-Risk Military Strategy," p. 41.

44. Ibid.

45. Jeff Moag, "US at High Risk of Being Unable to Carry Out Two War Strategy Until 2006," *Inside the Pentagon*, 10:38, 22 September 1994, pp. 1, 6.

46. Vago Muradian, "Airlift Woes Laid Out," *Air Force Times*, 19 December 1994, p. 22.

47. General Accounting Office, "Strategic Airlift: Further Air Base Reductions in Europe Could Jeopardize Capability," GAO/NLIAD-94-138, June 1994, pp. 3–5.

48. This is a major conclusion of the *Gulf War Air Power Survey* (ed. Eliot Cohen [Washington, DC, 1994]), written at the direction of Secretary of the Air Force Donald Rice.

49. *Defense Daily*, 3 March 1994, p. 326.

50. Tony Cappaccio, "Declassified Testimony Raises More Questions About Bomber Force," *Defense Week*, 7 November 1994, p. 5.

51. Steve Watkins, "More Smart Bombs," *Air Force Times*, 20 June 1994, p. 30.

52. Ibid.

53. John Gaffney, "Air Delivered Precision Guided Weapons," Hicks and Associates White Paper, March 1994, Washington, DC.

54. Bruce Auster, *US News and World Report*, 28 June 1993, p. 29.

55. David Morrison, "Bottoming Out," *National Journal*, 17 September 1994, pp. 2126–2130.

56. *Defense Daily*, 2 March 1994, p. 318.

57. Department of the Navy, *The United States Navy in Desert Shield/Desert Storm* (Washington, DC, 1991). Data were arrived at by combining OCA and Theater Strike sortie count on p. D-9.

58. Dave Deptula, Col., USAF, interview by author, Washington, DC, on 13 October 1994. Colonel Deptula was an air power planner in the "Black Hole" during the Gulf War.

59. CENTCOM Master Attack Plan, January 1991. Statistics derived from briefing memo.

60. Steve Ramsdale, Capt., USN, interview with P. Mason Carpenter, Maj., USAF, 21 January 1994, Washington, DC.

61. Mike Ryan, Brig. Gen., USMC, as quoted at Naval Aviation Seminar, 4 October 1994, Alexandria, VA.

62. Lockheed Corporation Briefing, "Military Force Structure Planning Study," 1994, Washington, DC.

63. "USAF Contends Navy Could Achieve Forward Presence with Fewer Carriers," *Inside the Pentagon*, 10:43, 27 October 1994.

64. James L. George, *The U.S. Navy in the 90s, Alternatives for Action* (Annapolis, MD, 1994), pp. 104–111.

65. *Congressional Record*, 15 July 1992, p. S9099.

66. Ibid.

67. *Congressional Record*, 17 August 1994, p. H8550.

68. General Accounting Office, "DoD Budget: Department of Defense Support for Domestic Civil Activities," GAO/NSIAD-94-41, November 1993, p. 2.

69. *Congressional Record*, 9 August 1994, p. S11001.

70. Todd Hoffman, "Cutting Nondefense Pork," BENS White Paper, October 1994.

71. Confidential remarks of a serving naval officer.

72. David Wood, "Malaise Casting a Spell over the Nation's Military," *New Orleans Times-Picayune*, 14 August 1994, p. A-13.

73. Unattributed, "Military Readiness, Capability Questioned," *Aerospace America*, October 1994.

74. Rep. Floyd Spence, "Spence Challenges DoD Claim of Improved Military Readiness," press release, 15 November 1994, Washington, DC.

75. Charles Aldlinger, "Perry Says Congress Must Pay for Peacekeeping," *Reuters*, 16 November 1994.

76. Jeanne Kirkpatrick, "What Price Peacekeeping?" *Washington Post*, 21 November 1994.

77. Wood, "Malaise Casting a Spell," p. A-13.

78. John G. Roos, "Redefining Readiness," *Armed Forces Journal International*, October 1994, p. 33.

79. Ibid.

80. Franklin C. Spinney, "Trip Report, VFA-81," 27 July 1994, p. 2.

81. "Training Readiness in the Department of Defense," Final Report, April 1994, Executive Summary.

82. Defense Science Board Task Force, "Technology for U.S. Rapid Deployment Forces," Final Report, 2 June 1982, p. 28.

83. Ibid.

84. Spinney, "Trip Report, VFA-81," p. 3.

85. Ibid., p. 9.

86. Franklin C. Spinney, "Anatomy of Decline: How Modes of Conduct Evolved During the Cold War Are Setting the Stage of a 'Hollow Military' or Higher Defense Budgets in the Mid-to-Late 1990's," White Paper, Washington, DC, 1994, p. 30.

87. Ibid., p. 35.

88. Remarks at U.S. Naval Institute symposium, "Naval Aviation Seminar: How Do We Get There from Here?" 4 October 1994, Washington, DC.

89. Spinney, "Anatomy of Decline," p. 36.

90. Spinney, "Trip Report, VFA-81," p. 5.

91. Spinney, "Anatomy of Decline," p. 28.

92. Ibid., p. 21.

93. Ibid., p. 17.

94. "Trends in National Defense Budget by Title," Center for Economic Conversion and Disarmament (Mountain View, CA).

95. Spinney, "Trip Report, VFA-81," p. 5.

96. "Training Readiness in the Department of Defense," Executive Summary, p. i.

97. James G. Andrus, Maj. Gen., USAF, "Aircraft Accident Investigation Board Report," 27 May 1994, vol. 13, p. 65.

98. Ibid.

99. Confidential interview, 20 October 1994.

100. John Gall, *Systemantics: How Systems Work and Especially How They Fail* (New York, 1977), p. 41.

101. "Training Readiness in the Department of Defense," p. 20.

102. Ibid., p. 32.

103. Ibid., p. 35.

104. Confidential interview, 20 October 1994.

105. T. R. Fehrenback, *This Kind of War, Korea: A Study in Unpreparedness* (New York, 1963), pp. 97–103.

106. Ibid., p. 108.

Chapter 5
The Clinton Defense Strategy

1. For a discussion of the military revolution, see Andrew F. Krepinevich, "Keeping Pace with the Military-Technological Revolution," *Issues in Science and Technology*, Summer 1994, and Andrew F. Krepinevich, "Cavalry to Computer: The Pattern of Military Revolutions," *National Interest*, Fall 1994.

2. The importance of this approach is highlighted in Richard Cheney, *Defense Strategy for the 1990s: The Regional Defense Strategy* (Washington, DC, 1993), p. 18. Cheney argues that the United States "must strike a careful balance between, on the one hand, the needs to demonstrate resolve, strengthen deterrence, and begin enhancing military capabilities, and, on the other hand, the imperative to avoid provocative steps. . . ."

3. Les Aspin, *Report on the Bottom-Up Review* (Washington, DC, 1993), p. iii.

4. Ibid.

5. Pat Towell and Carroll J. Doherty, "Inman, a Seasoned 'Operator,' Chosen as Aspin's Successor," *Congressional Quarterly*, 51:50, December 1993, p. 3467.

6. In fact, the Clinton national security strategy of engagement and enlargement omits these dangers when discussing U.S. defense missions. See William J. Clinton, *A National Security Strategy of Engagement and Enlargement* (Washington, DC, 1994), pp. 6–7.

7. Aspin, *Bottom-Up Review*, p. iii; and Clinton, *National Security Strategy*, p. 7.

8. Aspin, *Bottom-Up Review*, p. 8.

9. Ibid., p. 6

10. Ibid.

11. Author's discussion with Secretary of Defense Les Aspin, August 1993.

12. Aspin, *Bottom-Up Review*, p. 19. Another factor may have contributed to the decision to move to "win-win": when the "win-hold-win" posture was leaked in the late spring of 1993, it met with significant opposition from the military services and the Congress. The addition of the carriers was ostensibly the result of strong and successful lobbying by the navy to convince Aspin that the carriers were essential to the forward presence mission.

13. Congressional Budget Office, *An Analysis of the President's Budgetary Proposals for Fiscal Year 1995* (Washington, DC, 1994), p. 44; and Steven Kosiak, *Defense Likely to Be Hit Hard by Balanced Budget Amendment* (Washington, DC, 1994).

14. Lecture by Anthony Lake, delivered at the Johns Hopkins School of Advanced International Studies, Washington, DC, 21 September 1993.

15. See, for example, "Address by Ambassador Madeline Albright," delivered at the National Defense University, Washington, DC, 23 September 1993. See also John M. Goshko, "U.S. Lists Stiff Conditions for Troop Role in U.N. Peace Keeping," *Washington Post*, 24 September 1993, p. A19; John Lancaster and Daniel Williams, "U.S. Shapes Terms for Role in Bosnia," *Washington Post*, 26 September 1993, p. A1.

16. Aspin, *Bottom-Up Review*, p. 13.

17. Ibid., p. 26.

18. Clinton, *National Security Strategy*, pp. 11–12.

19. Aspin, *Bottom-Up Review*, p. 7.

20. The Joint Chiefs of Staff recommended during the Bush administration that the United States maintain sufficient forces to wage two major regional conflicts simultaneously (Directorate for Force Structure, Resources, and Assessment [J-8], the Joint Staff," 1992 Joint Military Net Assessment [Washington, DC, 1992] pp. 9-1 through 9-12).

21. Some of the more interesting, albeit less charitable, descriptions of the Bottom Up Review force structure are "Son of Base Force" and "Bush Light."

22. General Colin Powell observed that "Desert Storm was that Cold War battle that didn't come, without trees and mountains. We got a nice desert, and we got a very, very incompetent enemy to work against." See Secretary of Defense Les Aspin and General Colin Powell, "Department of Defense Bottom-Up Review," Department of Defense News Conference, 1 September 1993, Washington, DC.

23. Aspin, *Bottom-Up Review*, p. 7.

24. Ibid., p. 15. These are very similar to the scenarios employed in the 1992 Joint Military Net Assessment, which supported the Bush Base Force. This, combined with the short time (less than three months) available to Aspin to conduct his "fundamental" review of U.S. defense requirements, indicates much more of an "evolutionary" response to the geopolitical and military revolutions than the radical change expected—and feared—by many senior military officials and congressional defense supporters.

25. For a detailed discussion of this issue, see Stephen P. Rosen, *Winning the Next War* (Ithaca, NY, 1991), and Allan R. Millett and Williamson Murray, eds., *Military Effectiveness*, Vol. II: *The Interwar Period* (London, 1988).

26. Furthermore, it is not clear that South Korea—with twice the population and ten times the GNP of North Korea—needs the same level of support that Saudi Arabia would require if attacked by Iran or Iraq. Referring to the marine division and five army divisions slated for the Korean contingency, a former army chief of staff declared, "If the [Korean army] needs tanks, why not give them tanks?"

27. David E. Sanger, "Despite Atom Accord, U.S. Asks: Does North Korea Have a Bomb?" *New York Times*, 9 January 1994, p. A1. According to the article, U.S. intelligence has concluded that North Korea has probably already fabricated at least one nuclear weapon. For a discussion of the pitfalls of relying on a canonical scenario, see Eliot A. Cohen, *Net Assessment: An American Approach* (Tel Aviv, 1990), pp. 18–19.

28. An excellent sample of innovative Third World thinking on this issue can be found in Brigadier V. K. Nair, *War in the Gulf: Lessons for the Third World* (New Delhi, no date).

29. Aspin, *Bottom-Up Review*, p. 15.

30. Ibid., p. 9; and Clinton, *National Security Strategy*, pp. 7–9, 13–14.

31. Aspin, *Bottom-Up Review*, p. 13.

32. Ibid., p. 22.

33. For a discussion of the dimensions of strategy, see Michael Howard, "The Forgotten Dimensions of Strategy," *Foreign Affairs*, Summer 1979.

34. Les Aspin, address before the Association of the United States Army, Washington, DC, 18 October 1993.

35. Ibid.

36. See, for example, Andrew F. Krepinevich, *The Army and Vietnam* (Baltimore, MD, 1986), pp. 27–55.

37. Aspin, Association of the United States Army address.

38. Ibid.

39. Aspin, *Bottom-Up Review*, pp. 22–23.

40. See Krepinevich, *Army and Vietnam*, p. 139. For instance, the initial ground forces sent to South Vietnam in 1965 to support the special operations forces and other advisory forces already on station included a marine expeditionary brigade, the army's 173d Airborne Brigade, and the 1st Cavalry Division (Airmobile).

41. Clinton, *National Security Strategy*, p. 10.

42. These tests, or factors, include: What is the threat to international peace and security? Does the operation serve U.S. interests as well as those of the international community? Are there clear objectives? Are the necessary resources available to achieve the objectives? What is the operation's end point, or completion date? Ibid., p. 13.

43. Caspar W. Weinberger, *Annual Report to the Congress* (Washington, DC, 1986), pp. 78–81.

44. Arguably, this was the case in successful U.S. interventions in Lebanon (1985), the Dominican Republic (1965), Grenada (1983), and Panama (1989).

45. Aspin, *Bottom-Up Review*, pp. 23–24.

46. Ibid., p. 24.

47. Ibid., p. 50.

48. Ibid., p. 8.

49. See General Accounting Office, *Navy Carrier Battle Groups: The Structure and Affordability of the Future Force* (Washington, DC, February 1993), p. 19. The annual cost could rise to as much as $3.4 billion if a broader range of indirect operations and support (O&S) and acquisition costs are included. See Paul Taibl and Steven Kosiak, *An Affordable Long-Term Defense* (Washington, DC, 1993), p. 27.

50. David C. Morrison, "How Many Carriers Are Enough?" *National Journal*, 25:36, 4 September 1993, p. 2162.

51. For a detailed presentation of carrier involvement in forward presence operations, see Adam B. Siegel, *The Use of Naval Forces in the Post-War Era: U.S. Navy and U.S. Marine Corps Crisis Response Activity, 1946–1990* (Alexandria, VA, 1991).

52. Keith B. Richburg, "Crew on Carrier Wonders If Somalia Is Place for Its Kind of Action," *Washington Post*, 10 November 1993, p. A31.

53. Rowan Scarborough, "Saddam Behind Bush Plot, Aspin Says," *Washington Times*, 23 June 1993, p. A1.

54. Clinton, *National Security Strategy*, pp. 11–13.

55. Ibid., p. 11.

56. Ibid., p. 12. The president's national security strategy declares that counterproliferation "will require improved defensive capabilities." It adds that "we are placing a high priority on improving our ability to locate, identify, and disable arsenals of weapons, and their delivery systems."

57. Thomas A. Keaney and Eliot A. Cohen, *Gulf War Air Power Survey Summary Report* (Washington, DC, 1993), pp. 84, 90. The report notes, for example, that the air force flew over 1,500 strikes against Iraqi Scud ballistic missiles without scoring a single confirmed kill and

that the UN's Security Council inspection teams sent to Iraq after the war actually identified and destroyed more of the Iraqi nuclear program than did the air force.

58. David C. Morrison, "Bottoming Out?" *National Journal*, 17 September 1994, p. 2128.

59. Aspin, *Bottom-Up Review*, p. 108.

60. Steven Kosiak, *The Defense Department's $50 Billion Question* (Washington, DC, 1993) p. 1.

61. General Accounting Office, "Future Years Defense Program: Optimistic Estimates Lead to Billions in Overprogramming," GAO/NSIAD-94-210, 29 July 1994.

62. John Mintz, "Defense Memo Warns of Cuts in Programs," *Washington Post*, 22 August 1994, p. 1.

63. John Deutch, "Future Defense Programs," Testimony before the Senate Armed Services Committee, 20 September 1994. It should be noted that substantial funding shortfalls are the rule and not the exception when it comes to defense programs over the last forty-five years. They indicate that the Defense Department is likely going to be faced with two basic choices. One is to make cuts in defense programs, operations and maintenance, or force structure, or in all of these categories. Given the very tight "fit" between strategy and resources in the Clinton program, this would result in a failure to meet strategic requirements. This is not as strange as it may seem. The United States, for example, did not have the resources to meet its "two-and-a-half war" defense posture of the 1960s. (Nor does the United States currently have the ability to meet its two-major-regional-contingencies defense posture.) A second choice would be to increase defense spending.

64. Ibid.

65. Les Aspin and Colin Powell, "Bottom-Up Review," briefing slides dated 1 September 1993.

66. For example, according to one Defense Department estimate, at its peak in FY 1984, the Defense Department spent only about 25 percent as much on strategic forces as it did on general purpose forces. Moreover, since FY 1984 strategic forces funding has fallen by 62 percent, while general purpose forces funding has fallen by 36 percent (Office of the Comptroller, *National Defense Budget Estimates for FY 1994* [Washington, DC, 1993], p. 63). The Nuclear Posture Review resulted in a decision to reduce the number of Trident ballistic missile submarines from eighteen to fourteen and the B-52 bomber force from as many as ninety-four to sixty-six aircraft. See Secretary of Defense William Perry et al., "Nuclear Posture Review," Defense Department Briefing, 22 September 1994.

67. Aspin, *Bottom-Up Review*, p. 108.

68. Congressional Budget Office, *Planning for Defense: Affordability and Capability of the Administration's Program* (Washington, DC, 1994), pp. 18–19.

Chapter 6
The Second Nuclear Age:
Insecurity, Proliferation, and the Control of Arms

1. See Francis Fukuyama, "The End of History?" *National Interest* 16, Summer 1989, especially p. 4.

2. The practicality of the control of arms is emphasized in Colin S. Gray, "Arms Control Does Not Control Arms," *Orbis* 37:3, Summer 1993, pp. 333–48. The reasons why arms control cannot work as advertised are advanced in Colin S. Gray, *House of Cards: Why Arms Control Must Fail* (Ithaca, NY, 1992).

3. They cannot quite say this in print, but the writings of some scholars of proliferation have begun to reveal a barely concealed professional triumphalism. The unwritten claim is in essence that "at last we have made it to the big time." The general reader can interpret the following sentence strictly for its accurate face value. "The radical change in global nuclear relationships produced by the collapse of the ideological divide in East-West relations and the dissolution of the former Soviet Union has put nuclear proliferation concerns and nonproliferation strategies at the core of international security policies" (John Simpson, "Nuclear Non-Proliferation in the Post–Cold War Era," *International Affairs* 70:1, January 1994, p. 17). Defense professionals can read that sentence somewhat differently, as a registration of claim to major-league status for an issue-area previously treated as minor league by most members of the defense community. Some commentators are prepared to go beyond the announcement that nuclear proliferation has arrived as a major-league topic and to make the arresting claim that it "does indeed appear as the last critical problem remaining for strategic studies to analyze" (Martin van Creveld, *Nuclear Proliferation and the Future of Conflict* [New York, 1993], p. viii). What makes that claim even more extraordinary is that van Creveld purports to be a historian.

4. For a leading example of an arch neorealist see Kenneth N. Waltz. He has astonishingly argued that deterrence is easy to achieve with nuclear weapons and that generally those weapons "are in fact a tremendous force for peace and afford nations that possess them the possibility of security at reasonable cost." See particularly his "Nuclear Myths and Political Realities," *The American Political Science Review*, 84:3, September 1990, pp. 731–45. See also his monograph, "The Spread of Nuclear Weapons: More May Be Better," *Adelphi Papers*, no. 171 (London, 1981). The folly in Waltz's argument is underlined in greater detail in Iklé's "Comment," *National Interest* 34, Winter 1993/94. The quotation is on p. 39.

5. Knowledge of the technical "basics" nonetheless is essential. Excellent recent terse guides include U.S. Congress, Office of Technology Assessment (OTA), *Technologies Underlying Weapons of Mass Destruction*, OTA-BP-ISC-115 (Washington, DC, 1993); and Gary T. Gardner, *Nuclear Proliferation: A Primer* (Boulder, CO, 1994), chaps. 1–3.

6. See Colin S. Gray, "Strategy in the Nuclear Age: The United States, 1945–1991," in Williamson Murray, MacGregor Knox, and Alvin Bernstein, eds., *The Making of Strategy: Rulers, States, and War* (Cambridge, 1994), pp. 579–613. Ken Booth, *Strategy and Ethnocentrism* (London, 1979); Gerald Segal, "Strategy and Ethnic Chic," *International Affairs* 60:1, Winter 1983/84, pp. 15–30; and van Creveld, *Nuclear Proliferation*, also are relevant.

7. See the well-balanced analysis in Eliot A. Cohen, "The Mystique of U.S. Air Power," *Foreign Affairs* 73:1, January/February 1994, pp. 109–24.

8. Eliot A. Cohen, "Comment," *National Interest* 34, Winter 1993/94, p. 37.

9. The pervasiveness of this technicist pull in arms control matters is well illustrated by the concluding observations in John H. Maurer, "Arms Control and the Washington Conference," in Erik Goldstein and Maurer Maurer, eds., *The Washington Conference, 1921–22: Naval Rivalry, East Asian Stability and the Road to Pearl Harbor* (London, 1994), p. 289. The importance of politics is emphasized also in Robin Ranger's *Arms and Politics, 1958–1978: Arms Control in a Changing Political Context* (Toronto, 1979) and Colin S. Gray's *Weapons Don't Make War: Policy, Strategy, and Technology* (Lawrence, KS, 1993).

10. See E. A. Thompson, *A History of Attila and the Huns* (Oxford, 1948), p. 180.

11. See Philippe Contamine, *War in the Middle Ages* (Oxford, 1984), pp. 137–50, 193–207; and Kelly DeVries, *Medieval Military Technology* (Lewiston, NY, 1992), pp. 143–63.

12. Kathleen C. Bailey's *Doomsday Weapons in the Hands of Many: The Arms Control Challenge of the '90s* (Urbana, IL, 1992), chap. 1, is on the mark.

13. Robert Jervis's *The Meaning of the Nuclear Revolution: Statecraft and the Prospect of Armageddon* (Ithaca, NY, 1989) is outstanding.

14. As Kathleen C. Bailey argues powerfully in *Strengthening Nuclear Nonproliferation* (Boulder, CO, 1993), chap. 11.

15. Quoted in Lawrence Freedman, *The Evolution of Nuclear Strategy* (London, 1981), p. 307.

16. See van Creveld, *Nuclear Proliferation*.

17. For balanced discussion, see Brad Roberts, "From Nonproliferation to Antiproliferation," *International Security*, 18:1, Summer 1993, pp. 139–73; and Bailey, *Strengthening Nuclear Nonproliferation*, chap. 12.

18. See Jack S. Levy's "The Causes of War: A Review of Theories," in Philip E. Tetlock et al., eds., *Behavior, Society, and Nuclear War*, Vol. 1 (New York, 1989), pp. 209–333, for plausible confirmation of this discouraging news.

19. David Kaiser's *Politics and War: European Conflict from Philip II to Hitler* (Cambridge, MA, 1990) risks overstating this point.

20. I am indebted to Richard K. Betts, "Paranoids, Pygmies, Pariahs, and Nonproliferation Revisited," *Security Studies*, 2:3–4, Spring/Summer 1993, p. 118.

21. Ibid., pp. 110–11.

22. On which broad subject see Gray, *Weapons Don't Make War*.

23. See the pathbreaking study, Grant T. Hammond, *Plowshares into Swords: Arms Races in International Politics, 1840–1991* (Columbia, SC, 1993).

24. Simpson, "Nuclear Non-Proliferation," pp. 22–26.

25. Ibid., p. 35.

26. Frederick Maurice, *British Strategy: A Study of the Application of the Principle of War* (London, 1929), p. 243.

27. Bailey, *Strengthening Nuclear Nonproliferation*, p. 34.

28. See Richard K. Betts, "Systems for Peace or Causes of War? Collective Security, Arms Control, and the New Europe," *International Security* 17:1, Summer 1992, pp. 5–43.

29. Gerhard L. Weinberg's *A World at Arms: A Global History of World War II* (Cambridge, 1994), pp. 23, 952 n. 51, is damning.

30. I have dwelt at some length on this matter in my *House of Cards*, chap. 6. The historical record shows that Germany, Italy, and Japan between the world wars, and the Soviet Union and Iraq by recent decades, persistently evaded the terms of legal arms control obligations. For example, a careful scholar of the interwar naval arms limitation regime has observed that "[t]he Japanese broke the rules seriously, systematically, and often clandestinely" (Robert

Gordon Kaufman, *Arms Control During the Pre-Nuclear Era: The United States and Naval Limitation Between the Two World Wars* [New York, 1990], p. 99). Robin Ranger's *The Naval Arms Control Record, 1919–1939; Axis Violations Versus Democratic Compliance Policy Failures* (Final Report for OASD/ISP [START]; Fairfax, VA, 1987) is a convincing indictment. For the most blatant of Soviet treaty evasions, see Sven F. Kraemer, "The Krasnoyarsk Saga," *Strategic Review*, 18:1, Winter 1990, pp. 25–38. As a member of the President's General Advisory Committee on Arms Control and Disarmament from 1982 until 1987, I saw the evidence for a pattern of Soviet arms control violation.

31. This is the central thesis in Gray, *House of Cards.*

32. Lewis A. Dunn, "Containing Nuclear Proliferation," *Adelphi Papers*, no. 263 (London, 1991), p. 70.

33. Simpson, "Nuclear Non-Proliferation," p. 36.

34. Scott D. Sagan's *The Limits of Safety: Organizations, Accidents, and Nuclear Weapons* (Princeton, NJ, 1993) is very much to the point. More specialized, but still on target, is Bruce G. Blair's *The Logic of Accidental Nuclear War* (Washington, DC, 1993).

35. Bernard Brodie, *War and Politics* (New York, 1973), subtitle to chap. 9.

36. Bernard Brodie, ed., *The Absolute Weapon: Atomic Power and World Order* (New York, 1946), p. 76.

37. Simpson, "Nuclear Non-Proliferation," p. 36.

38. I am critical only of the value of the taboo hypothesis, not of the motives of its deluded perpetrators. It is high time for the hypotheses of a nuclear taboo to be subjected to critical enquiry and skeptical comment.

39. See the concluding quote at the end of MacGregor Knox's chapter in this volume.

40. See Weinberg, *World at Arms*, chap. 1.

41. Ibid., pp. 558–60; and Victor A. Utgoff, *The Challenge of Chemical Weapons: An American Perspective* (New York, 1991).

42. Although the example of North Korea certainly suggests otherwise.

43. Les Aspin, *Annual Report to the President and the Congress 1994* (Washington, DC, 1994), pp. 35–36.

44. Article IX, 3 of the Non-Proliferation Treaty identifies a nuclear weapons state as "one which has manufactured and exploded a nuclear weapon or other nuclear explosive device prior to 1 January 1967."

45. Not least from the former Soviet Union. See Oleg Bukharin, "Nuclear Safeguards and Security in the Former Soviet Union," *Survival*, 36:4, Winter 1994–95, pp. 53–72. Also pertinent is Wolfgang K. H. Panofsky, *Options for the Long-Term Disposition of Nuclear Materials*, CSTS-35-93 (Livermore, CA, 1993).

46. It is now open season on future roles for nuclear weapons. For a representative sample of current wisdom, see Stephen J. Cimbala, "Nuclear Weapons in the New World Order," *Journal of Strategic Studies*, 16:2, June 1993, pp. 173–99; Michael Quinlan, "The Future of Nuclear Weapons: Policy for Western Possessors," *International Affairs*, 69:3, July 1993, pp. 485–96; Michael McGuire, "Is There a Future for Nuclear Weapons?" *International Affairs*, 70:2, April 1994, pp. 211–28; and Lawrence Freedman, "Great Powers, Vital Interests and Nuclear Weapons," *Survival*, 36:4, Winter 1994–95, pp. 35–52.

47. Sun Tzu, *The Art of War*, trans. Ralph D. Sawyer (Boulder, CO, 1994), p. 179; Carl von Clausewitz, *On War*, trans. Michael Howard and Peter Paret (Princeton, NJ, 1976), pp. 119–21.

Chapter 7
Strategy and Resources:
Trends in the U.S. Defense Budget

1. Mackubin Thomas Owens, "The Evolution of U.S. Military Strategy Since World War II: An Overview" and "The Political Economy of National Defense," in his *Strategy and Force Planning* (Newport, RI, 1995).

2. Samuel P. Huntington (*The Common Defense: Strategic Programs in National Politics* [New York, 1961], pp. 3–5) divides military policy into two categories, strategy and structure:

> Strategy concerns the units and use of force. . . . A strategic concept identifies a particular need and implicitly or explicitly prescribes decisions on the uses, strengths, and weapons of the armed services. Structural decisions, on the other hand, are made in the currency of domestic politics. They deal with the procurement, allocation, and organization of the men, money, and material which go into the strategic units and uses of force. . . .
>
> In practice no sharp line exists between the strategic and structural elements in a military policy decision. This is particularly true of the overall magnitude of the effort. This is determined by many strategic and structural decisions on force levels, budgets, personnel, and by other decisions which are not directly part of military policy at all. The determination of the resources available to the government and the allocation of those resources . . . is indeed the crux of national policy.

3. Les Aspin, *Report on the Bottom-Up Review* (Washington, DC, 1993), p. iii.

4. Ibid.

5. "Budget authority" refers to funds that government agencies may spend, both in the year they are authorized and in future years, by entering into obligations for the provision of goods and services. "Outlays" refer to the actual expenditure of funds.

6. Defense spending is characterized by a substantial lag between budget authority and outlays, because the Department of Defense has a longer payout schedule than most other departments of government. As John Hamre, the Pentagon Comptroller, observes, "We're the only branch of government, largely, that buys things. Most everybody else either writes a paycheck to a beneficiary or to an employee" (Elizabeth A. Palmer, "Defense Reductions: A Case of Delayed Gratification," *Congressional Quarterly Weekly Report* [CQWR], 23 July 1994, p. 1998). The relationship between defense budget authority and outlays is illustrated by Figure 7–10. The flow of the federal budget as a whole (FY 1994) is shown by Figure 7–11.

7. Keith Berner and Paul Graney, "Defense Budget for FY 1995: Authorization and Appropriation," *Congressional Research Service [CRS] Issue Brief 94-017*, 6 October 1994, p. CRS-1.

8. Keith Berner and Paul Graney, "Defense Budget for FY 1995: Data Summary," in *CRS Report for Congress 94-128 FAN*, 18 February 1994, p. CRS-23.

9. The conference report on the FY 1995 defense budget (H. Rept. 103-701) authorized the expenditure of $264.1 billion. It was signed into law by the president on 5 October 1994 (Public Law 103-337). The conference report on the FY 1995 Defense Appropriation Bill (H. Rept. 103-747) provides $243.7 billion. It was signed into law on 30 September 1994 (Public Law 1013-335). The two amounts differ because the Defense Authorization Act covers activities not funded by the Defense Appropriation Act, specifically the nuclear weapons programs of the Department of Energy, military construction, and other defense-related activ-

Figure 7–10. DoD Budget Authority and Outlays: FY 1980–1999

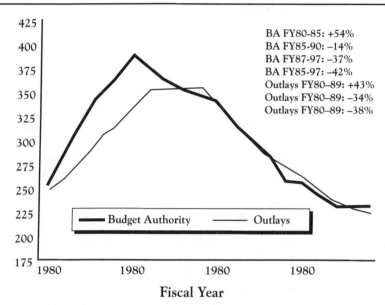

BA FY80-85: +54%
BA FY85-90: –14%
BA FY87-97: –37%
BA FY85-97: –42%
Outlays FY80–89: +43%
Outlays FY80–89: –34%
Outlays FY80–89: –38%

Fiscal Year

*Excludes Desert Shield/Desert Storm costs; FY95–99, Administration projection.

Figure 7–11. Relation of Budget Authority to Outlays: 1994 (in Billions of Dollars)

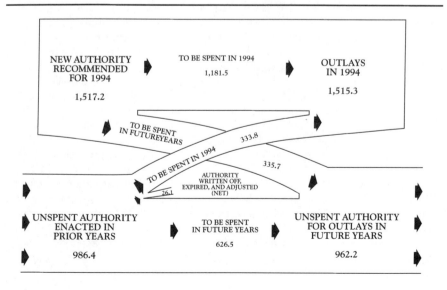

ities (civil defense programs within the Federal Emergency Management Agency, operation of the Selective Service System, and strategic stockpile programs of the General Services Administration). There is a separate appropriations bill for military construction. The Department of Energy's defense programs are appropriated in the Energy and Water Appropriations Act; and the other activities in the Appropriations Act for HUD and Independent Agencies. Meanwhile, the Department of Defense Appropriations Act includes funding of military personnel, which the Department of Defense Authorization Act does not.

10. Ann Devroy and Bradley Graham, "Clinton Seeks to Boost Defense by $25 Billion," *Washington Post*, 2 December 1994, p. A1; Pat Towell, "President to Seek Increase in Military Budget," *CQWR*, 3 December 1994, p. 3454.

11. Table from *CQWR*, 3 December 1994, p. 3454.

12. Devroy and Graham, "Clinton Seeks to Boost Defense," p. A15.

13. Congressional Budget Office (CBO), "Planning for Defense: Affordability and Capability of the Administration's Program" (Washington, DC, March 1994), p. 3.

14. Michael Wines, "Whose Deficit, and How Big?" *New York Times*, 30 October 1994.

15. CBO, "Reducing Entitlement Spending" (Washington, DC, September 1994), p. x–xi.

16. Ibid., p. 2.

17. Ibid., p. xi.

18. Ibid., p. 1.

19. CBO, "Planning for Defense," pp. 3–4.

20. Colin L. Powell, *National Military Strategy of the United States* (Washington, DC, 1992), p. 7.

21. David C. Morrison, "Bottoming Out?" *National Journal*, September 1994, p. 2127.

22. John T. Correll, "Revelations and Moonshine," *Air Force Magazine*, September 1994, p. 5; Eric Schmitt, "Some Doubt U.S. Ability to Fight Wars on 2 Fronts," *New York Times*, 17 October 1994.

23. Schmitt, "Some Doubt U.S. Ability," p. A8.

24. Howard Banks, "Parkinson's Law Revisited," *Forbes*, 15 August 1994, p. 81.

25. CBO, "Planning for Defense," pp. 23–28.

26. William Clinton, *A National Security Strategy of Engagement and Enlargement* (Washington, DC, 1994), p. 7.

27. Ibid., pp. 7, 13–14.

28. Mackubin Thomas Owens, "A Crash Course in Strategic Reality," *Strategic Review*, 21:4, Fall 1993, p. 6.

29. Pat Towell, "Clinton Must Match Budget with Pentagon Promises," *CQWR*, 23 July 1994, p. 1994.

30. Morrison, "Bottoming Out?" p. 2130

31. Baker Spring, "Clinton's Defense Budget Falls Far Short," *Heritage Foundation Backgrounder Update*, no. 217, 15 March 1994, p. 2

32. General Accounting Office, National Security and International Affairs Division, "Future Years Defense Program: Optimistic Estimates Lead to Billions in Overprogramming," GAO/NSIAD-94-210 (Washington, DC, 29 July 1994), p. 2

33. Dov S. Zakheim and Jeffrey M. Ranney, "Matching Defense Strategies to Resources," *International Security*, 18:1, Summer 1993, pp. 51–78. "[Operational and support] costs refer to those programs, activities, or costs funded in the DoD military pay (less retired pay accrual funds), operations & maintenance, revolving management funds, military construction, and family housing appropriation accounts" (p. 53).

34. Ibid., p. 54.

35. Ibid., pp. 72–73; Spring, "Clinton's Defense Budget Falls Far Short," p. 2.

36. Zakheim and Ranney, "Matching Defense Strategies to Resources," pp. 74–75.

37. CBO Memorandum, "Long-term Costs of the Administration's Bottom Up Review Forces," November 1994, three reports: "The Costs of the Administration's Plan for the Army Through the Year 2010"; "The Costs of the Administration's Plan for the Air Force Through the Year 2010"; and "The Costs of the Administration's Plan for the Navy Through the Year 2010."

38. Joint Chiefs of Staff, *JCS Publication 1: The Dictionary of Military and Associated Terms* (Washington, DC, January 1986).

39. William J. Perry, "Statement Before the Senate Armed Services Committee in Connection with the Fiscal Year 1995 Budget for the Department of Defense," 8 February 1994, p. 3.

40. General Edward C. Meyer, "Testimony Before the Subcommittee on Investigations, House Armed Services Committee," 29 May 1980, p. 18.

41. CBO, "Trends in Selected Indicators of Military Readiness, 1980 through 1993" (hereafter, CBO, "Trends in Military Readiness") (Washington, DC, March 1994), pp. 2–5.

42. Office of the Under Secretary of Defense for Acquisition and Technology, "Report of the Defense Science Board Task Force on Readiness" (Washington, DC, June 1994), p. i.

43. CBO, "Trends in Military Readiness," p. x.

44. Office of Undersecretary of Defense, "Report of Task Force on Readiness," pp. ii–iv, 11, 15, 19, 20, 34.

45. CBO, "Trends in Military Readiness," p. xii.

46. There are four C-ratings: C-1, fully combat ready; C-2, substantially combat ready; C-3, marginally combat ready; and C-4, not combat ready.

47. CBO, "Trends in Military Readiness," p. 11.

48. Larry Di Rita, et al., "Thumbs Down to the Bottom-Up Review," *Heritage Foundation Backgrounder Update*, no. 957, 24 September 1993; pp. 4–5; John Luddy, "Stop the Slide Toward a Hollow Military," *Heritage Foundation Backgrounder Update*, no. 209, 14 January 1994; Spring, "Clinton's Defense Budget Falls Far Short," p. 3; Spring, "The Army's Budget Choice: A Force Too Small or Hollow," *Heritage Foundation Backgrounder Update*, no. 219, 28 March 1994; Di Rita, "Clinton's Bankrupt National Security Strategy," *Heritage Foundation Backgrounder Update*, no. 1000, 27 September 1994, p. 3–6; Pat Towell, "Keeping the Fighting Edge: Monitoring Vital Signs," *CQWR*, 23 July 1994, p. 1996.

49. Banks, "Parkinson's Law Revisited," p. 82.

50. Ibid.; "Stretching Defense," *Wall Street Journal*, 1 September 1994, p. A12.

51. Eric Schmitt, "G.O.P. Military Power Assails Troop Readiness," *New York Times*, 17 November 1994, p. A22. Some argue that the army overstated the readiness problems of these divisions in order to influence the debate over service shares of the defense budget. "Interviews . . . disclose that the commanders of the three divisions with lowered readiness ratings painted the gloomiest picture possible, helping the army's uniformed leadership in Washington argue for more money in a long-running rivalry with the navy and air force" (Eric Schmitt, "Ready for Combat? The Assessment Isn't Simple," *New York Times*, 20 December 1994, p. B7).

52. Schmitt, "G.O.P. Military Power," p. A22.

53. Ibid.

54. Berner and Graney, "Defense Budget for 1995: Data Summary," p. CRS-11.

55. CBO, "Planning for Defense," pp. 10–11.

56. Ibid., pp. 11–12.

57. Perry, "Statement Before Senate Armed Services Committee," p. 4.

58. Philip Finnegan and Jason Glashow, "Budget Shortfall Impedes Weapon Projects," *Defense News*, 26 September–2 October 1994, p. 26.

59. CBO, "Planning for Defense," p. 11.

60. Morrison, "Bottoming Out?" p. 2130; Eric Schmitt, "Pentagon, Buoying Troops, Will Cut Arms Development," *New York Times*, 23 August 1994, p. A18; Pat Towell, "Measure Heralds a Tug of War Between People/Programs," *CQWR*, 10 September 1994, p. 2527.

61. Morrison, "Bottoming Out?" p. 2130.

62. David Silverberg, "Eating the Seed Corn," *Armed Forces Journal International*, September 1994, p. 6.

63. Pat Towell, "President to Seek Increase in Military Budget," *CQWR*, December 3, 1994, p. 3454.

64. Di Rita, "Clinton's Bankrupt National Security Strategy," pp. 7–8.

65. Devroy and Graham, "Clinton Seeks to Boost Defense," p. A15.

66. John Morrocco, "Senate Panel Knocks Weapons Cut Plan," *Aviation Week & Space Technology*, 26 September 1994, p. 22. Cf. Steven Greenhouse, "Republicans Plan to Guide Foreign Policy by Purse Strings," *New York Times*, 13 November 1994, p. 12.

67. "[Senator Sam Nunn said] 'I think we . . . have to take an increasingly critical look at non-defense related spending,' including environmental cleanup and humanitarian assistance operations" (Morrocco, "Senate Panel Knocks Weapons Cut Plan," p. 22).

68. General Accounting Office, "1995 Budget: Potential Reduction to the Operations and Maintenance Programs" (Washington, DC, 6 September 1994).

69. General Accounting Office, "DoD Budget: Department of Defense Support for Domestic Civil Activities" (Washington, DC, November 1993).

70. John Luddy, "This Is Defense? Non-Defense Spending in the Defense Budget," *Heritage Foundation FYI*, 30 March 1994.

71. Banks, "Parkinson's Law Revisited," p. 82.

72. William W. Kaufmann, "'Hollow Forces?' Current Issues of U.S. Military Readiness and Effectiveness," *Brookings Review*, Fall 1994, p. 26.

73. Morrison, "Bottoming Out?" p. 2127.

74. Andrew F. Krepinevich, *The Bottom Up Review: An Assessment* (Washington, DC, 1994), p. 59.

75. Cf. Robert J. Art, "Defense Policy," in Art and Seyom Brown, *U.S. Foreign Policy: The Search for a New Role* (New York, 1993), pp. 112–13; and Colin Gray, "Global Security and Economic Well-being: A Strategic Perspective," *Political Studies* 42:1, March 1994, p. 36.

Chapter 8
Peacekeeping and Power Projection? Conventional Forces for the Twenty-first Century

1. Colin L. Powell, *National Military Strategy of the United States* (Washington, DC, 1994), p. 7.

2. William Clinton, *National Security Strategy of the United States*, 1994, p. 8.

3. Anthony Lake, "From Containment to Enlargement," Speech by the Assistant to the President for National Security Affairs, Johns Hopkins University, School of Advanced International Studies, Washington, DC, September 1993, p. 6.

4. Ibid., p. 6.

5. General Gordon R. Sullivan, transcript of "Address to the 1994 Annual AUSA Convention," Washington, DC, 18 October 1994, p. 4.

6. In addition, 7,000 troops of the 24th Infantry Division redeployed to Kuwait as a response to troop buildups in southern Iraq in fall 1994.

7. Les Aspin, *Annual Report to the President and the Congress, FY 1994* (Washington, DC, 1994), p. 131.

8. Anthony Lake, "Press Briefing by National Security Advisor Tony Lake and Director for Strategic Plans and Policy General Wesley Clark," Office of the Press Secretary, The White House, 5 May 1994.

9. Les Aspin, *Report on the Bottom-Up Review* (Washington, DC, 1993), p. 1.

10. Ibid., p. 11.

11. Ibid., p. 20.

12. Aspin, *Annual Report 1994*, p. 71.

13. Ibid., p. 255.

14. Ibid., p. 42.

15. President Clinton's *National Security Strategy of Engagement and Enlargement* (Washington, DC, 1994) was submitted in accordance with Section 603 of the Goldwater-Nichols Defense Reorganization Act of 1986.

16. Ibid., p. ii.

17. Ibid. p. 6.

18. Ibid., p. ii.

19. Secretary of Defense Perry published an article at this same time that laid out the criteria for the commitment of American forces abroad. See William Perry, "Military Action: When to Use It and How to Ensure Its Effectiveness," in Janne E. Nolan, ed., *Global Engagement: Cooperation and Security in the 21st Century* (Washington, DC, 1994).

20. Aspin, *Bottom-Up Review*, p. 2; and Clinton, *National Security Strategy*, p. 3.

21. Clinton, *National Security Strategy*, p. 10.

22. Aspin, *Annual Report 1994*, p. 70; Aspin, *Bottom-Up Review*, p. 23. For more on this, see Michael Burton and Jeffrey S. Lantis, "American Policy and the Future of United Nations Peacekeeping," prepared for the Mershon Center Study Group on the Uses of Multilateral Force in the Quest for Peace, The Ohio State University, 1993.

23. The White House, "The Clinton Administration's Policy on Reforming Multilateral Peace Operations," Executive Summary, May 1994, p. 2.

24. See Jeffrey Smith, "U.S. Plans Wider Role in U.N. Peacekeeping," *Washington Post*, 18 June 1993, p. 1; Smith, *Washington Post Weekly Edition*, 18 August 1994, p. 4.

25. Anthony Lake, "Press Briefing by National Security Advisor Anthony Lake and Director for Strategic Plans and Policy General Wesley Clark," Office of the Press Secretary, The White House, 5 May 1994.

26. William Matthews, "Budget Blues," *Army Times*, 21 February 1994, p. 16.

27. Testimony of Defense Secretary Aspin and Chairman of the Joint Chiefs of Staff Colin Powell before hearings of the House and Senate Armed Services Committees on the FY 1994 Defense Authorization Bill, April 1994, as quoted in Alan Tonelson, "Superpower Without a Sword," *Foreign Affairs*, April/May 1994, p. 61.

28. Aspin, *Annual Report 1994*, p. 29.

29. "Pentagon and GAO at Odds over Shortfall," *Jane's Defence Weekly*, 10 August 1994, p. 4.

30. Ibid., p. 4. A general overview of the administration's projected needs in economic cuts was originally laid out in Economic Strategy Institute, *An Economic Strategy for America: A Blueprint for Economic Revitalization* (Washington, DC, 1992).

31. Aspin, *Annual Report 1994*, p. 17.

32. Matthews, "Budget Blues," p. 16.

33. John M. Collins, *U.S. Military Force Reductions: Capabilities* (Washington, DC, 1992).

34. When defining strategic mobility requirements for the twenty-first century, army officials have been quick to note that they "are not there yet." Lift capability estimates state the need to close three full divisions and their logistical support within thirty days of the initiation of the conflict and to bring up five divisions and necessary support within seventy-five days. The plan called for eleven new surge ships, eight new pre-positioning ships, nineteen additional roll-on/roll-off transports for rapid reinforcement missions, and a push to continue with the troubled C-17 acquisition plan; General David M. Maddox, CINC-Europe and Seventh Army, Washington DC, 24 August 1994.

35. General Hoar, as quoted in William Matthews, "The Bottom's Out," *Army Times*, 20 June 1994, p. 12.

36. William Perry, interview in *Jane's Defence Weekly*, 2 July 1994, p. 40.

37. Aspin, *Bottom-Up Review*, p. 2.

38. Clinton, *National Security Strategy*, p. ii.

39. The White House, "Reforming Multilateral Peace Operations," Executive Summary, p. 3.

40. Matthews, "The Bottom's Out," *Army Times*, 20 June 1994, p. 12.

41. See Edward F. Brunner, *U.S. Forces in Europe: Military Implications of Alternative Force Levels* (Washington, DC, 1992). See also Christopher Smart, *Europe's Next Wars: Security Challenges from the Baltic to the Adriatic* (Boulder, CO, 1993).

42. Adam Daniel Rothfeld, "The CSCE: Towards a Security Organization," in *SIPRI Yearbook: World Armaments and Disarmament, 1993* (Stockholm, 1993).

43. Jason Glashow and Robert Holzer, "Roles Commission List Leaves Off Reserve and Guard Issues," *Defense News*, 3–9 October 1994, p. 10.

44. Ibid., p. 10.

45. Peter D. Feaver and Kurt M. Campbell, "Rethinking Key West: Service Roles and Mission After the Cold War," *American Defense Annual 1993* (New York, 1994), pp. 155–73.

Chapter 9
Great Powers No More

1. The attempt to play a "separate power role," Acheson noted, was "about played out" (speech at West Point, 5 December 1962, cited in Laslo Boyd, *Britain's Search for a Role* [Lexington, MA, 1975], p. 1).

2. Paul Kennedy, *The Rise and Fall of the Great Powers: Economic Change and Military Conflict from 1500 to 2000* (London, 1988). See also David Calleo, *Beyond American Hegemony: The Future of the Western Alliance* (New York, 1987).

3. This is the message of Joseph Nye, *Bound to Lead: The Changing Nature of American Power* (New York, 1990).

4. John B. Wolf, *The Emergence of the Great Powers, 1685–1715* (New York, 1951).

5. See the essays in Herbert Butterfield and Martin Wight's *Diplomatic Investigations* (Cambridge, MA, 1968).

6. E. H. Carr, *The Twenty Years' Crisis, 1919–1939*, 2d ed. (London, 1946).

7. See the essays in David Reynolds, ed., *The Origins of the Cold War in Europe: International Perspectives* (New Haven, CT, 1994).

8. On the McCarthy era see Richard Fried, *Nightmare in Red* (Oxford, 1990).

9. See Phil Williams, *The Senate and U.S. Troops in Europe* (London, 1985), chaps. 3 and 4.

10. Michael R. Beschloss, *Kennedy v Khrushchev: The Crisis Years 1960–63* (London, 1991).

11. For a definitive history of the end of the Cold War see Raymond L. Grathoff, *The Great Transition: American Soviet Relations and the End of the Cold War* (Washington, DC, 1994). See also, Michael Beschloss and Strobe Talbott, *At the Highest Levels: The Inside Story of the End of the Cold War* (New York, 1993).

12. Charles Krauthammer, "The Unipolar Moment," *Foreign Affairs: America and the World*, 70:1, 1990/91.

13. Lawrence Freedman, "Order and Disorder in the New World," *Foreign Affairs: America and the World*, 71:1, 1991/92. See also Larry Berman and Bruce Jentleson, "Bush and the Post–Cold War World: New Challenges for American Leadership," in Colin Campbell and Bert Rockman, eds., *The Bush Presidency: First Appraisals* (Chatham, NJ, 1991).

14. Christopher Layne, "The Unipolar Illusion: Why New Great Powers Will Rise," *International Security*, 17:4, Spring, 1993.

Index

About the Contributors

Eliot A. Cohen is professor of strategic studies at the Paul H. Nitze School of Advanced International Studies, the Johns Hopkins University. He is the co-author of *Military Misfortunes: The Anatomy of Failure in War* and has written many other books and articles on defense policy and military history. From 1991 to 1993 Professor Cohen was the director of the Gulf War Air Power Survey, a comprehensive, multivolume study of the 1991 war with Iraq.

Lawrence Freedman is professor and head of the Department of War Studies at King's College, London. In addition to many articles on defense and foreign policy, he is most recently the co-author of *The Gulf Conflict 1990–91*. Professor Freedman held several positions in research and strategic studies before his appointment to the Chair of War Studies at King's College in April 1982. In 1990, Professor Freedman also became honorary director of the University of London's Centre for Defence Studies.

John R. Galvin is distinguished visiting policy analyst at the Mershon Center, The Ohio State University. Prior to his retirement from the U.S. Army, General Galvin was the Supreme Allied Commander, Europe and the Commander in Chief, U.S. European Command. He is author of numerous articles on strategy and tactics, leadership, and history, and his latest book is *The Minute Men*, on the American Revolution.

Robert W. Gaskin is vice president for policy and programs at Business Executives for National Security, a defense-oriented, public policy organization in Washington, DC. He served in the air force for twenty-eight years, retiring in 1992 as a colonel. Mr. Gaskin's last assignment was at the Pentagon. In this position he created the concept of the joint force air component commander (JFACC) and played a key role in firmly establishing this into joint doctrine. Then-Colonel Gaskin also served as the Assistant Director of Net Assessment under Dr. Andrew Marshall and wrote the definitive assessment of the military balance on the Korean Peninsula. He has lectured at the Air War College, the Army's School for Advanced Military Science, the Army War College, the National War College, the Navy War College, as well as at Harvard and Georgetown Universities.

Colin S. Gray is professor of international politics and director of the Centre for Security Studies at the University of Hull. Before taking his current appointment in 1993, he was the founding president of the National Institute for Public Policy in Washington, DC. Professor Gray's many publications include *Nuclear Strategy and National Style* (1986), *War, Peace, and Victory* (1990), *The Leverage of Sea Power* (1993), and *Weapons Don't Make War* (1993).

MacGregor Knox is Stevenson Professor of International History at the London School of Economics and Political Science. He graduated from Harvard College in 1967, served in South Vietnam with the 173d Airborne Brigade in 1969, and received a Ph.D. in history from Yale University in 1976. He is the author of, among other works, *Mussolini Unleashed: Politics and Strategy in Fascist Italy's Last War, 1939–1941* (Cambridge University Press, 1982) and co-editor (with Williamson Murray and Alvin Bernstein) of *The Making of Strategy: Rulers, States, and War* (Cambridge University Press, 1994). He is currently writing a comparative history of the Italian and German dictatorships.

Andrew F. Krepinevich is the director of the Defense Budget Project, an independent research organization in Washington, DC. His extensive strategic planning and management experience includes executive posts with the Department of Defense's Office of Net Assessment and the staffs of three secretaries of defense. Dr. Krepinevich's numerous publications include *The Army and Vietnam* (1987) and comprehensive revisions of the Department of Defense's *Annual Report to the Congress* (1987–89) and *Soviet Military Power* (1988 and 1989).

Jeffrey S. Lantis is assistant professor of political science at The College of Wooster. His recent publications include "Bottom's Up for the Defense Budget?" in the *American Defense Annual 1994* and "United Germany in the United Nations: Promise for the Future?" in *German Politics and Society* (1993).

Mackubin T. Owens is professor of strategy and defense economics at the Naval War College, adjunct professor of international relations at Boston University, and the editor-in-chief of *Strategic Review*. He previously served as national security advisor to Senator Bob Kasten and as the director of legislative affairs, Nuclear Weapons Programs, Department of Energy. Awarded the Silver Star for U.S. Marine Corps service during the Vietnam War, Professor Owens is the author of numerous articles in periodicals including *International Security*, *Orbis*, and *Comparative Strategy*.

Brian R. Sullivan is senior research professor and senior fellow at the Institute for National Strategic Studies at National Defense University. At INSS, he has contributed to studies dealing with the emerging international system, including *Project 2025* and *Project 2015*. He has taught military history at Yale University and strategy at the Naval War College. During the Gulf War, Professor Sullivan advised the Defense Department on special and psychological operations. He received the Silver Star and the Purple Heart while a Marine Corps officer in Vietnam. He is the co-author of *Il Duce's Other Woman* and many articles on Italian military history.

About the Editor

Williamson Murray, presently the Horner Professor of Strategy at the Marine Corps University in Quantico, Virginia, is professor emeritus of history at Ohio State University. He served in the U.S. Air Force, active and reserve, including service in Vietnam and with the Air Staff. A prolific author, Professor Murray has written *The Change in the European Military Balance of Power, 1938–1939* (Princeton University Press, 1984), *Luftwaffe* (Nautical and Aviation Press, 1985), *German Military Effectiveness* (Nautical and Aviation Press, 1992), and, most recently, *Air War in the Persian Gulf* (Nautical and Aviation Press, 1995), as well as numerous articles. In collaboration with Professor Allan R. Millett, he edited the three-volume set *Military Effectiveness—The First World War, The Interwar Period, The Second World War* (Unwin Hyman, 1988)—and *Calculations, Net Assessment, and the Coming of World War II* (The Free Press, 1992). Professor Murray also co-edited with MacGregor Knox and Alvin Bernstein *The Making of Strategy: Rulers, States, and War* (Cambridge University Press, 1994). He has been a distinguished visiting professor at West Point (1983) and the Naval War College (1985–86), as well as a Secretary of the Navy Fellow at the Naval War College (1991–92). Professor Murray is also (1994–95) the Centennial Visiting Professor at the London School of Economics and Political Science.